Tharg's

TERROR TALES

presents

NECRONAUTS &
A LOVE LIKE BLOOD

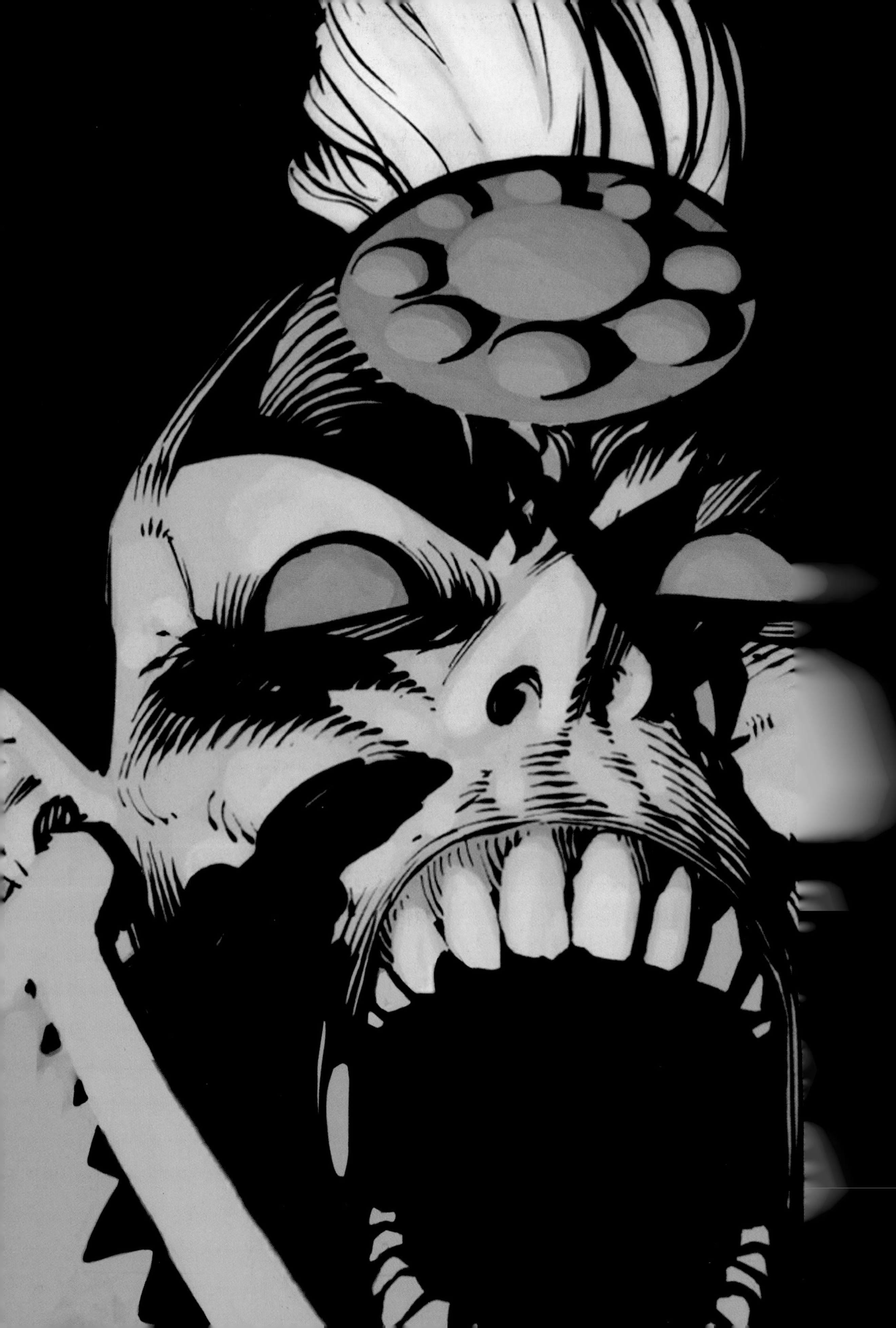

BORAG THUNGG EARTHLETS

My name is Tharg the Mighty, editor of the Galaxy's Greatest Comic, *2000 AD*. I came from Quaxxan in the Betelgeuse system in order to spread the cosmic gift of Thrill-power amongst your miserable little species. For years you have been entertained by a legion of my creative minions. The likes of Alan Moore, Grant Morrison, John Wagner, Brian Bolland, Kevin O'Neill and Simon Bisley have brought you epic tales of sci-fi and fantasy. But recently my Thrill-vaults have been darkened by tales of unmitigated evil!

Read on if you dare, and experience the creepiest comic strips ever committed to print.

SPLUNDIG VUR THRIGG!

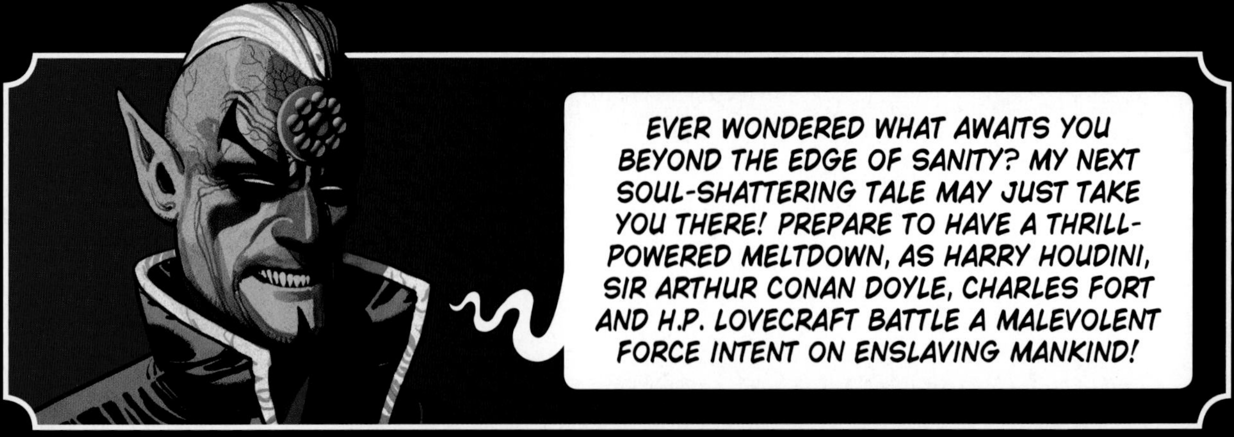
EVER WONDERED WHAT AWAITS YOU BEYOND THE EDGE OF SANITY? MY NEXT SOUL-SHATTERING TALE MAY JUST TAKE YOU THERE! PREPARE TO HAVE A THRILL-POWERED MELTDOWN, AS HARRY HOUDINI, SIR ARTHUR CONAN DOYLE, CHARLES FORT AND H.P. LOVECRAFT BATTLE A MALEVOLENT FORCE INTENT ON ENSLAVING MANKIND!

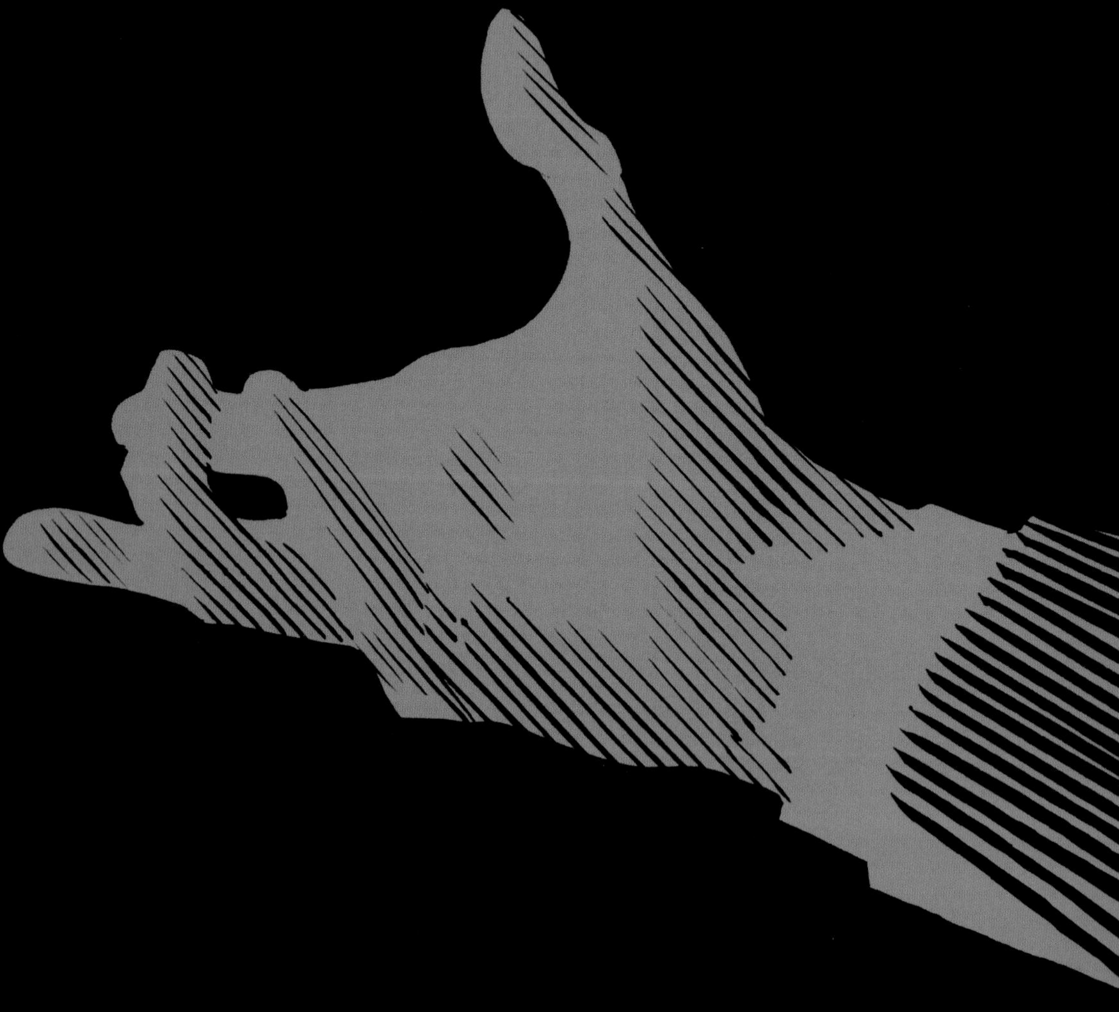

NECRONAUTS

Script: Gordon Rennie
Art: Frazer Irving
Letters: Tom Frame

Originally published in *2000 AD* Progs 2001, 1223-1230

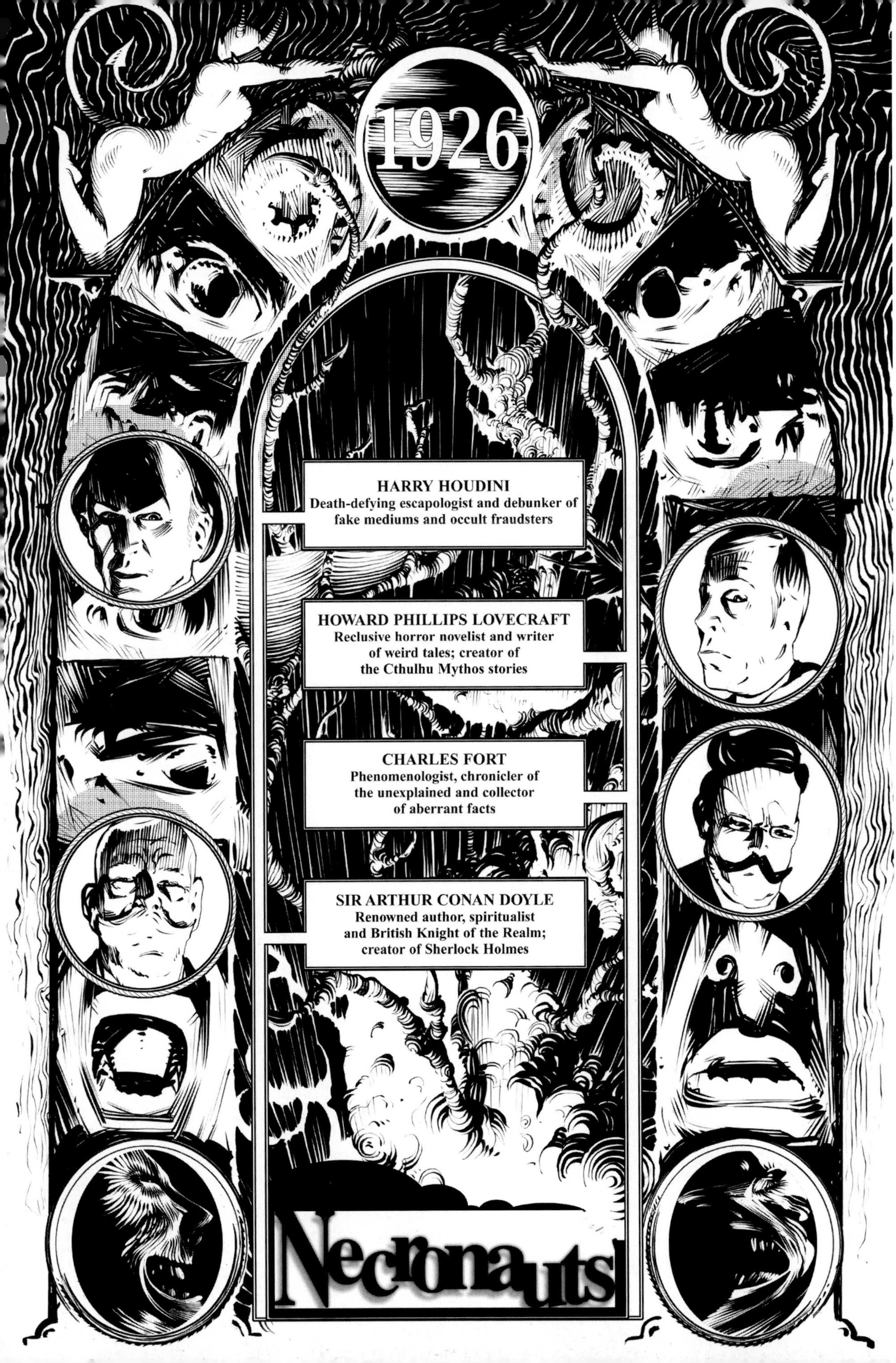

1926
HARRY HOUDINI
Death-defying escapologist and debunker of fake mediums and occult fraudsters
HOWARD PHILLIPS LOVECRAFT
Reclusive horror novelist and writer of weird tales; creator of the Cthulhu Mythos stories
CHARLES FORT
Phenomenologist, chronicler of the unexplained and collector of aberrant facts
SIR ARTHUR CONAN DOYLE
Renowned author, spiritualist and British Knight of the Realm; creator of Sherlock Holmes
Necronauts

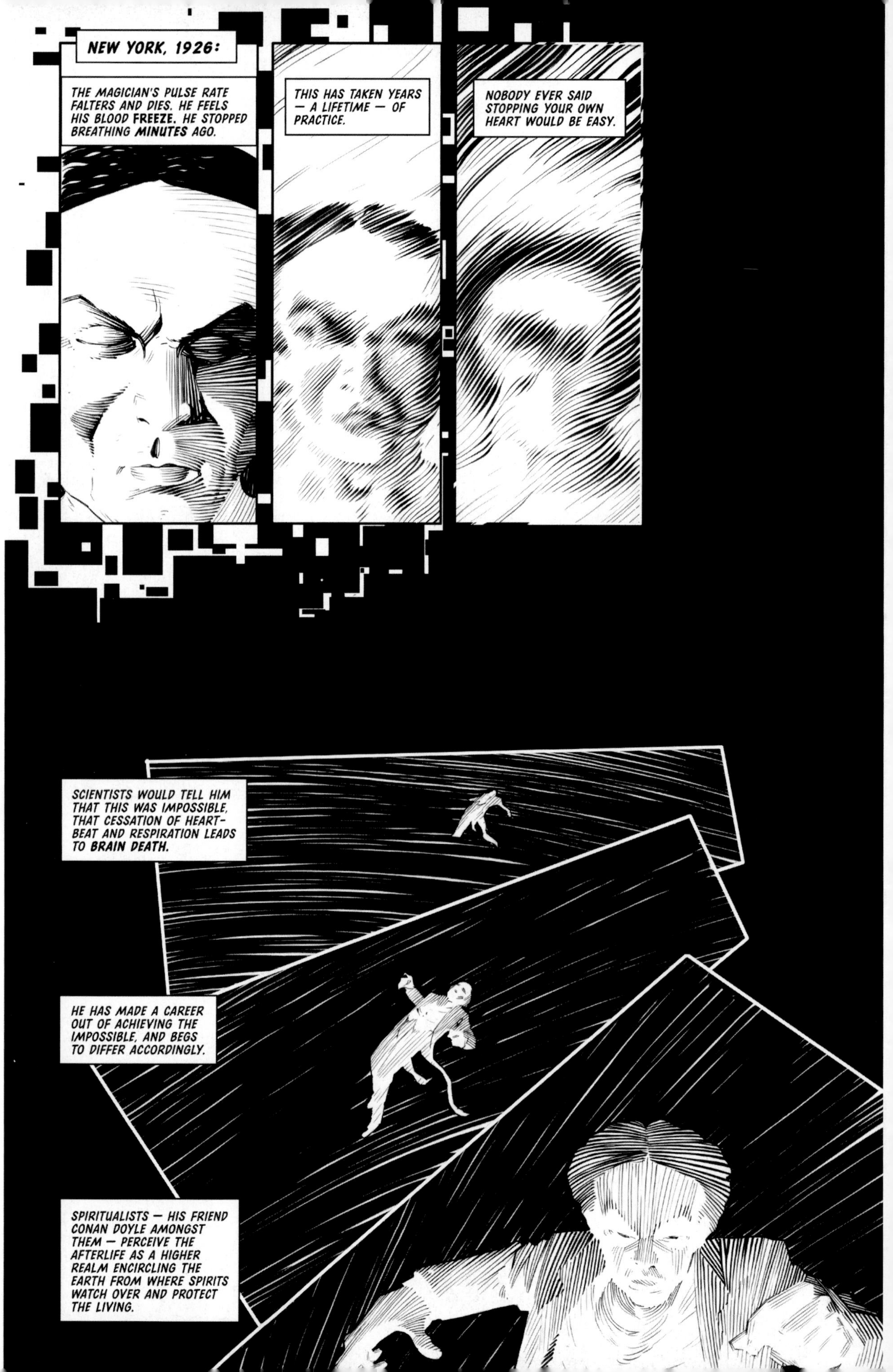
NEW YORK, 1926:
THE MAGICIAN'S PULSE RATE FALTERS AND DIES. HE FEELS HIS BLOOD FREEZE. HE STOPPED BREATHING MINUTES AGO.
THIS HAS TAKEN YEARS — A LIFETIME — OF PRACTICE.
NOBODY EVER SAID STOPPING YOUR OWN HEART WOULD BE EASY.
SCIENTISTS WOULD TELL HIM THAT THIS WAS IMPOSSIBLE, THAT CESSATION OF HEART-BEAT AND RESPIRATION LEADS TO BRAIN DEATH.
HE HAS MADE A CAREER OUT OF ACHIEVING THE IMPOSSIBLE, AND BEGS TO DIFFER ACCORDINGLY.
SPIRITUALISTS — HIS FRIEND CONAN DOYLE AMONGST THEM — PERCEIVE THE AFTERLIFE AS A HIGHER REALM ENCIRCLING THE EARTH FROM WHERE SPIRITS WATCH OVER AND PROTECT THE LIVING.

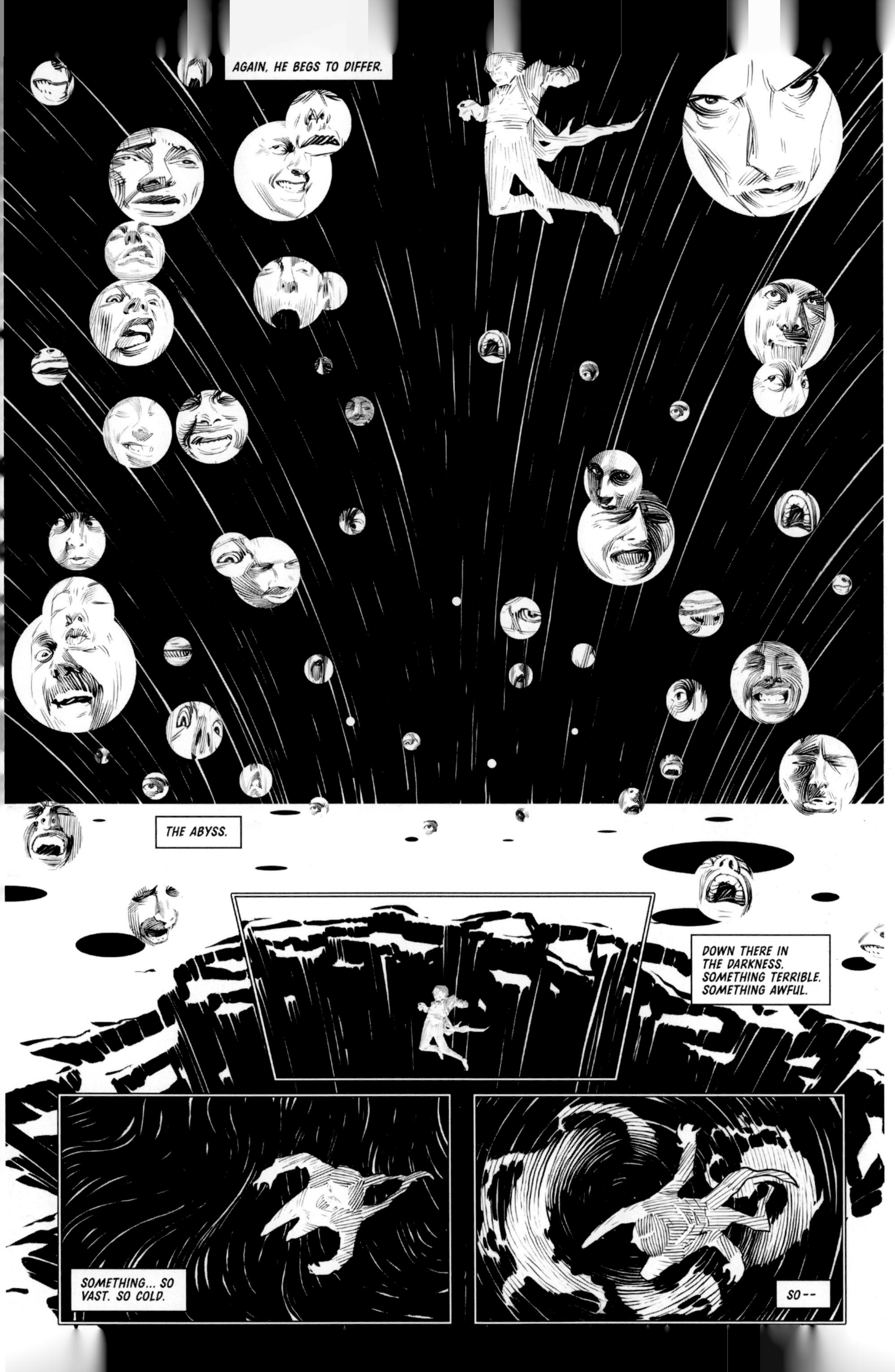
AGAIN, HE BEGS TO DIFFER.
THE ABYSS.
DOWN THERE IN THE DARKNESS. SOMETHING TERRIBLE. SOMETHING AWFUL.
SOMETHING... SO VAST. SO COLD.
SO--

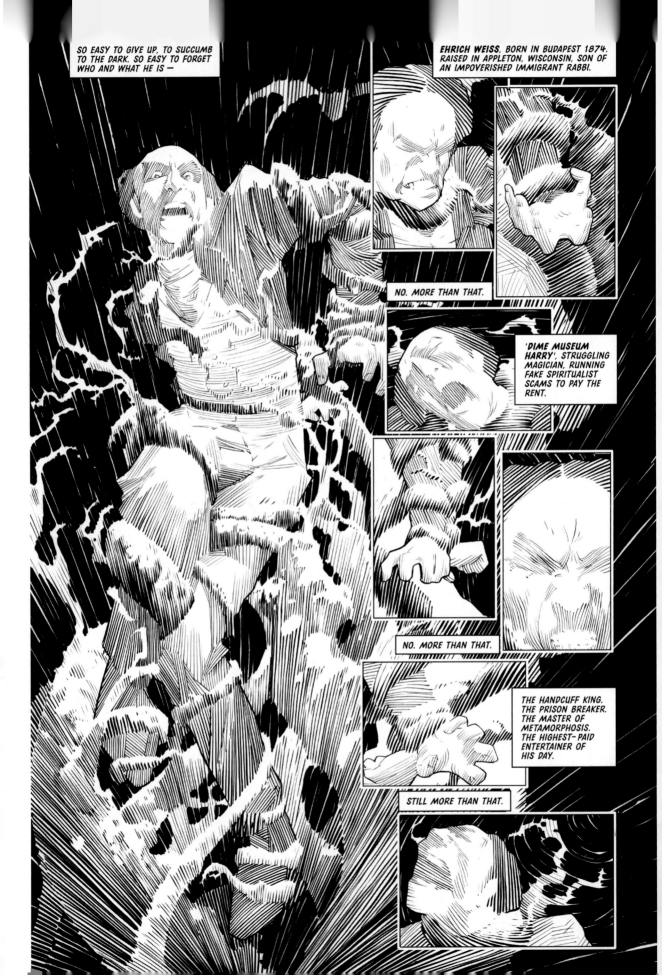

SO EASY TO GIVE UP, TO SUCCUMB TO THE DARK. SO EASY TO FORGET WHO AND WHAT HE IS —

EHRICH WEISS, BORN IN BUDAPEST 1874. RAISED IN APPLETON, WISCONSIN, SON OF AN IMPOVERISHED IMMIGRANT RABBI.

NO. MORE THAN THAT.

'DIME MUSEUM HARRY', STRUGGLING MAGICIAN, RUNNING FAKE SPIRITUALIST SCAMS TO PAY THE RENT.

NO. MORE THAN THAT.

THE HANDCUFF KING. THE PRISON BREAKER. THE MASTER OF METAMORPHOSIS. THE HIGHEST-PAID ENTERTAINER OF HIS DAY.

STILL MORE THAN THAT.

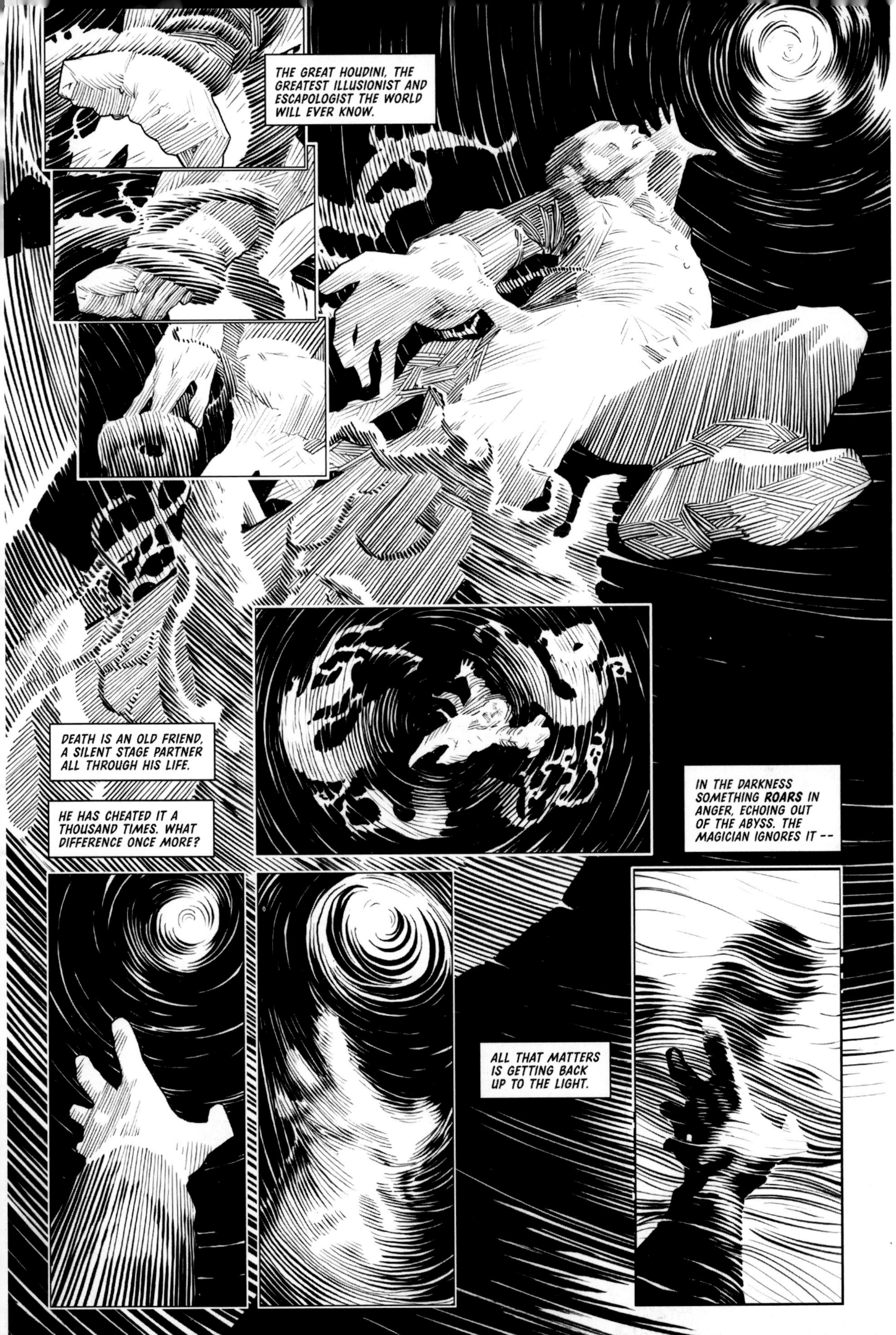
THE GREAT HOUDINI, THE GREATEST ILLUSIONIST AND ESCAPOLOGIST THE WORLD WILL EVER KNOW.
DEATH IS AN OLD FRIEND, A SILENT STAGE PARTNER ALL THROUGH HIS LIFE.
HE HAS CHEATED IT A THOUSAND TIMES. WHAT DIFFERENCE ONCE MORE?
IN THE DARKNESS SOMETHING ROARS IN ANGER, ECHOING OUT OF THE ABYSS. THE MAGICIAN IGNORES IT --
ALL THAT MATTERS IS GETTING BACK UP TO THE LIGHT.

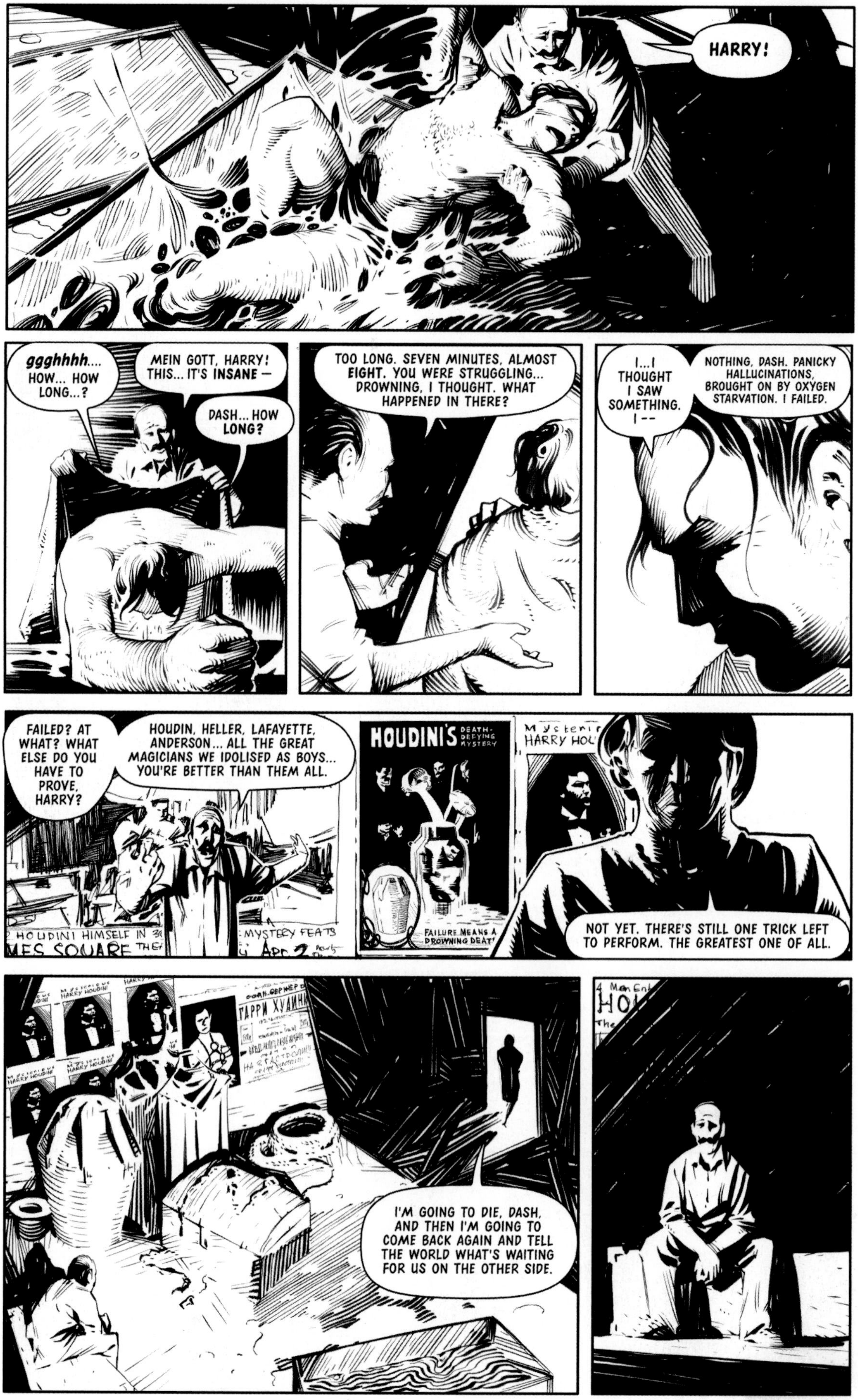
HARRY!
ggghhhh.... HOW... HOW LONG...?
MEIN GOTT, HARRY! THIS... IT'S INSANE —
DASH... HOW LONG?
TOO LONG. SEVEN MINUTES, ALMOST EIGHT. YOU WERE STRUGGLING... DROWNING, I THOUGHT. WHAT HAPPENED IN THERE?
I...I THOUGHT I SAW SOMETHING. I --
NOTHING, DASH. PANICKY HALLUCINATIONS, BROUGHT ON BY OXYGEN STARVATION. I FAILED.
FAILED? AT WHAT? WHAT ELSE DO YOU HAVE TO PROVE, HARRY?
HOUDIN, HELLER, LAFAYETTE, ANDERSON... ALL THE GREAT MAGICIANS WE IDOLISED AS BOYS... YOU'RE BETTER THAN THEM ALL.
HOUDINI HIMSELF IN
MYSTERY FEATS
HOUDINI'S DEATH-DEFYING MYSTERY
FAILURE MEANS A DROWNING DEAT
NOT YET. THERE'S STILL ONE TRICK LEFT TO PERFORM. THE GREATEST ONE OF ALL.
I'M GOING TO DIE, DASH, AND THEN I'M GOING TO COME BACK AGAIN AND TELL THE WORLD WHAT'S WAITING FOR US ON THE OTHER SIDE.

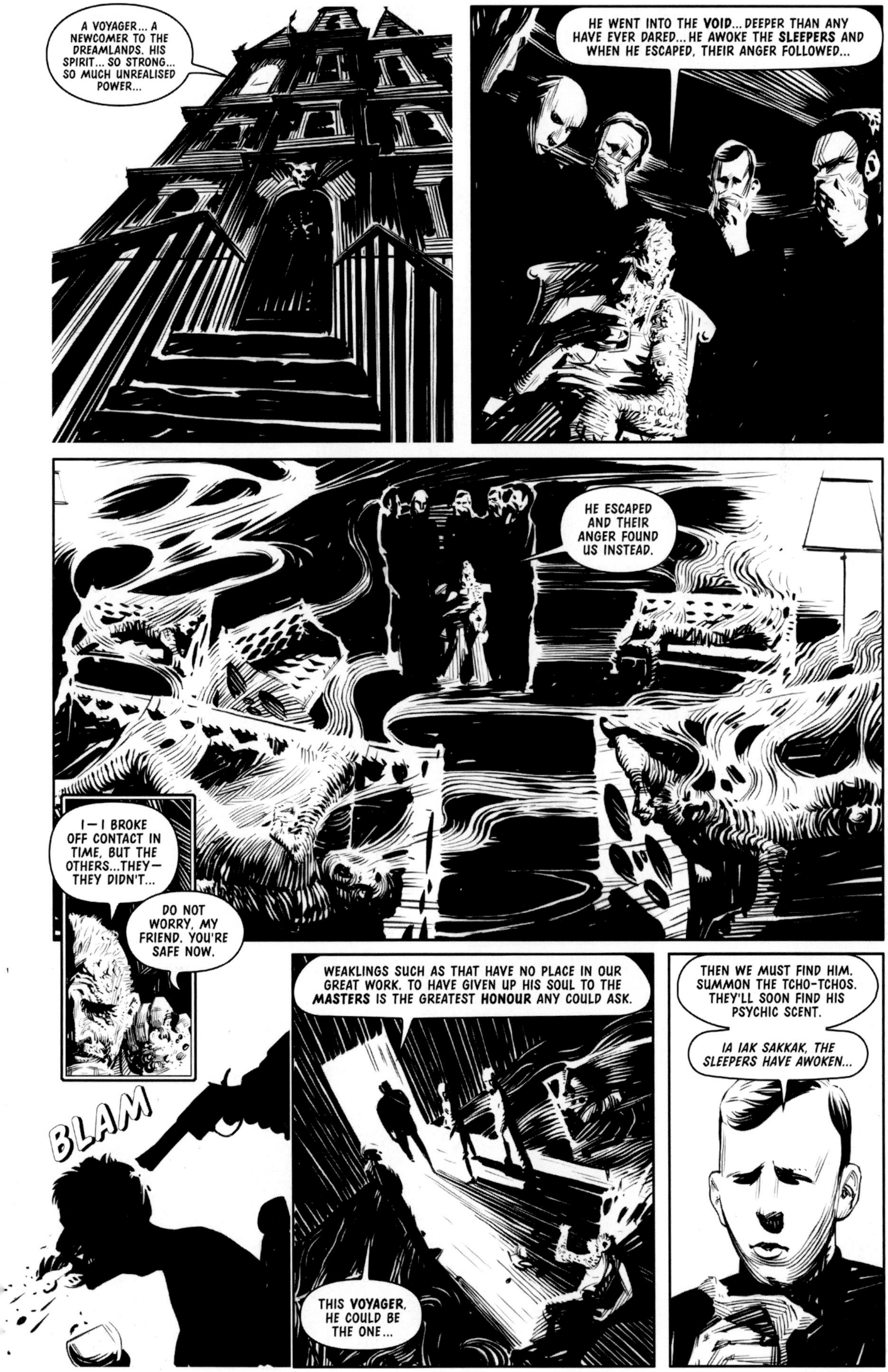
A VOYAGER... A NEWCOMER TO THE DREAMLANDS. HIS SPIRIT... SO STRONG... SO MUCH UNREALISED POWER...
HE WENT INTO THE VOID... DEEPER THAN ANY HAVE EVER DARED... HE AWOKE THE SLEEPERS AND WHEN HE ESCAPED, THEIR ANGER FOLLOWED...
HE ESCAPED AND THEIR ANGER FOUND US INSTEAD.
I— I BROKE OFF CONTACT IN TIME, BUT THE OTHERS...THEY— THEY DIDN'T...
DO NOT WORRY, MY FRIEND, YOU'RE SAFE NOW.
BLAM
WEAKLINGS SUCH AS THAT HAVE NO PLACE IN OUR GREAT WORK. TO HAVE GIVEN UP HIS SOUL TO THE MASTERS IS THE GREATEST HONOUR ANY COULD ASK.
THIS VOYAGER, HE COULD BE THE ONE...
THEN WE MUST FIND HIM. SUMMON THE TCHO-TCHOS. THEY'LL SOON FIND HIS PSYCHIC SCENT.
IA IAK SAKKAK, THE SLEEPERS HAVE AWOKEN...

PROVIDENCE RHODE ISLAND, ONCE UPON A MIDNIGHT DREARY:

The most merciful thing in all the world, I think, is the inability of the human mind to correlate all its contents. We live on a placid island of ignorance in the midst of black seas of infinity, and it was not meant that we should voyage far.

The sciences, each straining in its own direction, have hitherto harmed us little; but some day the piecing together of disassociated knowledge will open up such terrifying vistas of reality, and of our frightful position therein, that we shall either go mad from the revelation or —

TAP

TAP
TAP

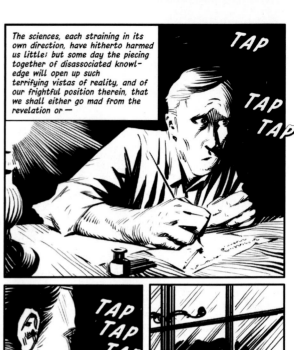

TAP
TAP
TAP

PREPARE YOURSELF, HOWARD. WE HAVE NEED OF YOU.

THE SLEEPERS, HOWARD. THE SLEEPERS HAVE AWOKEN, AND WE HAVE NEED OF YOU IN NEW YORK.

...ANOTHER VOICE... THIS ONE VERY FAINT, BUT VERY INSISTENT... A MESSAGE FOR SOMEONE HERE...

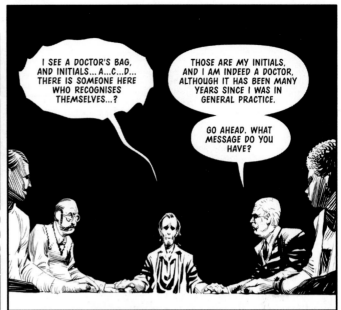

I SEE A DOCTOR'S BAG, AND INITIALS... A...C...D... THERE IS SOMEONE HERE WHO RECOGNISES THEMSELVES...?

THOSE ARE MY INITIALS, AND I AM INDEED A DOCTOR, ALTHOUGH IT HAS BEEN MANY YEARS SINCE I WAS IN GENERAL PRACTICE.

GO AHEAD. WHAT MESSAGE DO YOU HAVE?

CONAN DOYLE...THE MAGICIAN...THE MAGICIAN HAS CROSSED THE GREAT DIVIDE AND HAS SEEN WHAT LAY HIDDEN THERE. THE SLEEPERS...HE HAS AWOKEN THE SLEEPERS—!

THEY HAVE SEEN HIM...HIS SPIRIT IS LIKE A CANDLE IN THE DARK TO THEM...HE IS THE LINK THAT WILL DRAW THEM BACK TO OUR WORLD...

THE MAGICIAN... YOU MUST HELP HIM, CONAN DOYLE. EVEN NOW, THEY ARE STIRRING IN THE VOID, REACHING UP TOWARDS THE LIGHT. THEY —

NO... PLEASE... I DON'T WANT TO SEE THAT... I DON'T WANT TO SEE ANY MORE...

NO! I DON'T WANT TO SEE THAT...

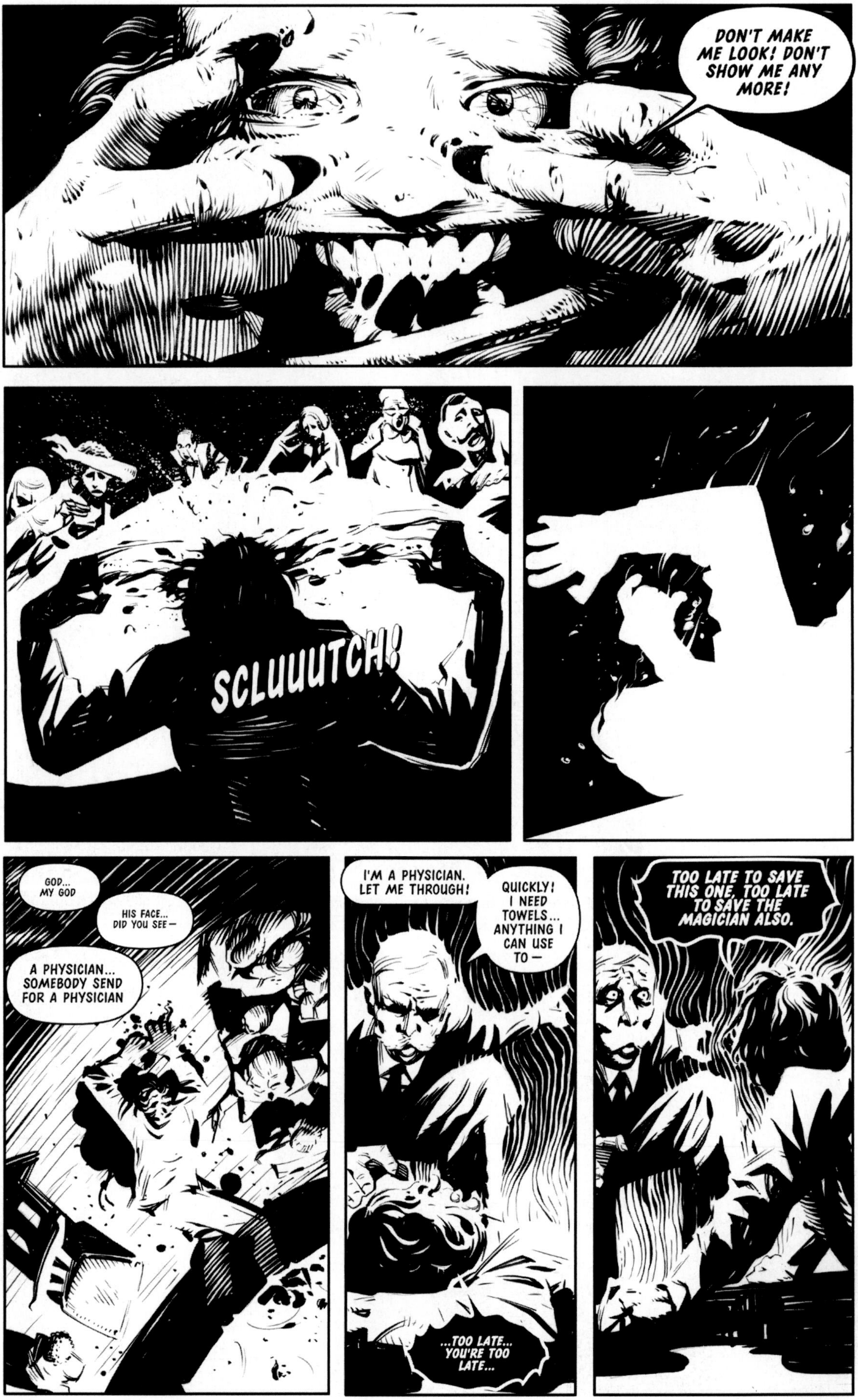
DON'T MAKE ME LOOK! DON'T SHOW ME ANY MORE!
SCLUUUTCH!
GOD... MY GOD
HIS FACE... DID YOU SEE—
A PHYSICIAN... SOMEBODY SEND FOR A PHYSICIAN
I'M A PHYSICIAN. LET ME THROUGH!
QUICKLY! I NEED TOWELS... ANYTHING I CAN USE TO—
...TOO LATE... YOU'RE TOO LATE...
TOO LATE TO SAVE THIS ONE, TOO LATE TO SAVE THE MAGICIAN ALSO.

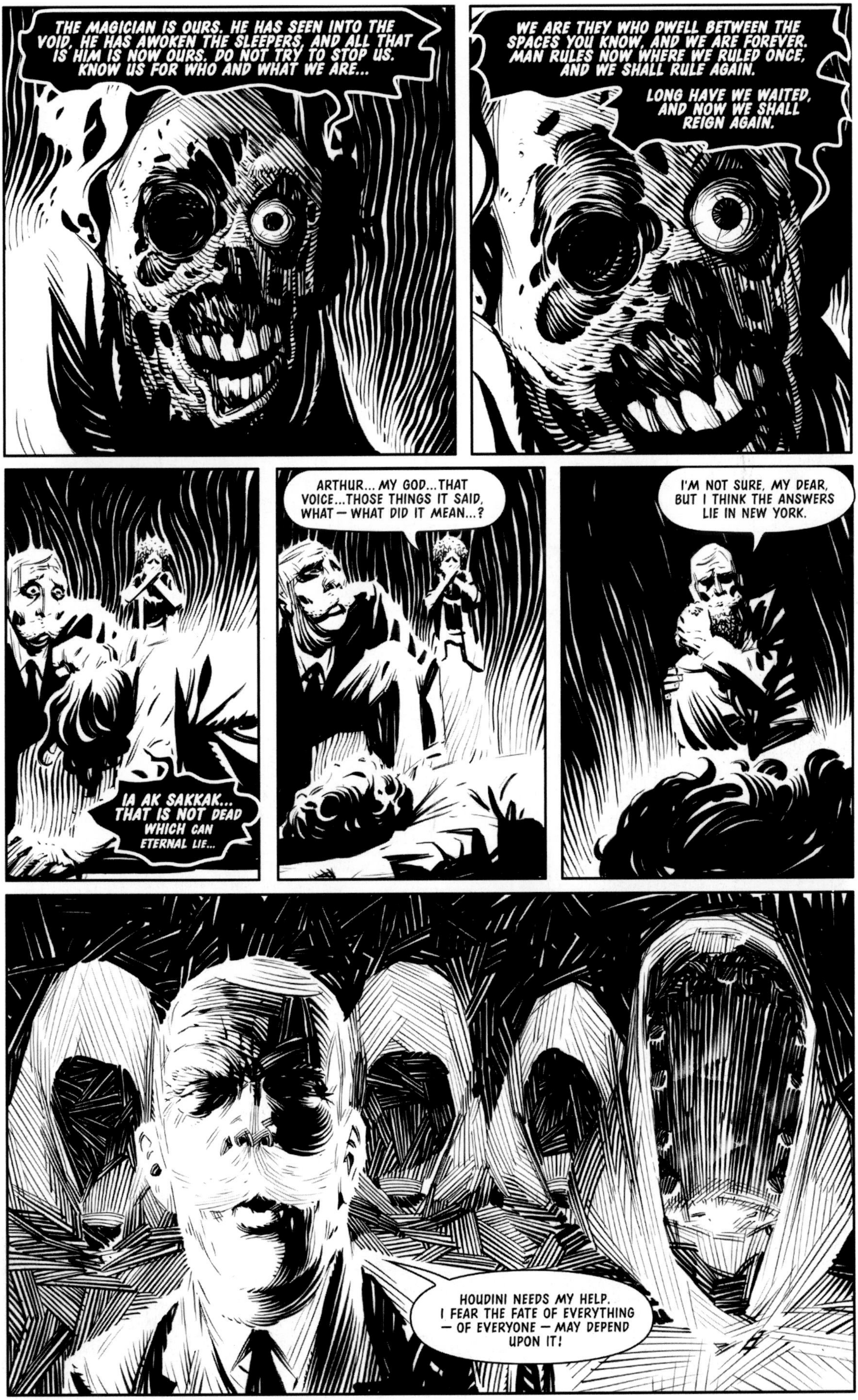
THE MAGICIAN IS OURS. HE HAS SEEN INTO THE VOID, HE HAS AWOKEN THE SLEEPERS, AND ALL THAT IS HIM IS NOW OURS. DO NOT TRY TO STOP US. KNOW US FOR WHO AND WHAT WE ARE...
WE ARE THEY WHO DWELL BETWEEN THE SPACES YOU KNOW, AND WE ARE FOREVER. MAN RULES NOW WHERE WE RULED ONCE, AND WE SHALL RULE AGAIN.
LONG HAVE WE WAITED, AND NOW WE SHALL REIGN AGAIN.
IA AK SAKKAK... THAT IS NOT DEAD WHICH CAN ETERNAL LIE...
ARTHUR... MY GOD... THAT VOICE... THOSE THINGS IT SAID, WHAT — WHAT DID IT MEAN...?
I'M NOT SURE, MY DEAR, BUT I THINK THE ANSWERS LIE IN NEW YORK.
HOUDINI NEEDS MY HELP. I FEAR THE FATE OF EVERYTHING — OF EVERYONE — MAY DEPEND UPON IT!

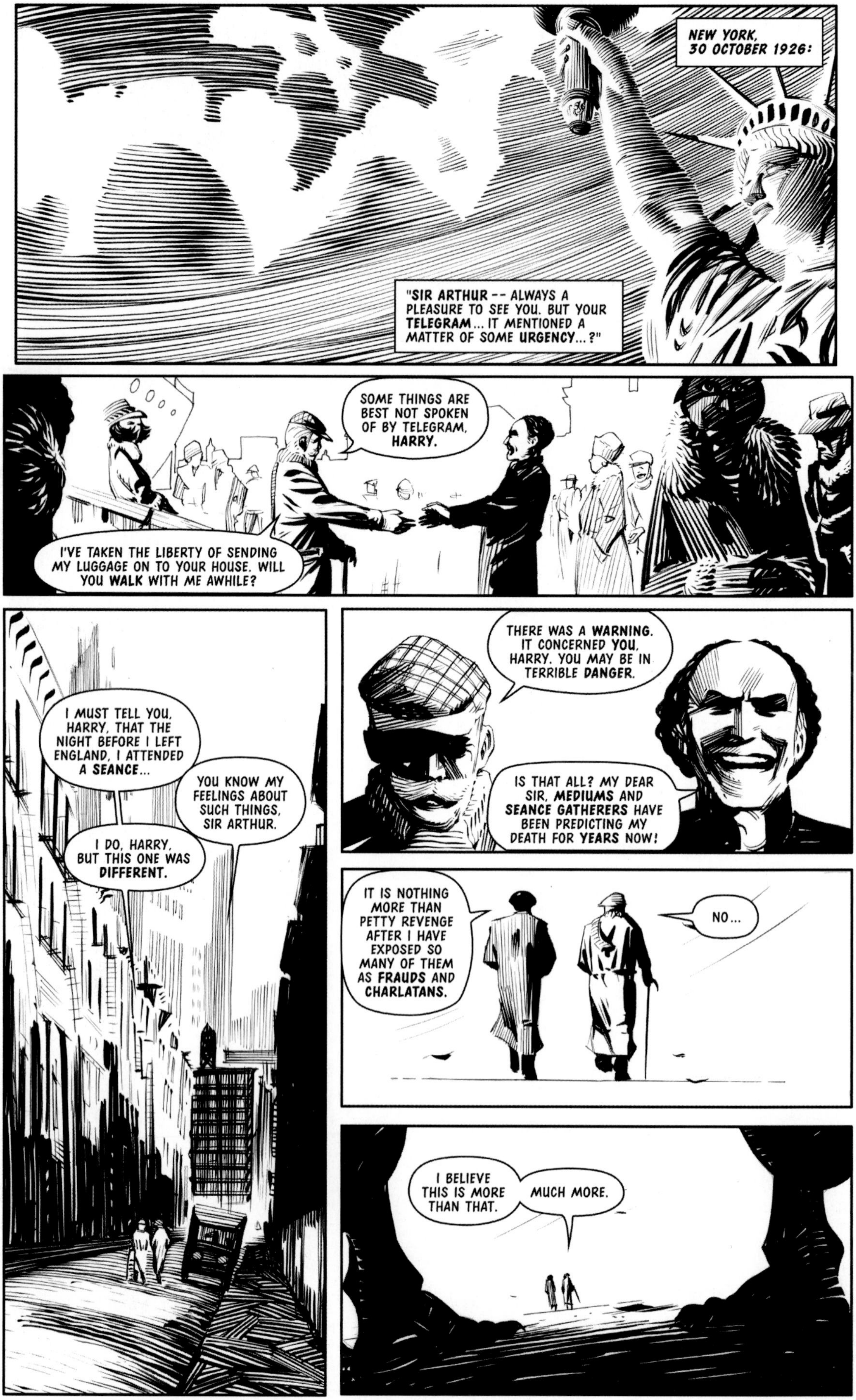
NEW YORK, 30 OCTOBER 1926:
"SIR ARTHUR -- ALWAYS A PLEASURE TO SEE YOU. BUT YOUR TELEGRAM... IT MENTIONED A MATTER OF SOME URGENCY...?"
SOME THINGS ARE BEST NOT SPOKEN OF BY TELEGRAM, HARRY.
I'VE TAKEN THE LIBERTY OF SENDING MY LUGGAGE ON TO YOUR HOUSE. WILL YOU WALK WITH ME AWHILE?
I MUST TELL YOU, HARRY, THAT THE NIGHT BEFORE I LEFT ENGLAND, I ATTENDED A SEANCE...
YOU KNOW MY FEELINGS ABOUT SUCH THINGS, SIR ARTHUR.
I DO, HARRY, BUT THIS ONE WAS DIFFERENT.
THERE WAS A WARNING. IT CONCERNED YOU, HARRY. YOU MAY BE IN TERRIBLE DANGER.
IS THAT ALL? MY DEAR SIR, MEDIUMS AND SEANCE GATHERERS HAVE BEEN PREDICTING MY DEATH FOR YEARS NOW!
IT IS NOTHING MORE THAN PETTY REVENGE AFTER I HAVE EXPOSED SO MANY OF THEM AS FRAUDS AND CHARLATANS.
NO...
I BELIEVE THIS IS MORE THAN THAT.
MUCH MORE.

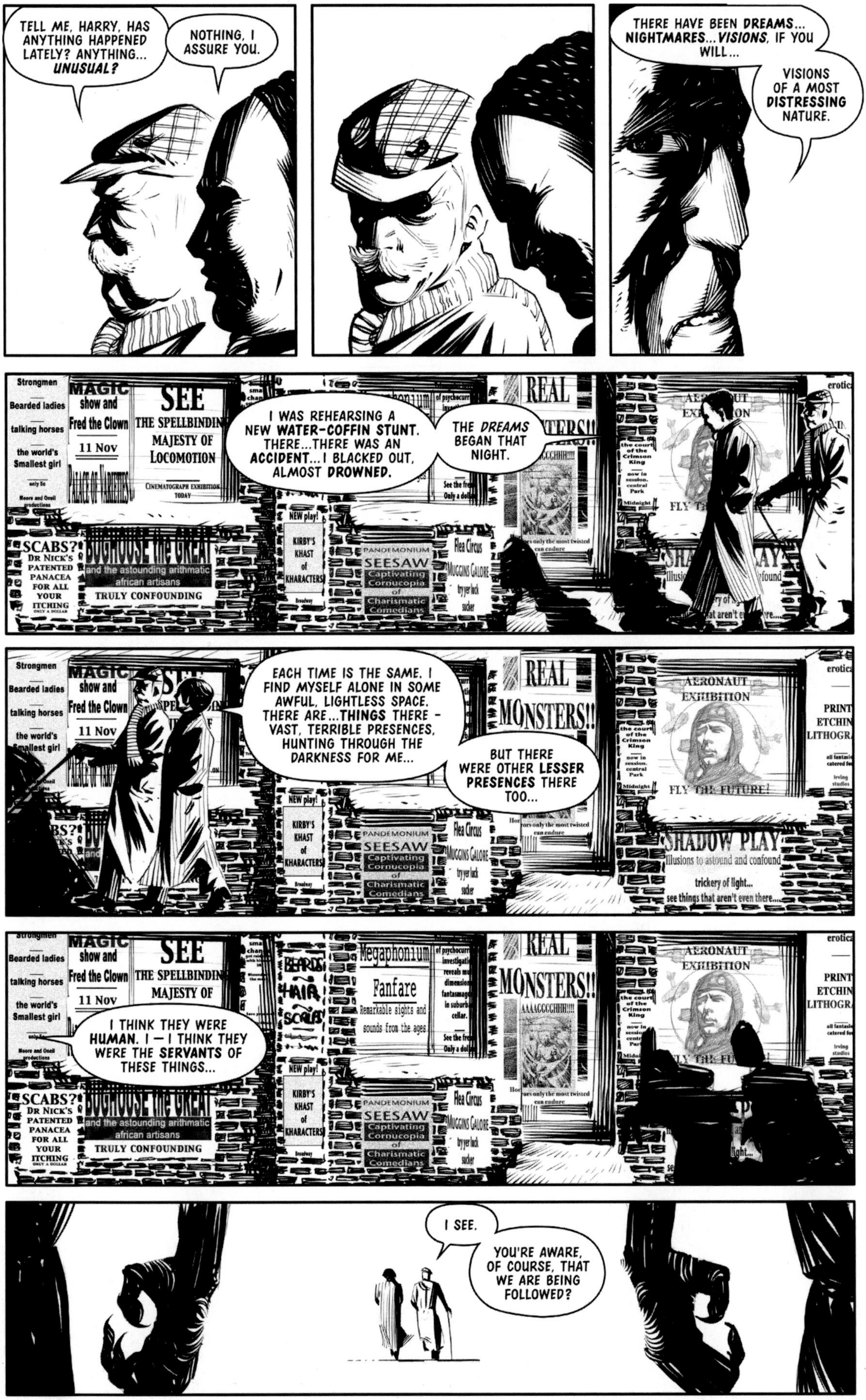
TELL ME, HARRY, HAS ANYTHING HAPPENED LATELY? ANYTHING... UNUSUAL?
NOTHING, I ASSURE YOU.
THERE HAVE BEEN DREAMS... NIGHTMARES... VISIONS, IF YOU WILL...
VISIONS OF A MOST DISTRESSING NATURE.
Strongmen
Bearded ladies
talking horses
the world's Smallest girl
MAGIC show and Fred the Clown 11 Nov
PALACE OF VARIETIES
SEE THE SPELLBINDING MAJESTY OF LOCOMOTION
CINEMATOGRAPH EXHIBITION TODAY
I WAS REHEARSING A NEW WATER-COFFIN STUNT. THERE...THERE WAS AN ACCIDENT...I BLACKED OUT, ALMOST DROWNED.
THE DREAMS BEGAN THAT NIGHT.
REAL MONSTERS!!
AERONAUT EXHIBITION
FLY THE FUTURE!
SCABS? DR NICK'S PATENTED PANACEA FOR ALL YOUR ITCHING ONLY A DOLLAR
BUGHOUSE the GREAT and the astounding arithmatic african artisans TRULY CONFOUNDING
NEW play! KIRBY'S KHAST of KHARACTERS Broadway
PANDEMONIUM SEESAW Captivating Cornucopia of Charismatic Comedians
Flea Circus MUGGINS GALORE try yer luck sucker
SHADOW PLAY illusions to astound and confound trickery of light... see things that aren't even there...
EACH TIME IS THE SAME. I FIND MYSELF ALONE IN SOME AWFUL, LIGHTLESS SPACE. THERE ARE...THINGS THERE - VAST, TERRIBLE PRESENCES, HUNTING THROUGH THE DARKNESS FOR ME...
BUT THERE WERE OTHER LESSER PRESENCES THERE TOO...
Megaphonium Fanfare Remarkable sights and sounds from the ages
I THINK THEY WERE HUMAN. I — I THINK THEY WERE THE SERVANTS OF THESE THINGS...
I SEE.
YOU'RE AWARE, OF COURSE, THAT WE ARE BEING FOLLOWED?

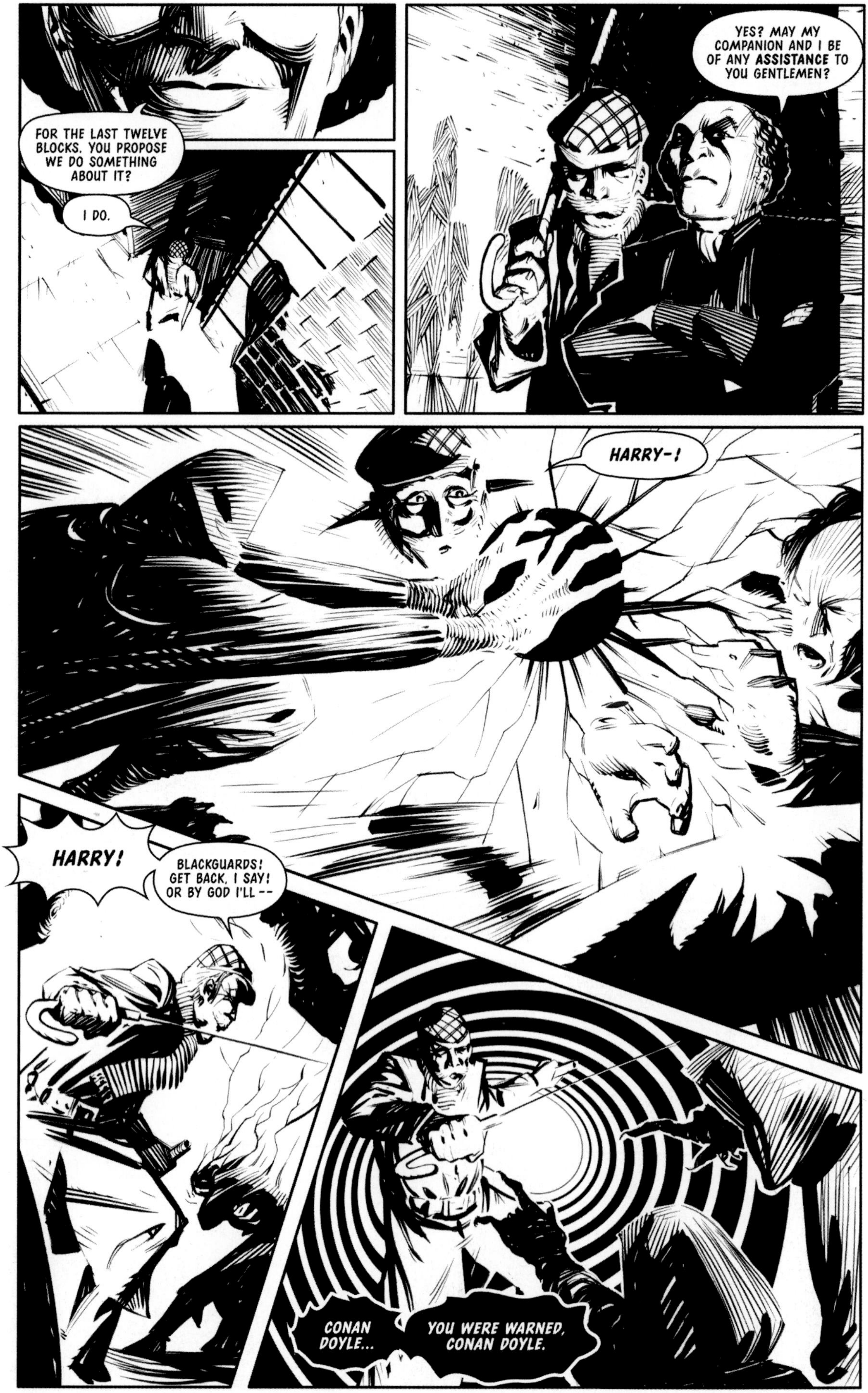
FOR THE LAST TWELVE BLOCKS. YOU PROPOSE WE DO SOMETHING ABOUT IT?
I DO.
YES? MAY MY COMPANION AND I BE OF ANY ASSISTANCE TO YOU GENTLEMEN?
HARRY-!
HARRY!
BLACKGUARDS! GET BACK, I SAY! OR BY GOD I'LL --
CONAN DOYLE...
YOU WERE WARNED, CONAN DOYLE.

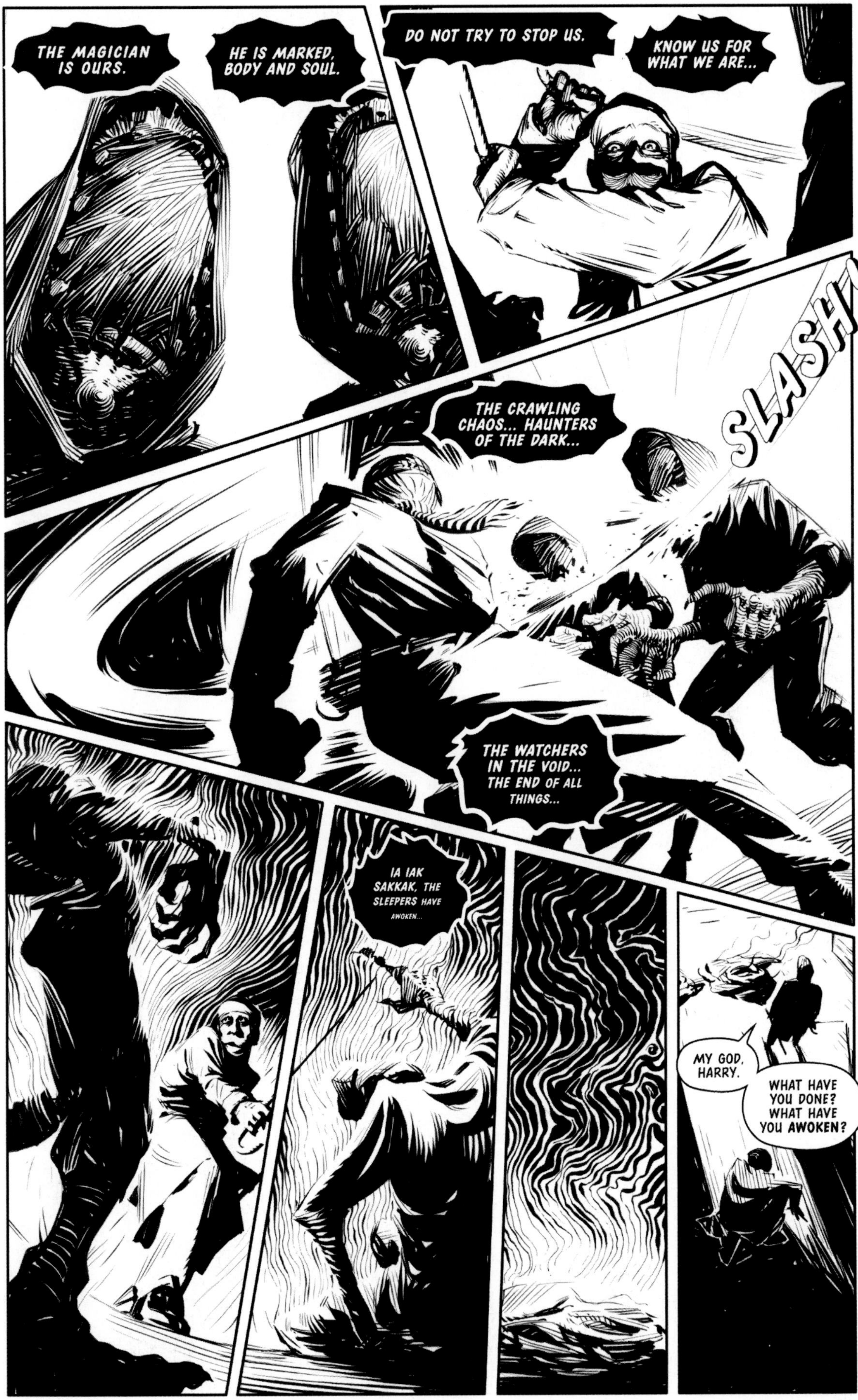
THE MAGICIAN IS OURS.
HE IS MARKED, BODY AND SOUL.
DO NOT TRY TO STOP US.
KNOW US FOR WHAT WE ARE...
SLASH!
THE CRAWLING CHAOS... HAUNTERS OF THE DARK...
THE WATCHERS IN THE VOID... THE END OF ALL THINGS...
IA IAK SAKKAK, THE SLEEPERS HAVE AWOKEN...
MY GOD, HARRY.
WHAT HAVE YOU DONE? WHAT HAVE YOU AWOKEN?

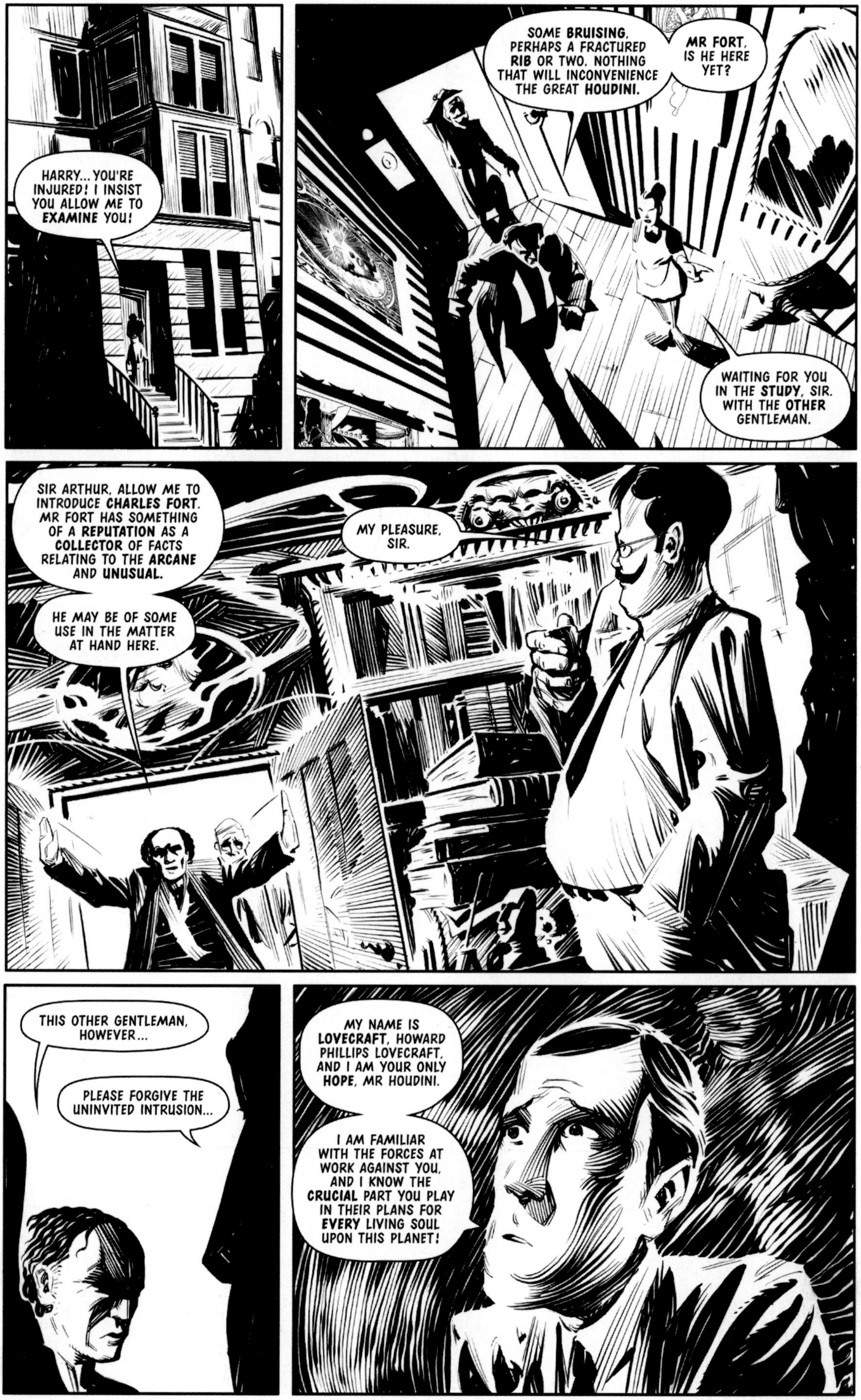
HARRY... YOU'RE INJURED! I INSIST YOU ALLOW ME TO EXAMINE YOU!
SOME BRUISING, PERHAPS A FRACTURED RIB OR TWO. NOTHING THAT WILL INCONVENIENCE THE GREAT HOUDINI.
MR FORT, IS HE HERE YET?
WAITING FOR YOU IN THE STUDY, SIR. WITH THE OTHER GENTLEMAN.
SIR ARTHUR, ALLOW ME TO INTRODUCE CHARLES FORT. MR FORT HAS SOMETHING OF A REPUTATION AS A COLLECTOR OF FACTS RELATING TO THE ARCANE AND UNUSUAL.
HE MAY BE OF SOME USE IN THE MATTER AT HAND HERE.
MY PLEASURE, SIR.
THIS OTHER GENTLEMAN, HOWEVER...
PLEASE FORGIVE THE UNINVITED INTRUSION...
MY NAME IS LOVECRAFT, HOWARD PHILLIPS LOVECRAFT, AND I AM YOUR ONLY HOPE, MR HOUDINI.
I AM FAMILIAR WITH THE FORCES AT WORK AGAINST YOU, AND I KNOW THE CRUCIAL PART YOU PLAY IN THEIR PLANS FOR EVERY LIVING SOUL UPON THIS PLANET!

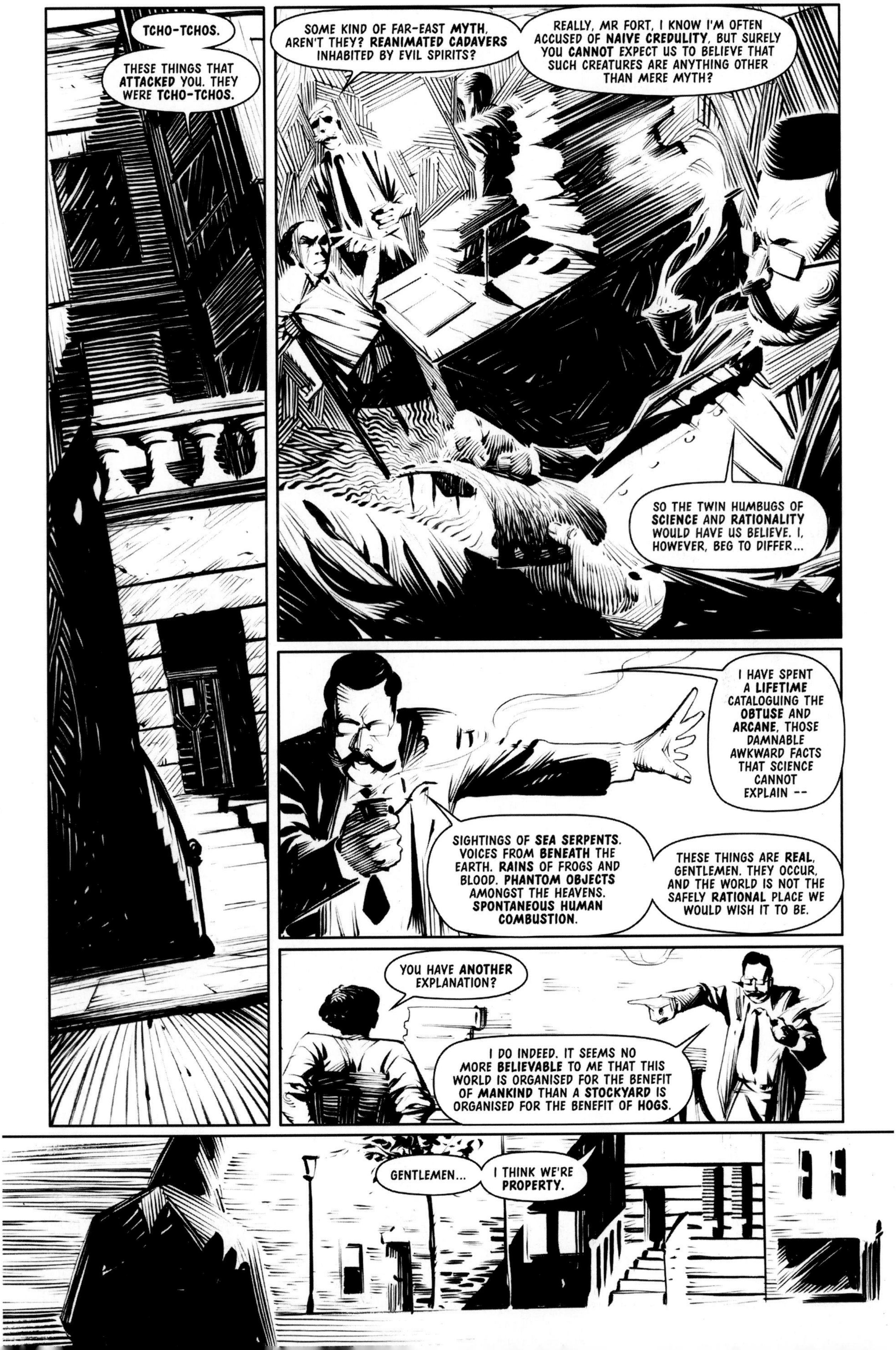
TCHO-TCHOS.
THESE THINGS THAT ATTACKED YOU. THEY WERE TCHO-TCHOS.
SOME KIND OF FAR-EAST MYTH, AREN'T THEY? REANIMATED CADAVERS INHABITED BY EVIL SPIRITS?
REALLY, MR FORT, I KNOW I'M OFTEN ACCUSED OF NAIVE CREDULITY, BUT SURELY YOU CANNOT EXPECT US TO BELIEVE THAT SUCH CREATURES ARE ANYTHING OTHER THAN MERE MYTH?
SO THE TWIN HUMBUGS OF SCIENCE AND RATIONALITY WOULD HAVE US BELIEVE. I, HOWEVER, BEG TO DIFFER...
I HAVE SPENT A LIFETIME CATALOGUING THE OBTUSE AND ARCANE, THOSE DAMNABLE AWKWARD FACTS THAT SCIENCE CANNOT EXPLAIN --
SIGHTINGS OF SEA SERPENTS. VOICES FROM BENEATH THE EARTH. RAINS OF FROGS AND BLOOD. PHANTOM OBJECTS AMONGST THE HEAVENS. SPONTANEOUS HUMAN COMBUSTION.
THESE THINGS ARE REAL, GENTLEMEN. THEY OCCUR, AND THE WORLD IS NOT THE SAFELY RATIONAL PLACE WE WOULD WISH IT TO BE.
YOU HAVE ANOTHER EXPLANATION?
I DO INDEED. IT SEEMS NO MORE BELIEVABLE TO ME THAT THIS WORLD IS ORGANISED FOR THE BENEFIT OF MANKIND THAN A STOCKYARD IS ORGANISED FOR THE BENEFIT OF HOGS.
GENTLEMEN...
I THINK WE'RE PROPERTY.

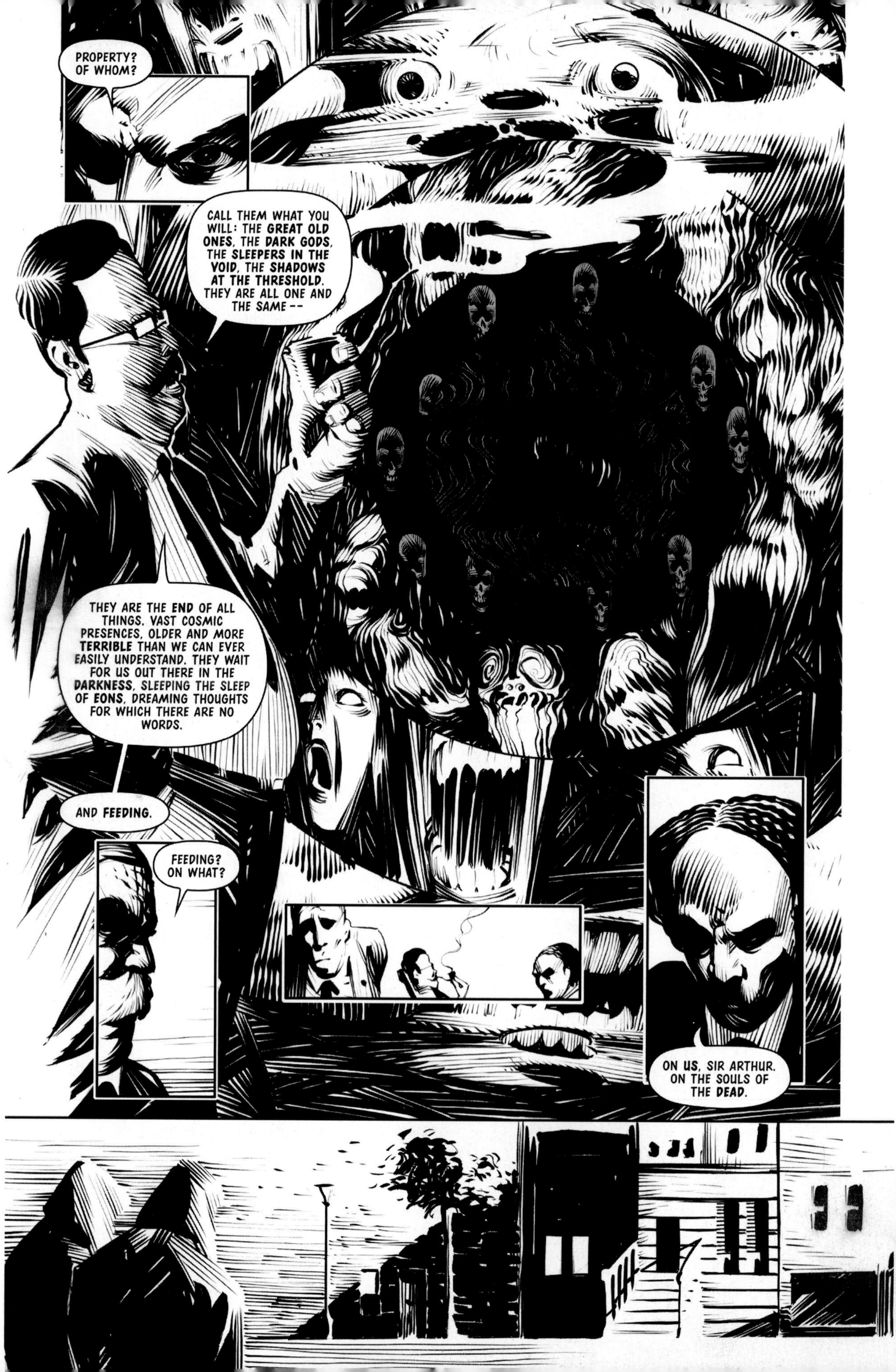
PROPERTY? OF WHOM?
CALL THEM WHAT YOU WILL: THE GREAT OLD ONES, THE DARK GODS, THE SLEEPERS IN THE VOID, THE SHADOWS AT THE THRESHOLD. THEY ARE ALL ONE AND THE SAME --
THEY ARE THE END OF ALL THINGS. VAST COSMIC PRESENCES, OLDER AND MORE TERRIBLE THAN WE CAN EVER EASILY UNDERSTAND. THEY WAIT FOR US OUT THERE IN THE DARKNESS, SLEEPING THE SLEEP OF EONS, DREAMING THOUGHTS FOR WHICH THERE ARE NO WORDS.
AND FEEDING.
FEEDING? ON WHAT?
ON US, SIR ARTHUR. ON THE SOULS OF THE DEAD.

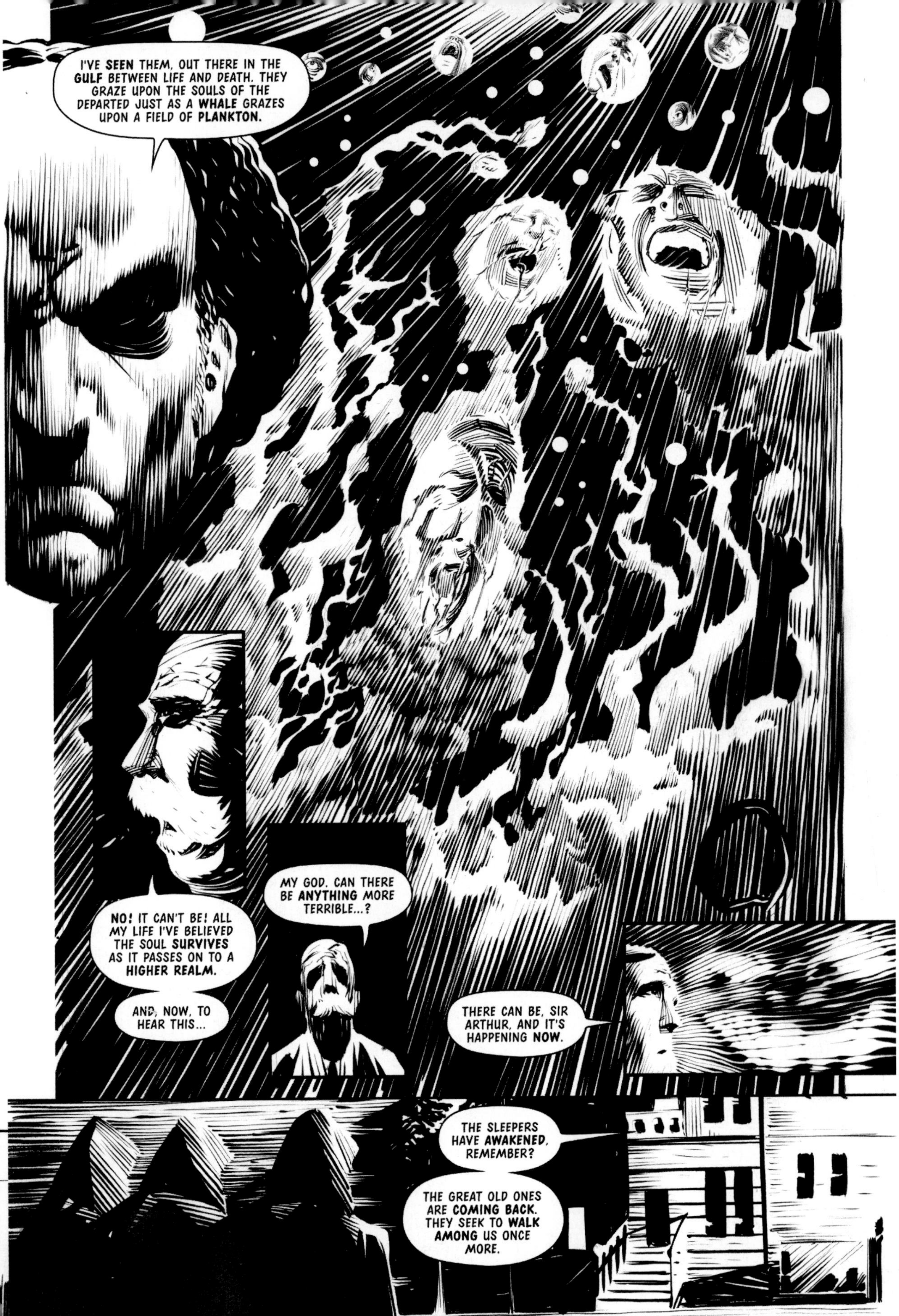
I'VE SEEN THEM, OUT THERE IN THE GULF BETWEEN LIFE AND DEATH. THEY GRAZE UPON THE SOULS OF THE DEPARTED JUST AS A WHALE GRAZES UPON A FIELD OF PLANKTON.
NO! IT CAN'T BE! ALL MY LIFE I'VE BELIEVED THE SOUL SURVIVES AS IT PASSES ON TO A HIGHER REALM.
AND, NOW, TO HEAR THIS...
MY GOD. CAN THERE BE ANYTHING MORE TERRIBLE...?
THERE CAN BE, SIR ARTHUR, AND IT'S HAPPENING NOW.
THE SLEEPERS HAVE AWAKENED, REMEMBER?
THE GREAT OLD ONES ARE COMING BACK. THEY SEEK TO WALK AMONG US ONCE MORE.

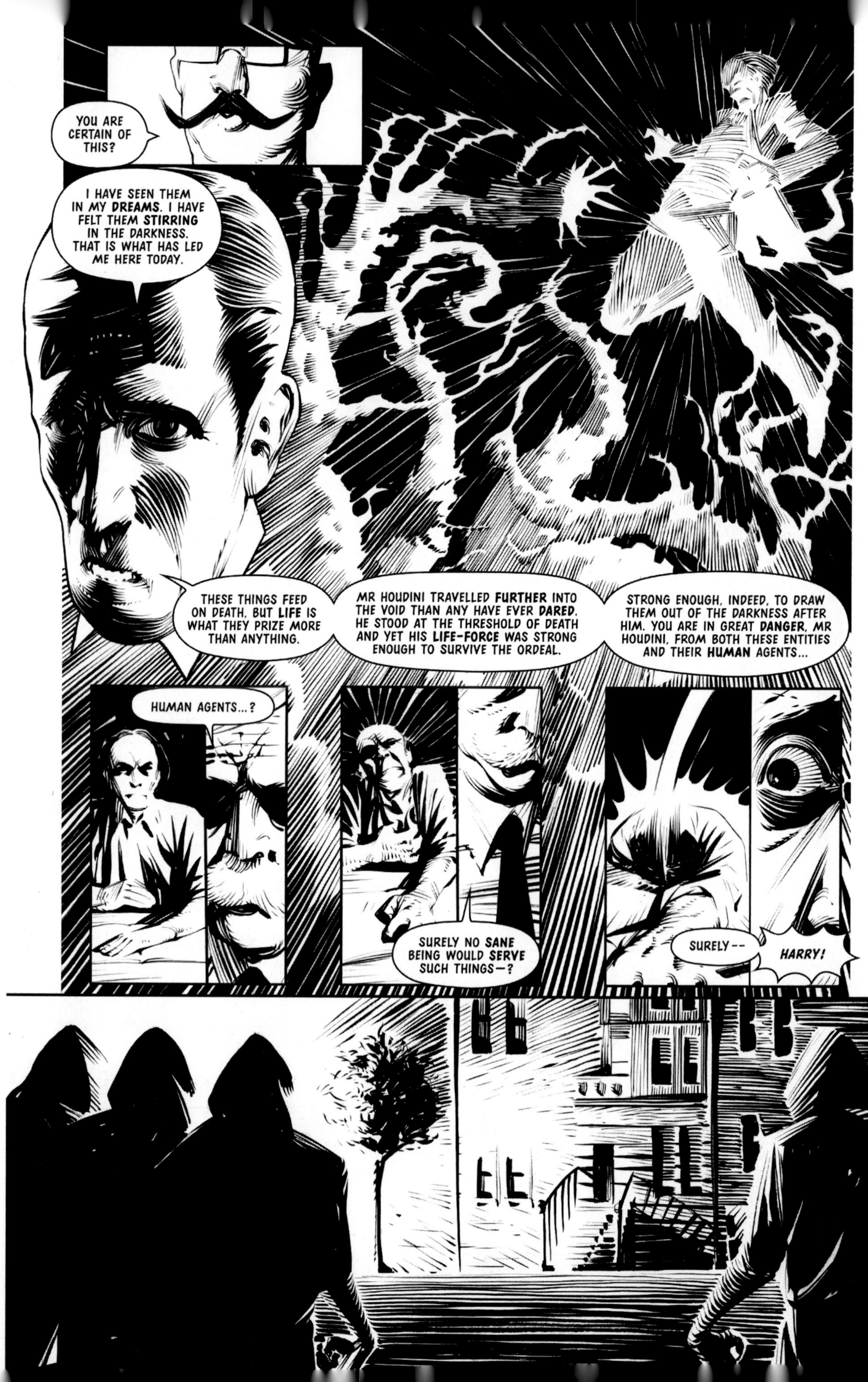
YOU ARE CERTAIN OF THIS?
I HAVE SEEN THEM IN MY DREAMS. I HAVE FELT THEM STIRRING IN THE DARKNESS. THAT IS WHAT HAS LED ME HERE TODAY.
THESE THINGS FEED ON DEATH, BUT LIFE IS WHAT THEY PRIZE MORE THAN ANYTHING.
MR HOUDINI TRAVELLED FURTHER INTO THE VOID THAN ANY HAVE EVER DARED. HE STOOD AT THE THRESHOLD OF DEATH AND YET HIS LIFE-FORCE WAS STRONG ENOUGH TO SURVIVE THE ORDEAL.
STRONG ENOUGH, INDEED, TO DRAW THEM OUT OF THE DARKNESS AFTER HIM. YOU ARE IN GREAT DANGER, MR HOUDINI, FROM BOTH THESE ENTITIES AND THEIR HUMAN AGENTS...
HUMAN AGENTS...?
SURELY NO SANE BEING WOULD SERVE SUCH THINGS—?
SURELY--
HARRY!

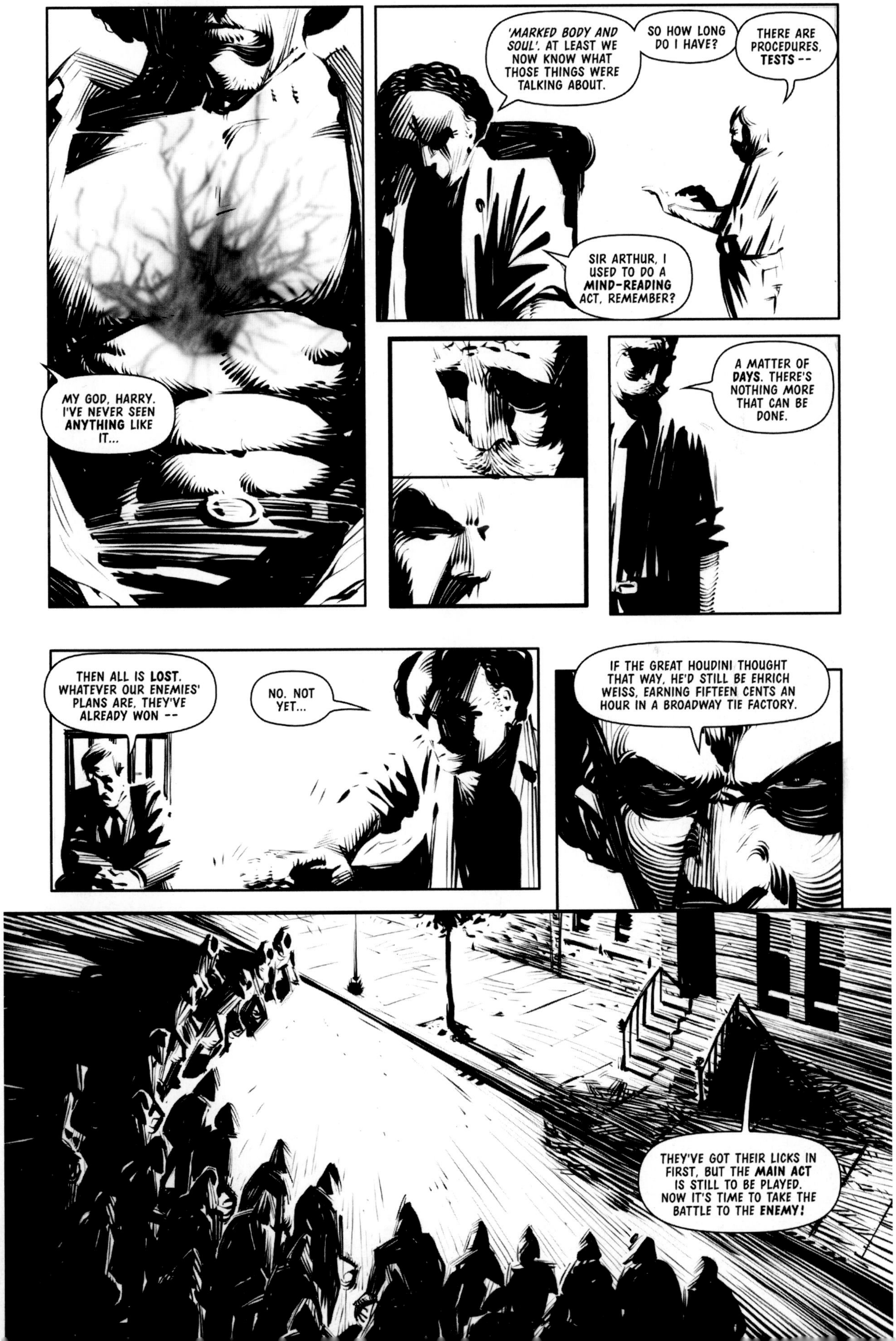

MY GOD, HARRY. I'VE NEVER SEEN ANYTHING LIKE IT...
'MARKED BODY AND SOUL'. AT LEAST WE NOW KNOW WHAT THOSE THINGS WERE TALKING ABOUT.
SO HOW LONG DO I HAVE?
THERE ARE PROCEDURES, TESTS --
SIR ARTHUR, I USED TO DO A MIND-READING ACT, REMEMBER?
A MATTER OF DAYS. THERE'S NOTHING MORE THAT CAN BE DONE.
THEN ALL IS LOST. WHATEVER OUR ENEMIES' PLANS ARE, THEY'VE ALREADY WON --
NO. NOT YET...
IF THE GREAT HOUDINI THOUGHT THAT WAY, HE'D STILL BE EHRICH WEISS, EARNING FIFTEEN CENTS AN HOUR IN A BROADWAY TIE FACTORY.
THEY'VE GOT THEIR LICKS IN FIRST, BUT THE MAIN ACT IS STILL TO BE PLAYED. NOW IT'S TIME TO TAKE THE BATTLE TO THE ENEMY!

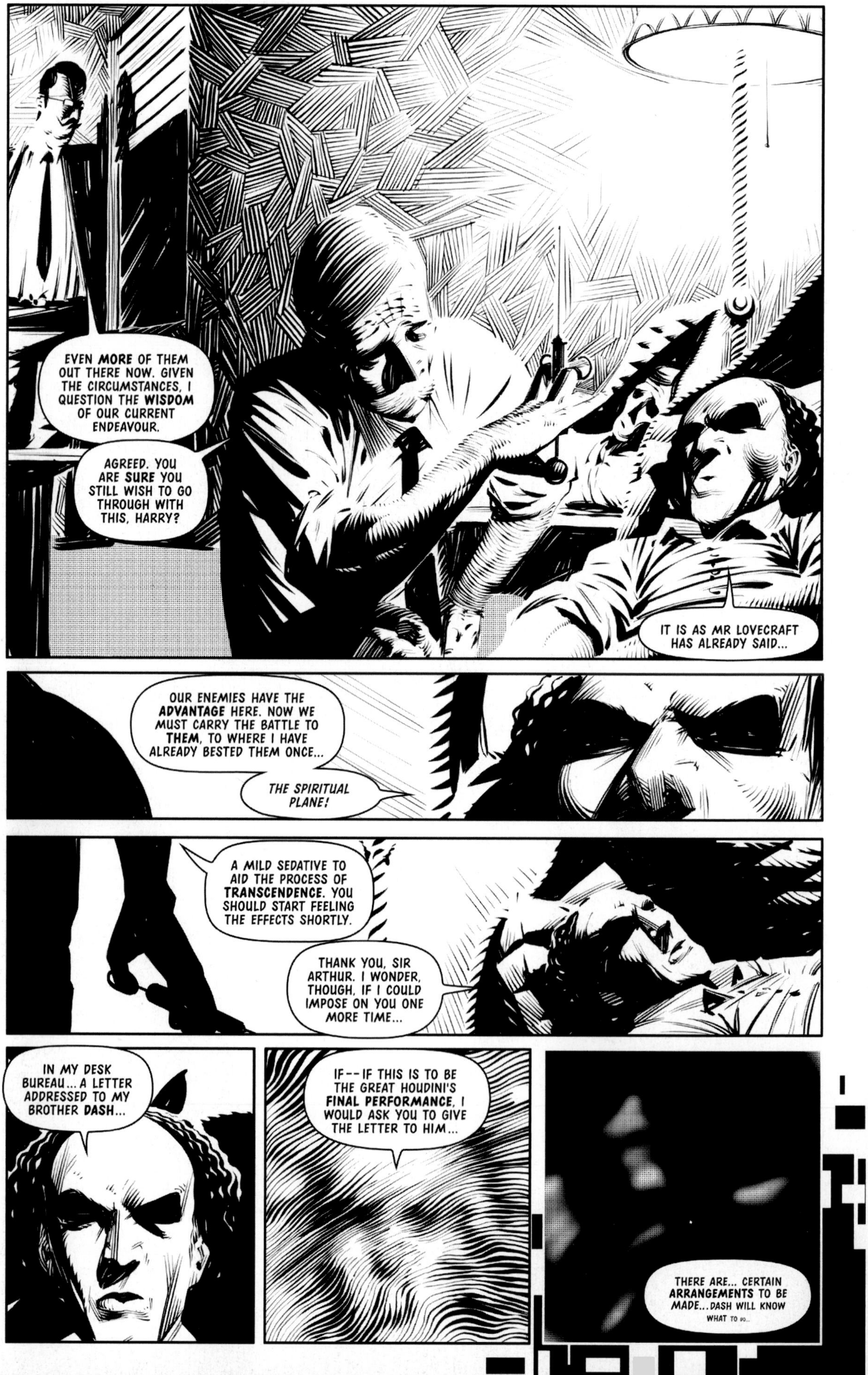
EVEN MORE OF THEM OUT THERE NOW. GIVEN THE CIRCUMSTANCES, I QUESTION THE WISDOM OF OUR CURRENT ENDEAVOUR.
AGREED. YOU ARE SURE YOU STILL WISH TO GO THROUGH WITH THIS, HARRY?
IT IS AS MR LOVECRAFT HAS ALREADY SAID...
OUR ENEMIES HAVE THE ADVANTAGE HERE. NOW WE MUST CARRY THE BATTLE TO THEM, TO WHERE I HAVE ALREADY BESTED THEM ONCE...
THE SPIRITUAL PLANE!
A MILD SEDATIVE TO AID THE PROCESS OF TRANSCENDENCE. YOU SHOULD START FEELING THE EFFECTS SHORTLY.
THANK YOU, SIR ARTHUR. I WONDER, THOUGH, IF I COULD IMPOSE ON YOU ONE MORE TIME...
IN MY DESK BUREAU... A LETTER ADDRESSED TO MY BROTHER DASH...
IF--IF THIS IS TO BE THE GREAT HOUDINI'S FINAL PERFORMANCE, I WOULD ASK YOU TO GIVE THE LETTER TO HIM...
THERE ARE... CERTAIN ARRANGEMENTS TO BE MADE...DASH WILL KNOW WHAT TO DO...

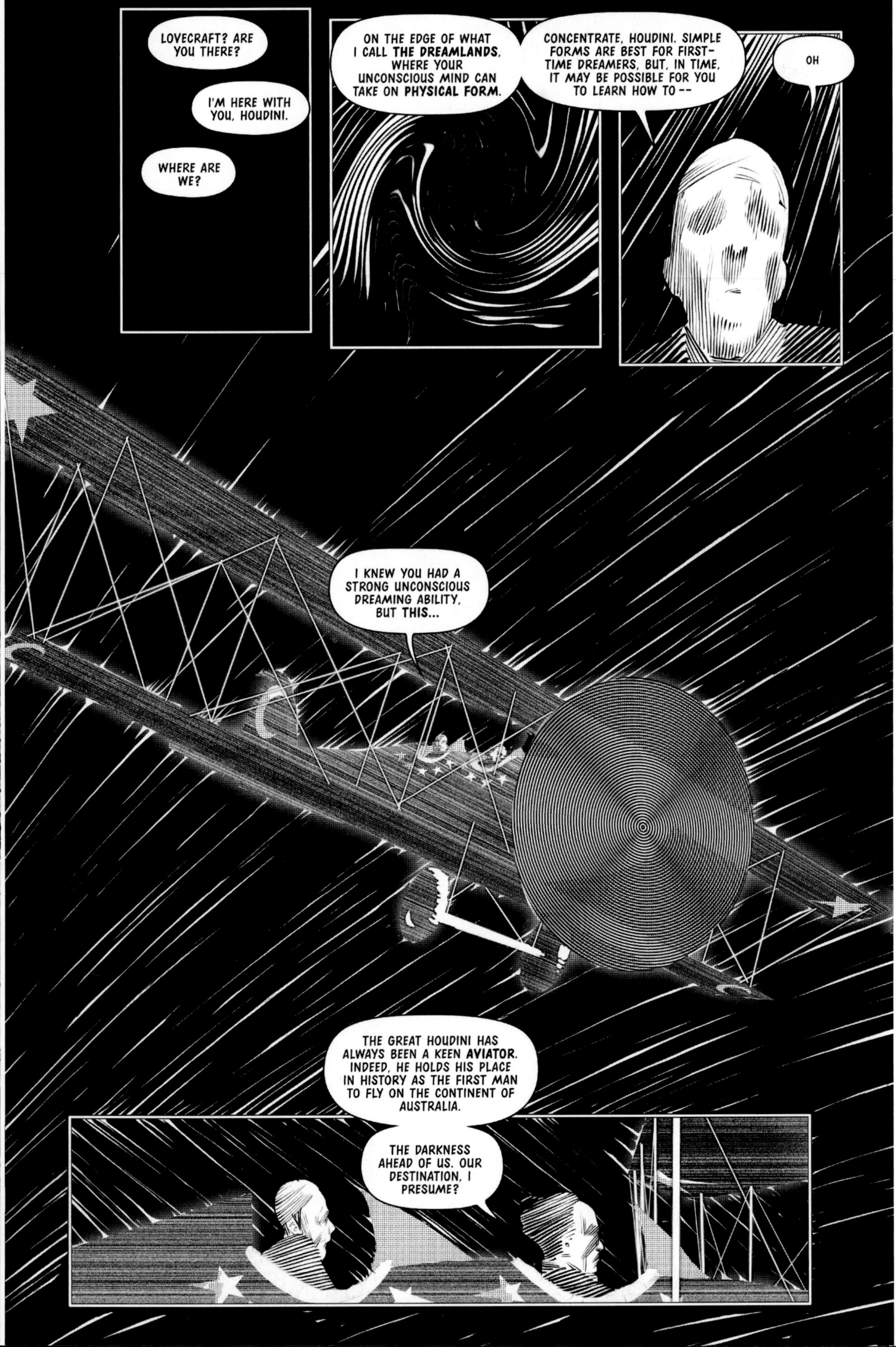

LOVECRAFT? ARE YOU THERE?
I'M HERE WITH YOU, HOUDINI.
WHERE ARE WE?
ON THE EDGE OF WHAT I CALL **THE DREAMLANDS**, WHERE YOUR UNCONSCIOUS MIND CAN TAKE ON **PHYSICAL FORM**.
CONCENTRATE, HOUDINI. SIMPLE FORMS ARE BEST FOR FIRST-TIME DREAMERS, BUT, IN TIME, IT MAY BE POSSIBLE FOR YOU TO LEARN HOW TO --
OH
I KNEW YOU HAD A STRONG UNCONSCIOUS DREAMING ABILITY, BUT **THIS**...
THE GREAT HOUDINI HAS ALWAYS BEEN A KEEN **AVIATOR**. INDEED, HE HOLDS HIS PLACE IN HISTORY AS THE FIRST MAN TO FLY ON THE CONTINENT OF AUSTRALIA.
THE DARKNESS AHEAD OF US. OUR DESTINATION, I PRESUME?

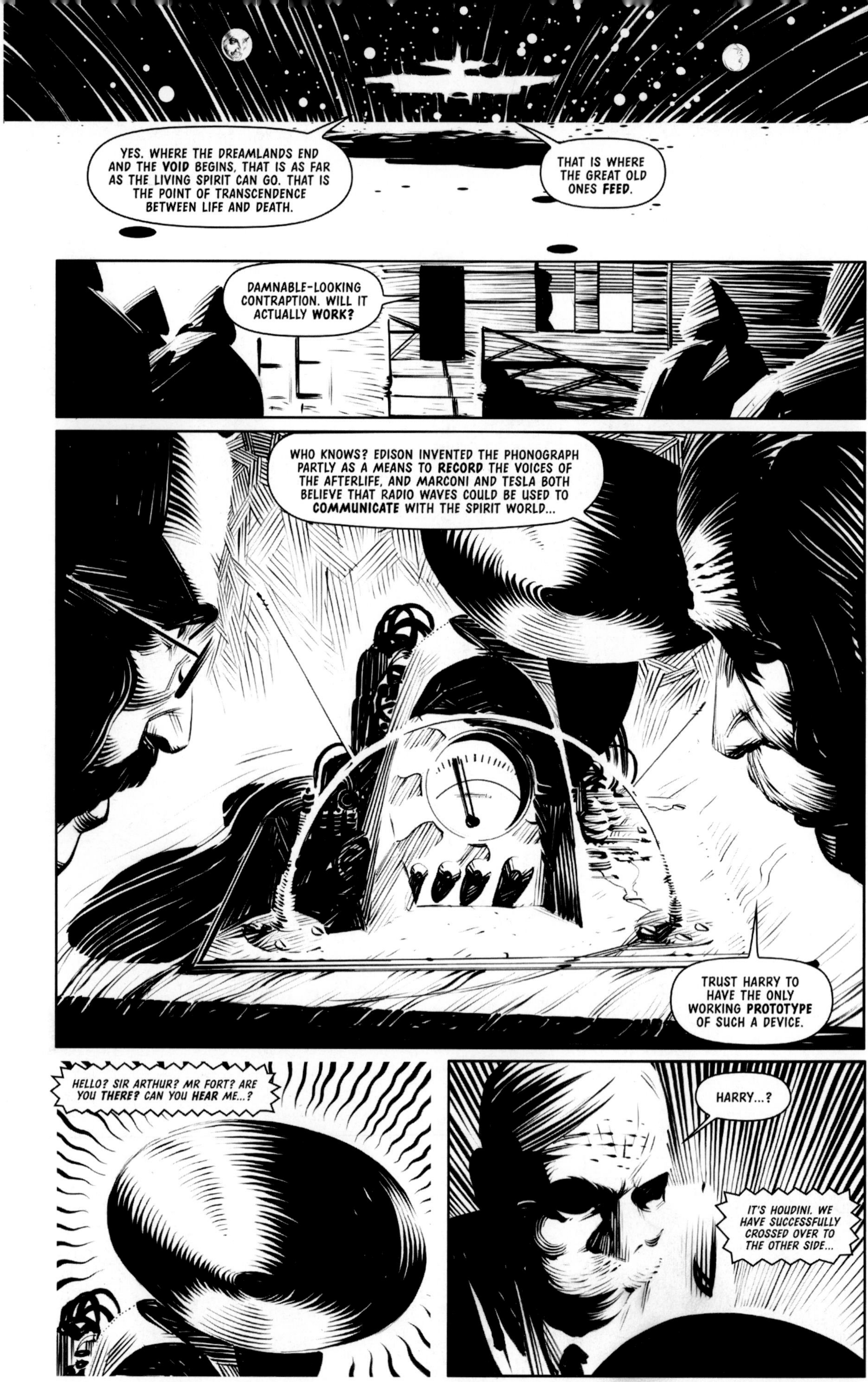
YES. WHERE THE DREAMLANDS END AND THE VOID BEGINS, THAT IS AS FAR AS THE LIVING SPIRIT CAN GO. THAT IS THE POINT OF TRANSCENDENCE BETWEEN LIFE AND DEATH.
THAT IS WHERE THE GREAT OLD ONES FEED.
DAMNABLE-LOOKING CONTRAPTION. WILL IT ACTUALLY WORK?
WHO KNOWS? EDISON INVENTED THE PHONOGRAPH PARTLY AS A MEANS TO RECORD THE VOICES OF THE AFTERLIFE, AND MARCONI AND TESLA BOTH BELIEVE THAT RADIO WAVES COULD BE USED TO COMMUNICATE WITH THE SPIRIT WORLD...
TRUST HARRY TO HAVE THE ONLY WORKING PROTOTYPE OF SUCH A DEVICE.
HELLO? SIR ARTHUR? MR FORT? ARE YOU THERE? CAN YOU HEAR ME...?
HARRY...?
IT'S HOUDINI. WE HAVE SUCCESSFULLY CROSSED OVER TO THE OTHER SIDE...

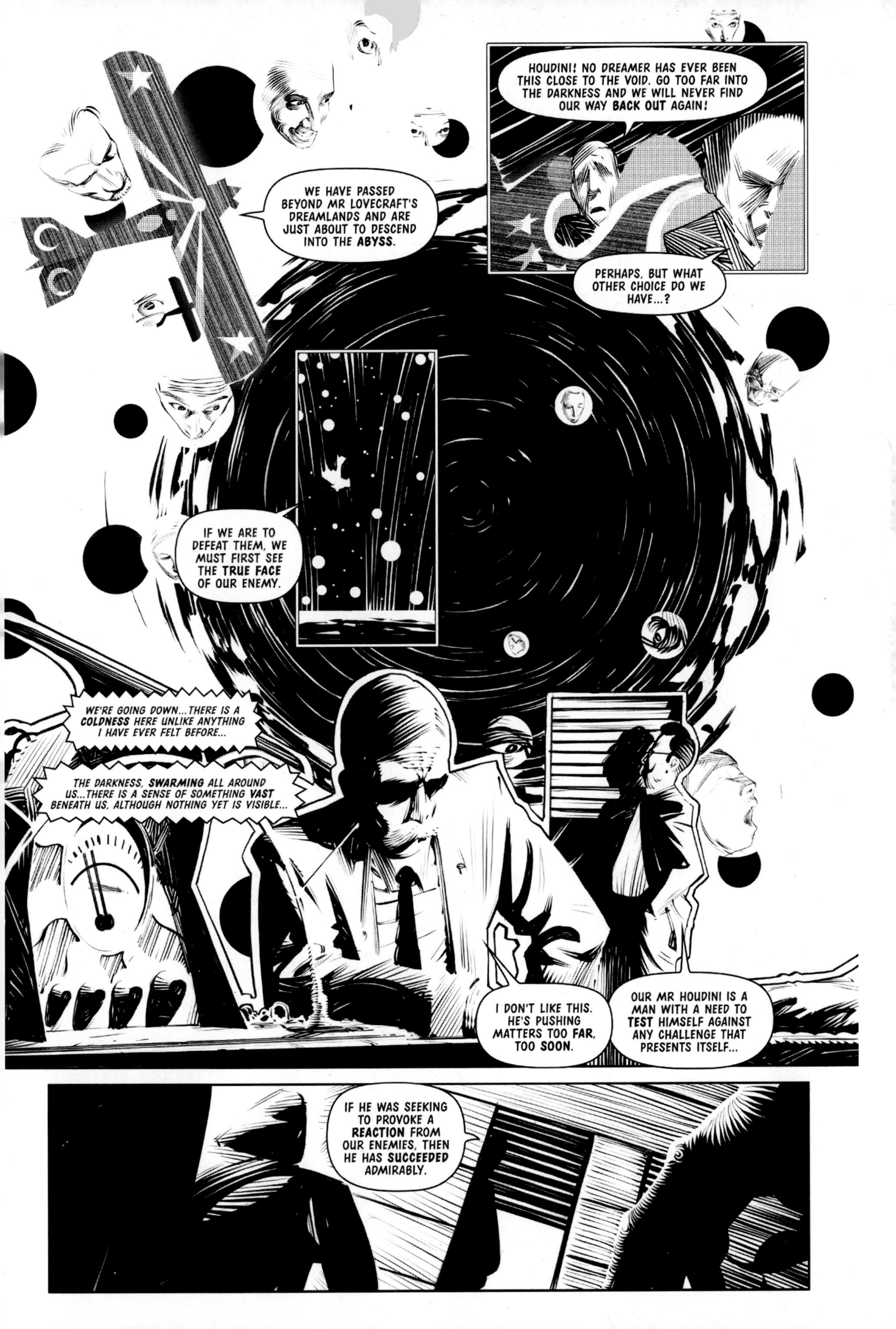

WE HAVE PASSED BEYOND MR LOVECRAFT'S DREAMLANDS AND ARE JUST ABOUT TO DESCEND INTO THE ABYSS.
HOUDINI! NO DREAMER HAS EVER BEEN THIS CLOSE TO THE VOID. GO TOO FAR INTO THE DARKNESS AND WE WILL NEVER FIND OUR WAY BACK OUT AGAIN!
PERHAPS, BUT WHAT OTHER CHOICE DO WE HAVE...?
IF WE ARE TO DEFEAT THEM, WE MUST FIRST SEE THE TRUE FACE OF OUR ENEMY.
WE'RE GOING DOWN... THERE IS A COLDNESS HERE UNLIKE ANYTHING I HAVE EVER FELT BEFORE...
THE DARKNESS, SWARMING ALL AROUND US... THERE IS A SENSE OF SOMETHING VAST BENEATH US, ALTHOUGH NOTHING YET IS VISIBLE...
I DON'T LIKE THIS. HE'S PUSHING MATTERS TOO FAR, TOO SOON.
OUR MR HOUDINI IS A MAN WITH A NEED TO TEST HIMSELF AGAINST ANY CHALLENGE THAT PRESENTS ITSELF...
IF HE WAS SEEKING TO PROVOKE A REACTION FROM OUR ENEMIES, THEN HE HAS SUCCEEDED ADMIRABLY.

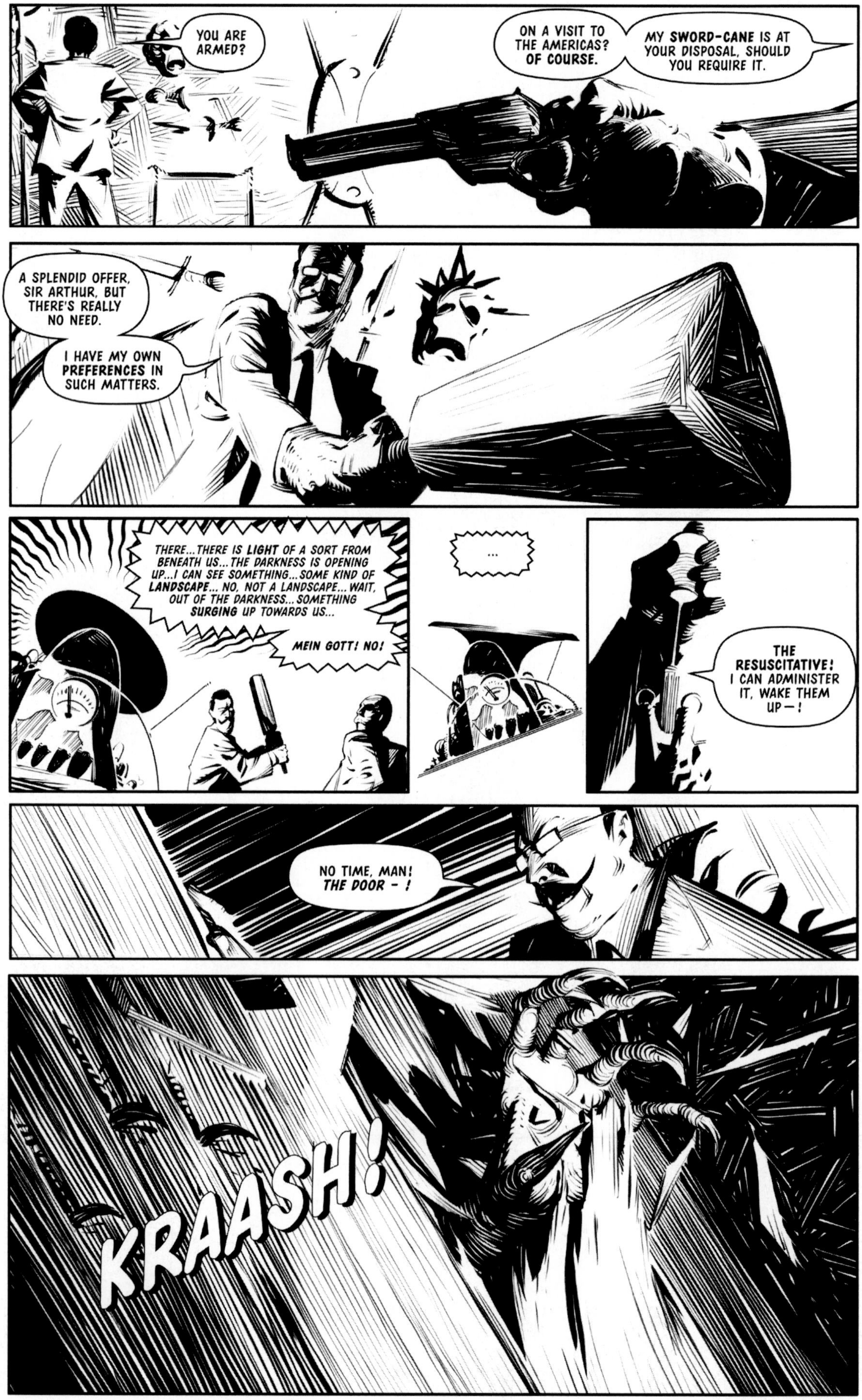
YOU ARE ARMED?
ON A VISIT TO THE AMERICAS? OF COURSE.
MY SWORD-CANE IS AT YOUR DISPOSAL, SHOULD YOU REQUIRE IT.
A SPLENDID OFFER, SIR ARTHUR, BUT THERE'S REALLY NO NEED.
I HAVE MY OWN PREFERENCES IN SUCH MATTERS.
THERE...THERE IS LIGHT OF A SORT FROM BENEATH US...THE DARKNESS IS OPENING UP...I CAN SEE SOMETHING...SOME KIND OF LANDSCAPE... NO, NOT A LANDSCAPE... WAIT, OUT OF THE DARKNESS...SOMETHING SURGING UP TOWARDS US...
MEIN GOTT! NO!
...
THE RESUSCITATIVE! I CAN ADMINISTER IT, WAKE THEM UP—!
NO TIME, MAN! THE DOOR - !
KRAASH!

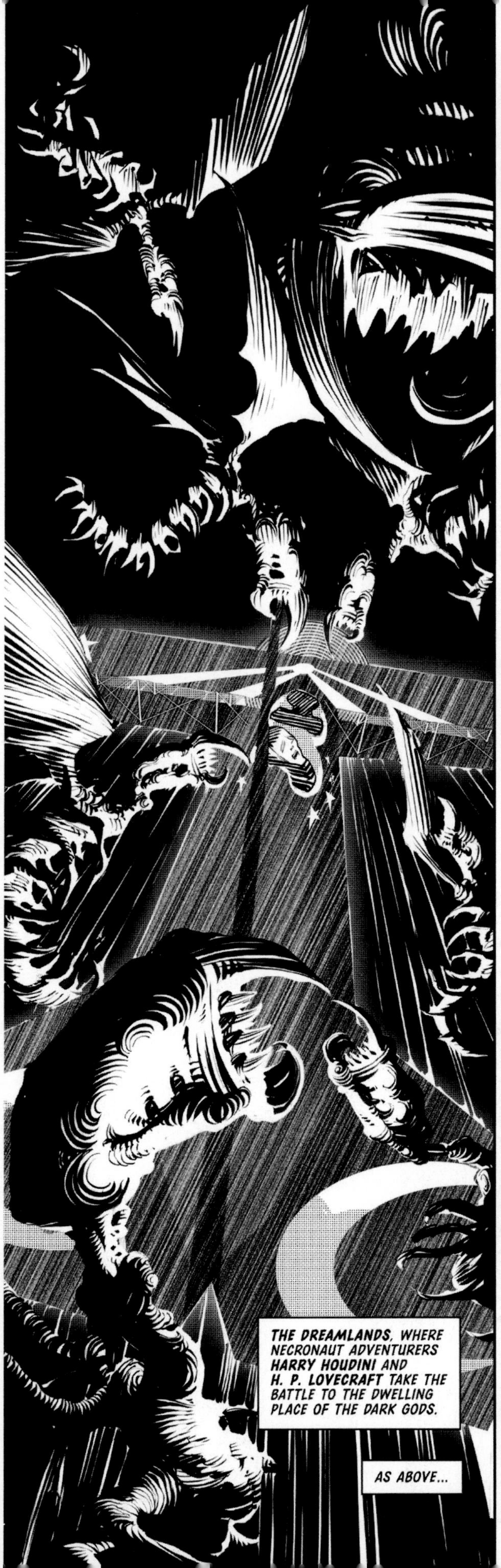
THE DREAMLANDS, WHERE NECRONAUT ADVENTURERS HARRY HOUDINI AND H. P. LOVECRAFT TAKE THE BATTLE TO THE DWELLING PLACE OF THE DARK GODS.
AS ABOVE...
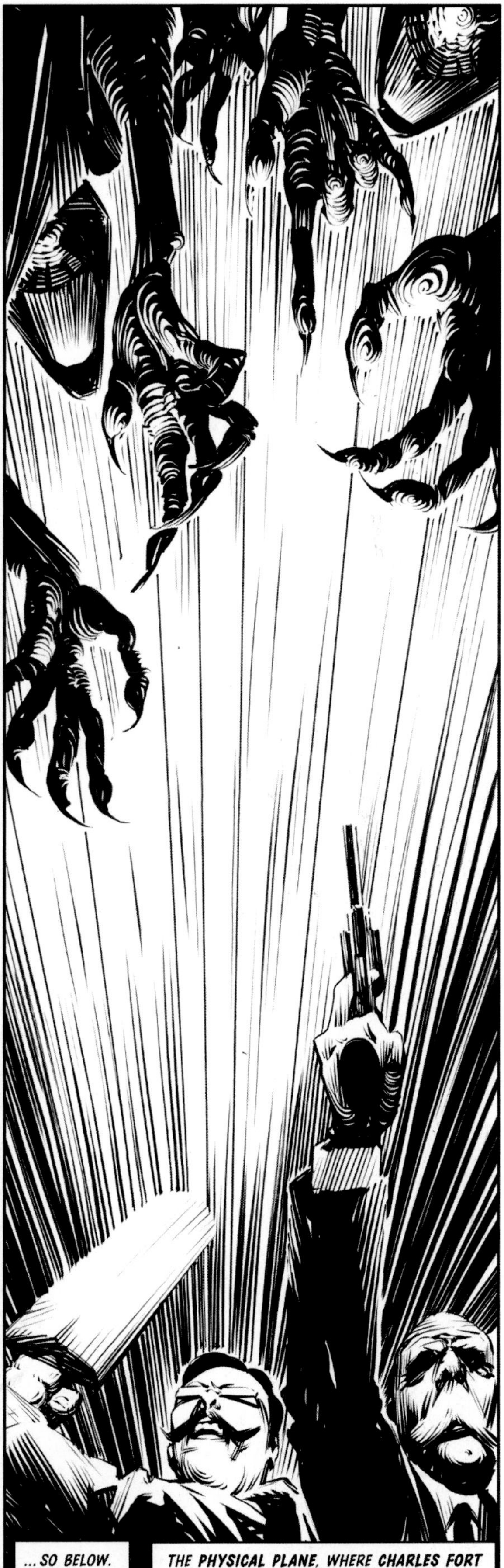
...SO BELOW.
THE PHYSICAL PLANE, WHERE CHARLES FORT AND SIR ARTHUR CONAN DOYLE FACE THEIR ENEMY'S EARTHLY SERVANTS.

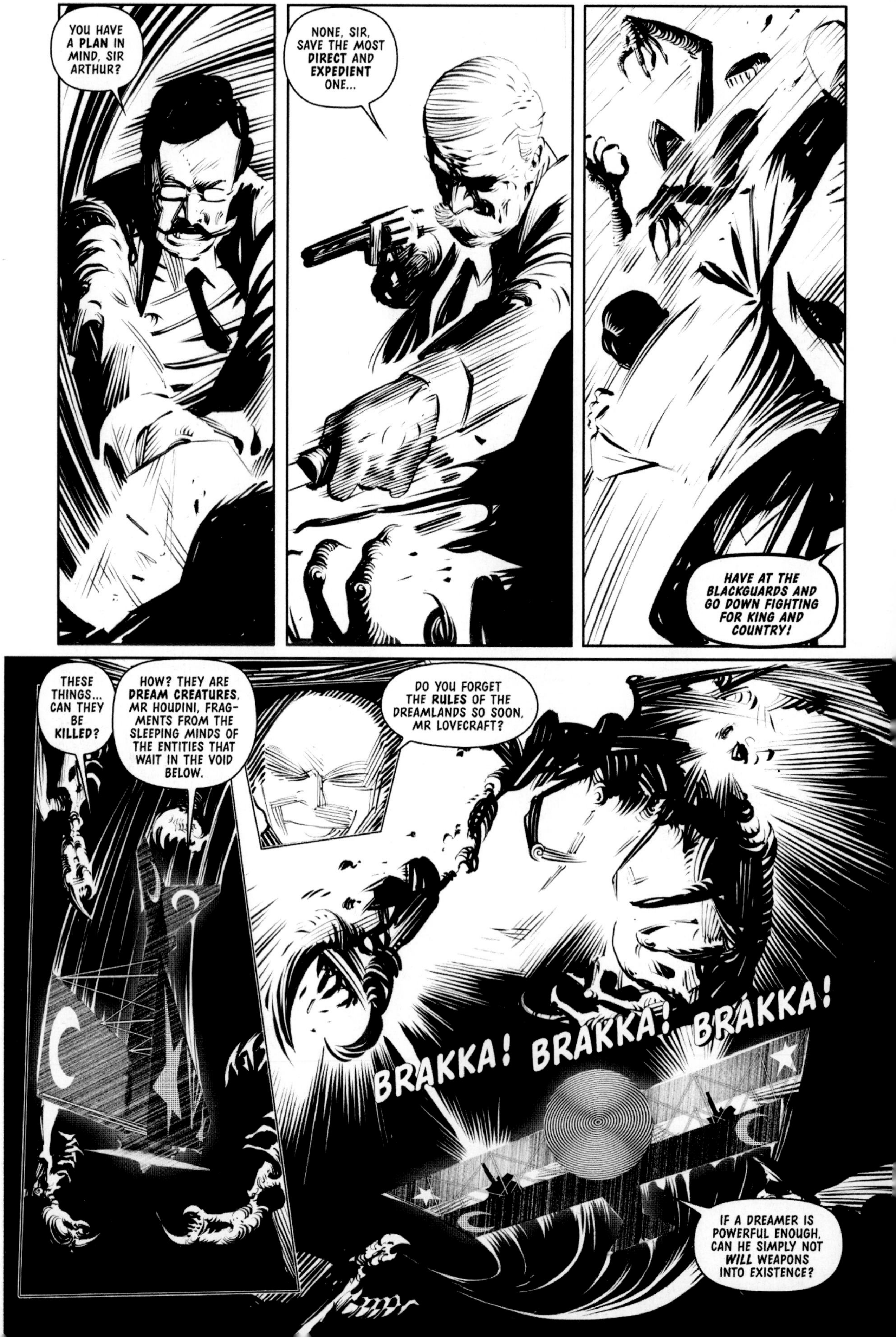

YOU HAVE A PLAN IN MIND, SIR ARTHUR?
NONE, SIR, SAVE THE MOST DIRECT AND EXPEDIENT ONE...
HAVE AT THE BLACKGUARDS AND GO DOWN FIGHTING FOR KING AND COUNTRY!
THESE THINGS... CAN THEY BE KILLED?
HOW? THEY ARE DREAM CREATURES, MR HOUDINI, FRAGMENTS FROM THE SLEEPING MINDS OF THE ENTITIES THAT WAIT IN THE VOID BELOW.
DO YOU FORGET THE RULES OF THE DREAMLANDS SO SOON, MR LOVECRAFT?
BRAKKA! BRAKKA! BRAKKA!
IF A DREAMER IS POWERFUL ENOUGH, CAN HE SIMPLY NOT WILL WEAPONS INTO EXISTENCE?

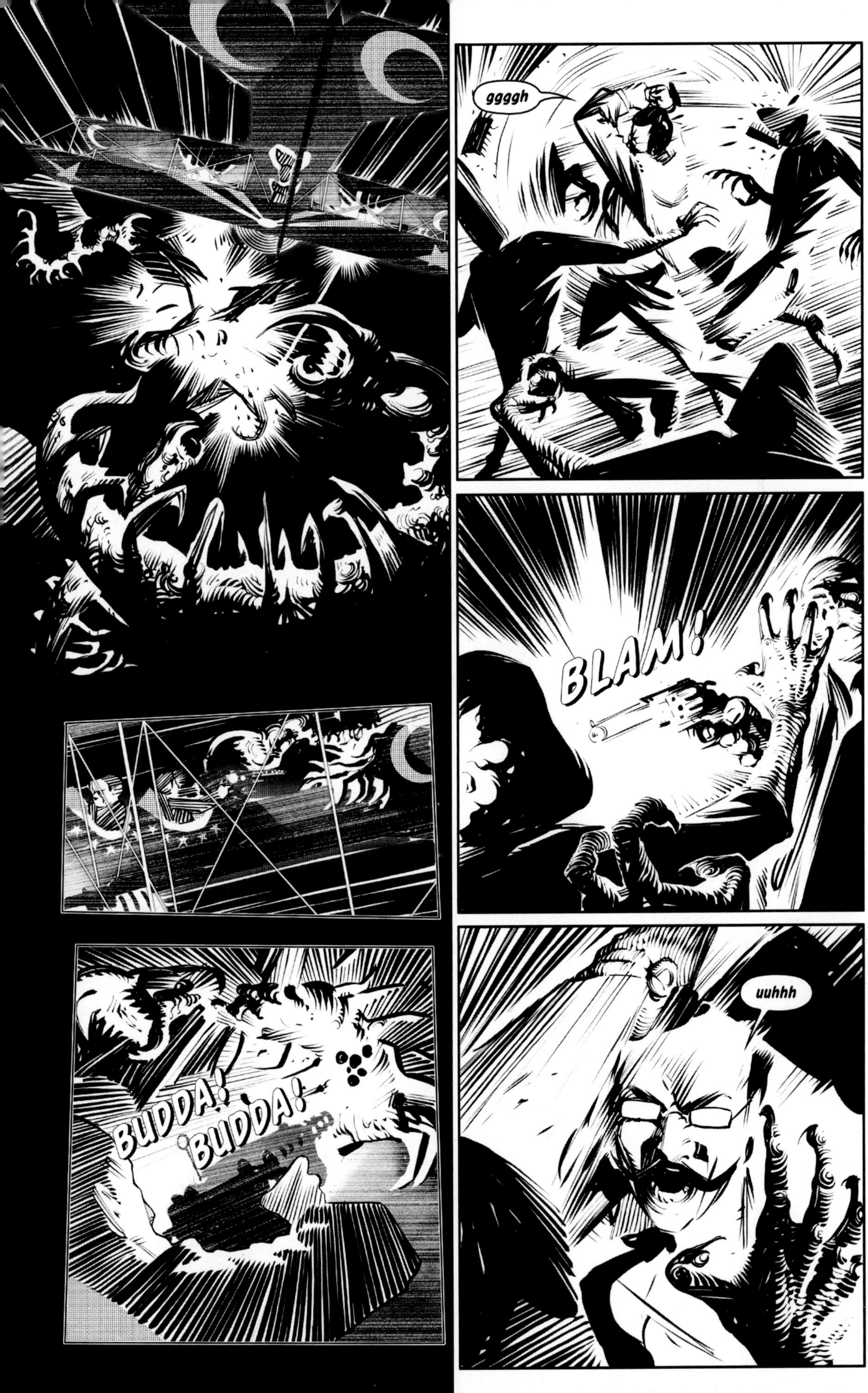
BUDDA! BUDDA!
gggh
BLAM!
uuhhh

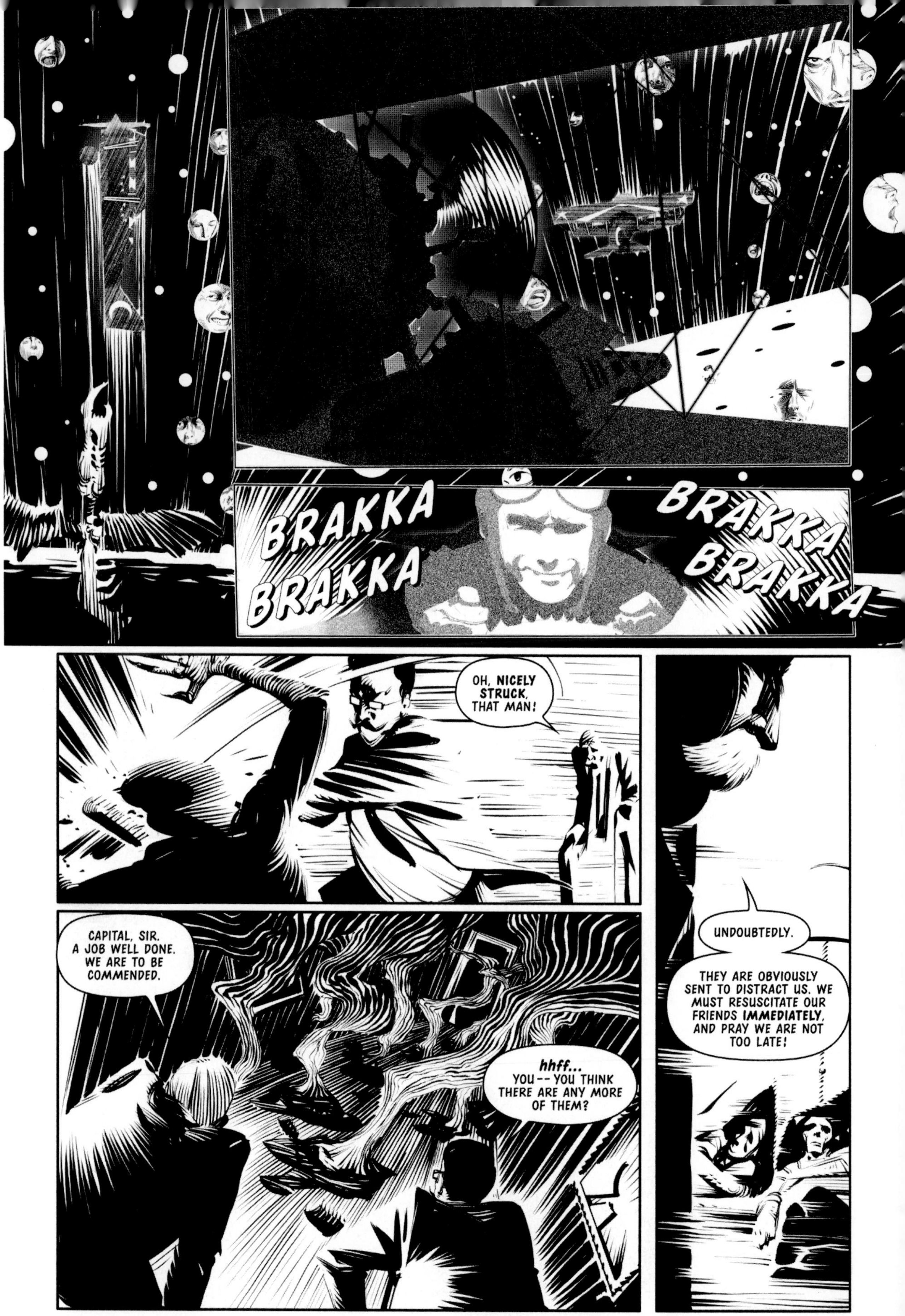
BRAKKA BRAKKA
BRAKKA BRAKKA
OH, NICELY STRUCK, THAT MAN!
CAPITAL, SIR. A JOB WELL DONE. WE ARE TO BE COMMENDED.
hhff... YOU-- YOU THINK THERE ARE ANY MORE OF THEM?
UNDOUBTEDLY.
THEY ARE OBVIOUSLY SENT TO DISTRACT US. WE MUST RESUSCITATE OUR FRIENDS IMMEDIATELY, AND PRAY WE ARE NOT TOO LATE!

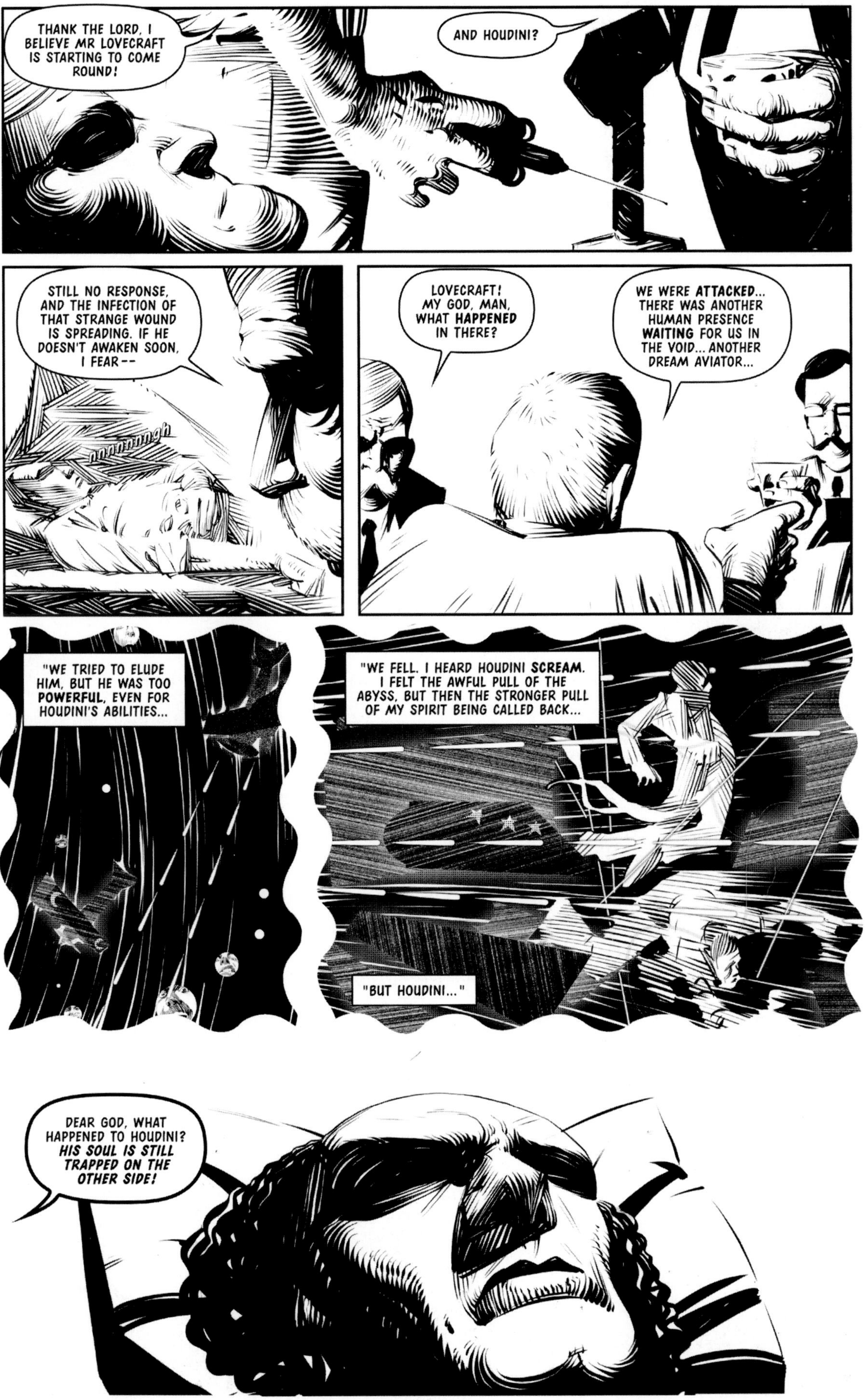
THANK THE LORD, I BELIEVE MR LOVECRAFT IS STARTING TO COME ROUND!
AND HOUDINI?
STILL NO RESPONSE, AND THE INFECTION OF THAT STRANGE WOUND IS SPREADING. IF HE DOESN'T AWAKEN SOON, I FEAR--
nnnnnnnngh
LOVECRAFT! MY GOD, MAN, WHAT **HAPPENED** IN THERE?
WE WERE **ATTACKED**... THERE WAS ANOTHER HUMAN PRESENCE **WAITING** FOR US IN THE VOID... ANOTHER DREAM AVIATOR...
"WE TRIED TO ELUDE HIM, BUT HE WAS TOO **POWERFUL**, EVEN FOR HOUDINI'S ABILITIES...
"WE FELL. I HEARD HOUDINI **SCREAM**. I FELT THE AWFUL PULL OF THE ABYSS, BUT THEN THE STRONGER PULL OF MY SPIRIT BEING CALLED BACK...
"BUT HOUDINI..."
DEAR GOD, WHAT HAPPENED TO HOUDINI? ***HIS SOUL IS STILL TRAPPED ON THE OTHER SIDE!***

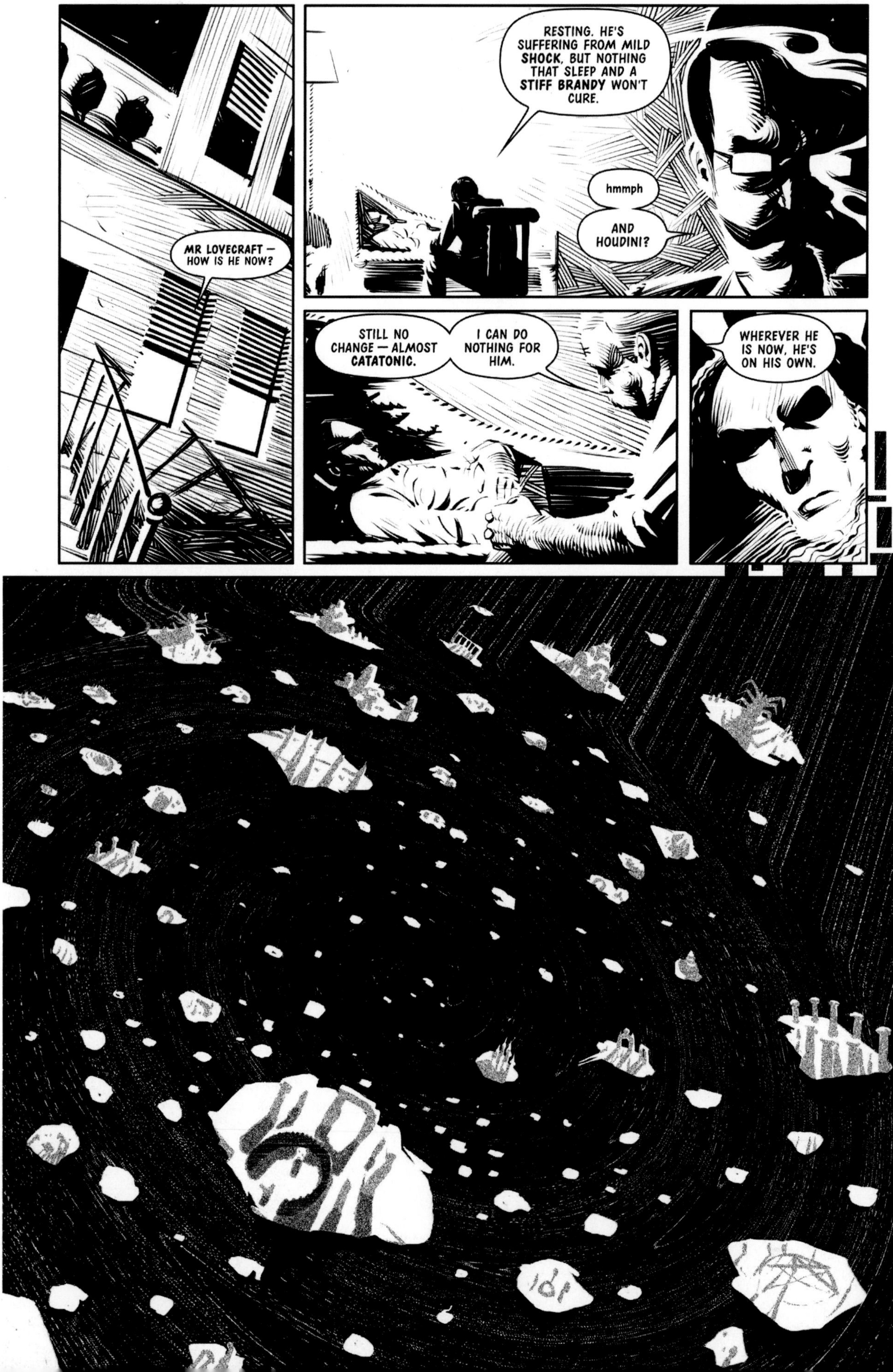
MR LOVECRAFT — HOW IS HE NOW?
RESTING. HE'S SUFFERING FROM MILD SHOCK, BUT NOTHING THAT SLEEP AND A STIFF BRANDY WON'T CURE.
hmmph
AND HOUDINI?
STILL NO CHANGE — ALMOST CATATONIC.
I CAN DO NOTHING FOR HIM.
WHEREVER HE IS NOW, HE'S ON HIS OWN.

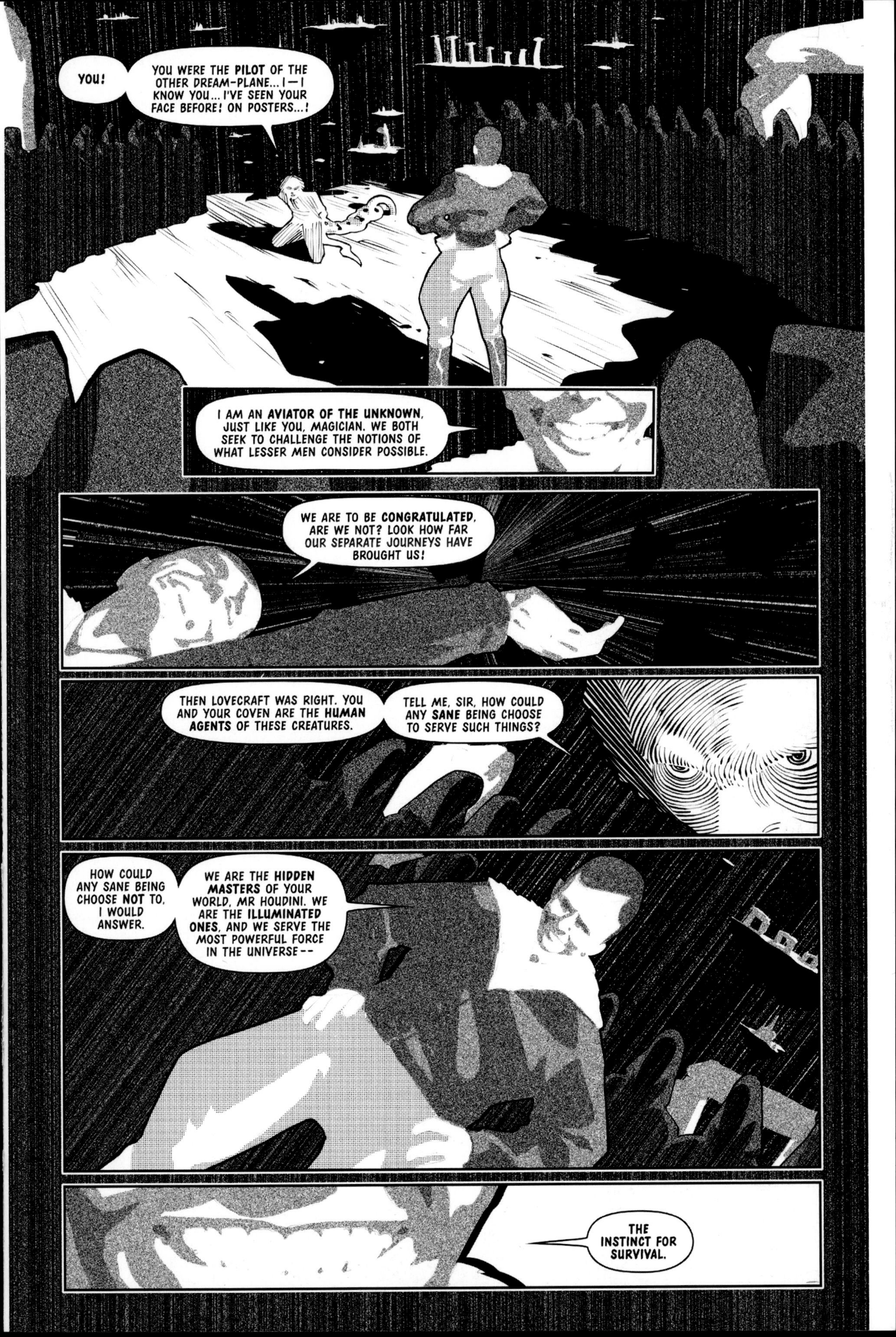
YOU!
YOU WERE THE PILOT OF THE OTHER DREAM-PLANE... I—I KNOW YOU... I'VE SEEN YOUR FACE BEFORE! ON POSTERS...!
I AM AN AVIATOR OF THE UNKNOWN, JUST LIKE YOU, MAGICIAN. WE BOTH SEEK TO CHALLENGE THE NOTIONS OF WHAT LESSER MEN CONSIDER POSSIBLE.
WE ARE TO BE CONGRATULATED, ARE WE NOT? LOOK HOW FAR OUR SEPARATE JOURNEYS HAVE BROUGHT US!
THEN LOVECRAFT WAS RIGHT. YOU AND YOUR COVEN ARE THE HUMAN AGENTS OF THESE CREATURES.
TELL ME, SIR, HOW COULD ANY SANE BEING CHOOSE TO SERVE SUCH THINGS?
HOW COULD ANY SANE BEING CHOOSE NOT TO, I WOULD ANSWER.
WE ARE THE HIDDEN MASTERS OF YOUR WORLD, MR HOUDINI. WE ARE THE ILLUMINATED ONES, AND WE SERVE THE MOST POWERFUL FORCE IN THE UNIVERSE--
THE INSTINCT FOR SURVIVAL.

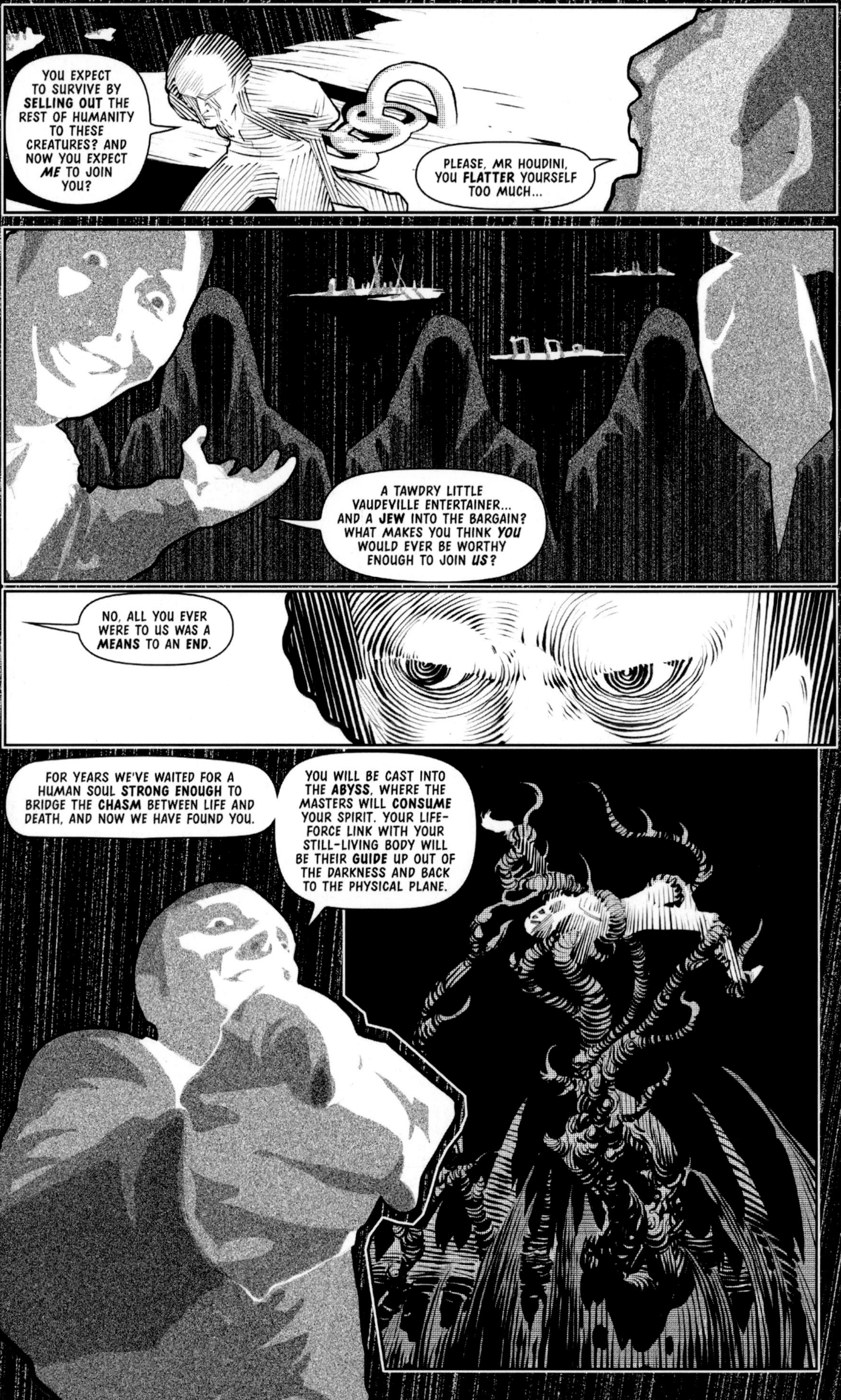
YOU EXPECT TO SURVIVE BY SELLING OUT THE REST OF HUMANITY TO THESE CREATURES? AND NOW YOU EXPECT ME TO JOIN YOU?
PLEASE, MR HOUDINI, YOU FLATTER YOURSELF TOO MUCH...
A TAWDRY LITTLE VAUDEVILLE ENTERTAINER... AND A JEW INTO THE BARGAIN? WHAT MAKES YOU THINK YOU WOULD EVER BE WORTHY ENOUGH TO JOIN US?
NO, ALL YOU EVER WERE TO US WAS A MEANS TO AN END.
FOR YEARS WE'VE WAITED FOR A HUMAN SOUL STRONG ENOUGH TO BRIDGE THE CHASM BETWEEN LIFE AND DEATH, AND NOW WE HAVE FOUND YOU.
YOU WILL BE CAST INTO THE ABYSS, WHERE THE MASTERS WILL CONSUME YOUR SPIRIT. YOUR LIFE-FORCE LINK WITH YOUR STILL-LIVING BODY WILL BE THEIR GUIDE UP OUT OF THE DARKNESS AND BACK TO THE PHYSICAL PLANE.

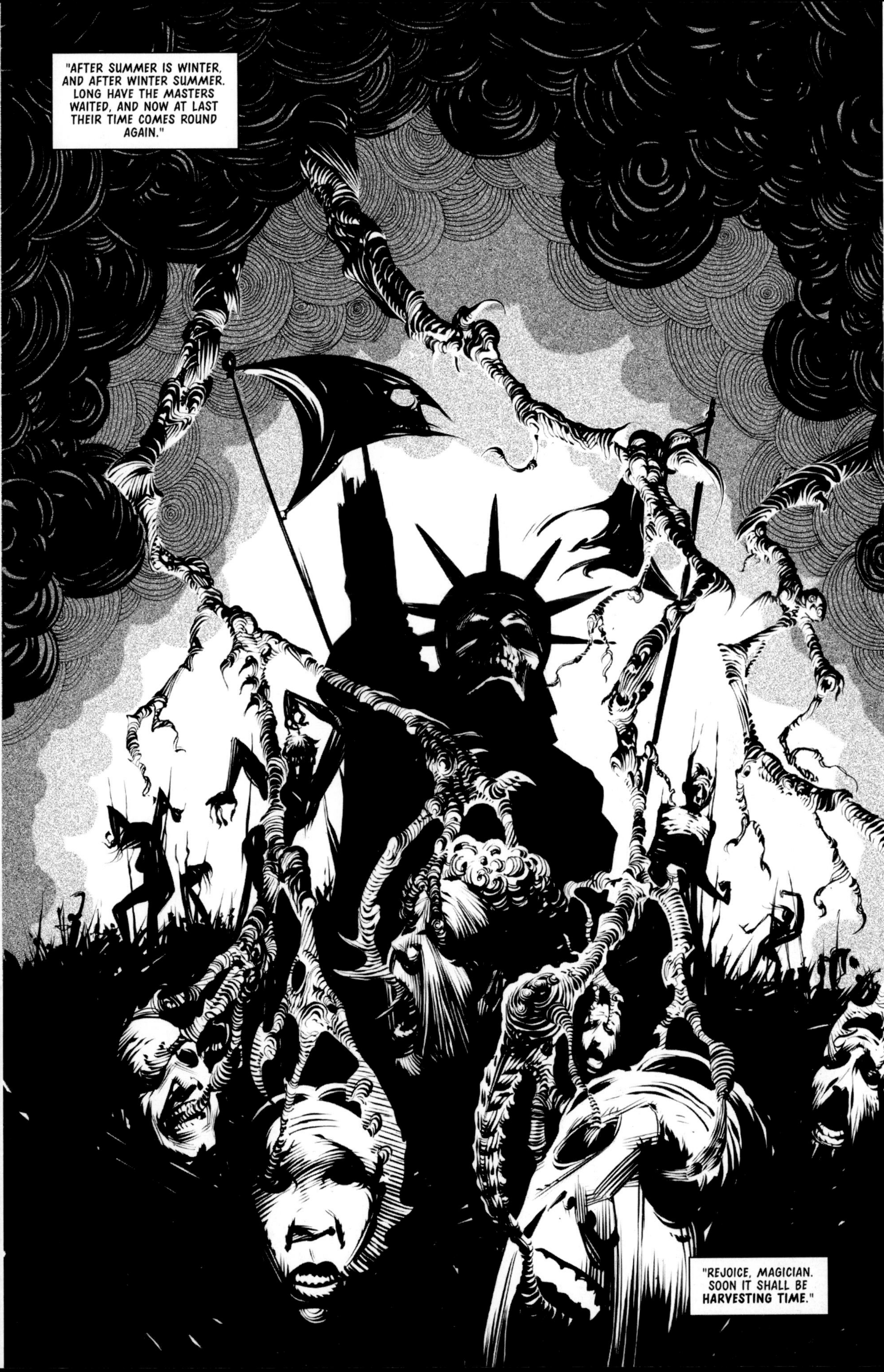
"AFTER SUMMER IS WINTER, AND AFTER WINTER SUMMER. LONG HAVE THE MASTERS WAITED, AND NOW AT LAST THEIR TIME COMES ROUND AGAIN."
"REJOICE, MAGICIAN. SOON IT SHALL BE HARVESTING TIME."

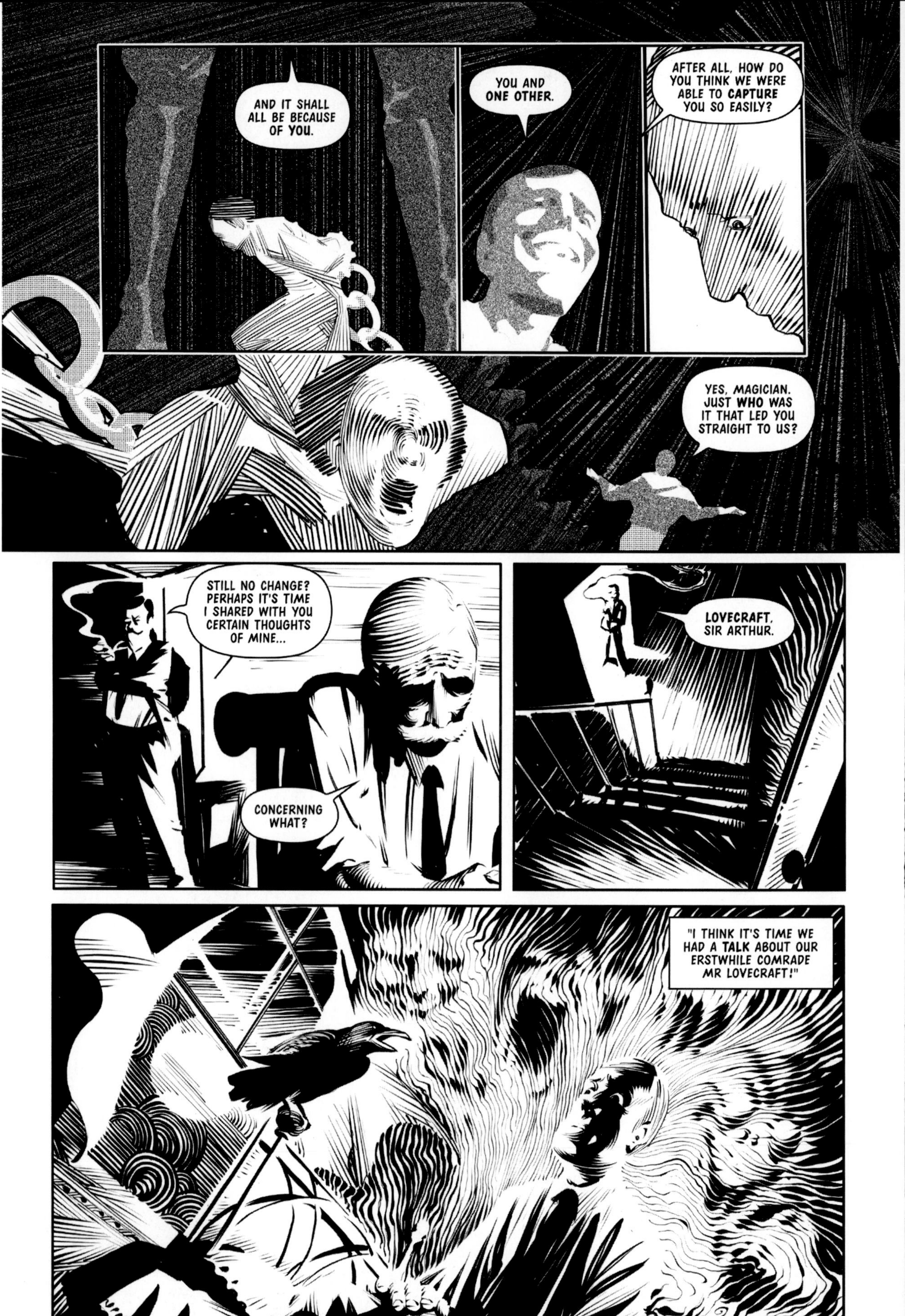
AND IT SHALL ALL BE BECAUSE OF YOU.
YOU AND ONE OTHER.
AFTER ALL, HOW DO YOU THINK WE WERE ABLE TO CAPTURE YOU SO EASILY?
YES, MAGICIAN. JUST WHO WAS IT THAT LED YOU STRAIGHT TO US?
STILL NO CHANGE? PERHAPS IT'S TIME I SHARED WITH YOU CERTAIN THOUGHTS OF MINE...
CONCERNING WHAT?
LOVECRAFT, SIR ARTHUR.
"I THINK IT'S TIME WE HAD A TALK ABOUT OUR ERSTWHILE COMRADE MR LOVECRAFT!"

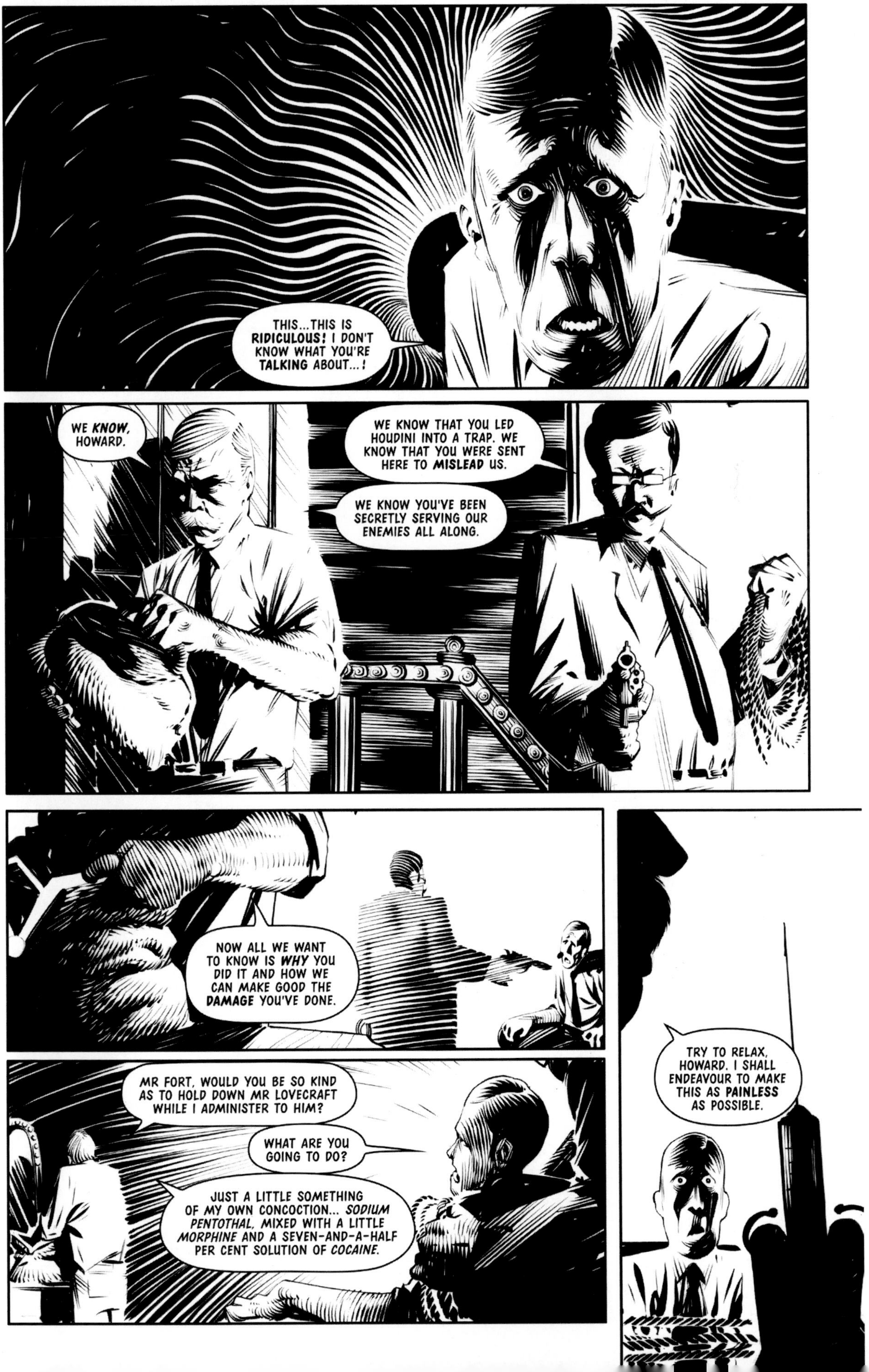
THIS...THIS IS RIDICULOUS! I DON'T KNOW WHAT YOU'RE TALKING ABOUT...!
WE KNOW, HOWARD.
WE KNOW THAT YOU LED HOUDINI INTO A TRAP. WE KNOW THAT YOU WERE SENT HERE TO MISLEAD US.
WE KNOW YOU'VE BEEN SECRETLY SERVING OUR ENEMIES ALL ALONG.
NOW ALL WE WANT TO KNOW IS WHY YOU DID IT AND HOW WE CAN MAKE GOOD THE DAMAGE YOU'VE DONE.
MR FORT, WOULD YOU BE SO KIND AS TO HOLD DOWN MR LOVECRAFT WHILE I ADMINISTER TO HIM?
WHAT ARE YOU GOING TO DO?
JUST A LITTLE SOMETHING OF MY OWN CONCOCTION... SODIUM PENTOTHAL, MIXED WITH A LITTLE MORPHINE AND A SEVEN-AND-A-HALF PER CENT SOLUTION OF COCAINE.
TRY TO RELAX, HOWARD. I SHALL ENDEAVOUR TO MAKE THIS AS PAINLESS AS POSSIBLE.

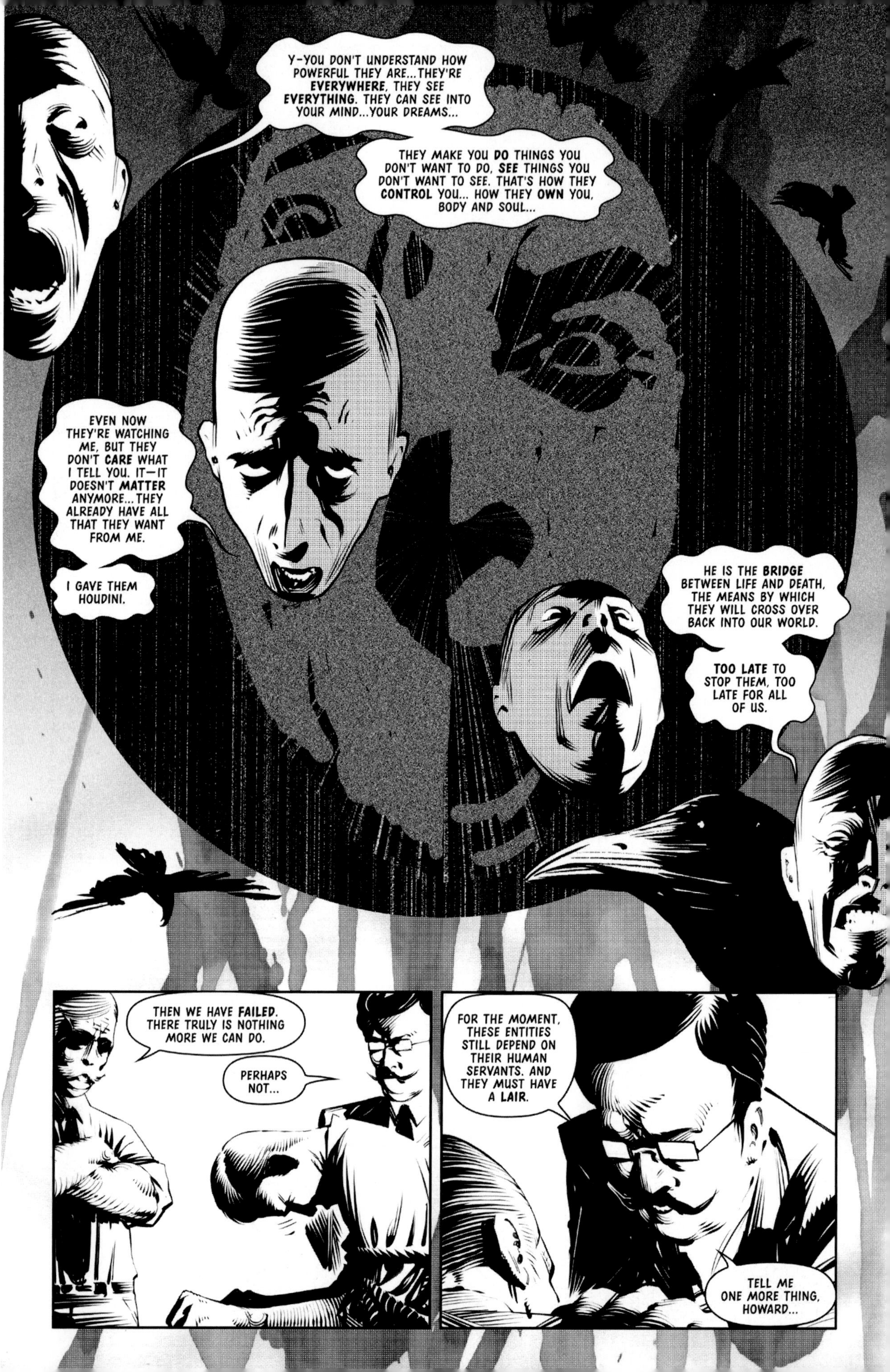
Y-YOU DON'T UNDERSTAND HOW POWERFUL THEY ARE...THEY'RE EVERYWHERE, THEY SEE EVERYTHING. THEY CAN SEE INTO YOUR MIND...YOUR DREAMS...
THEY MAKE YOU DO THINGS YOU DON'T WANT TO DO, SEE THINGS YOU DON'T WANT TO SEE. THAT'S HOW THEY CONTROL YOU... HOW THEY OWN YOU, BODY AND SOUL...
EVEN NOW THEY'RE WATCHING ME, BUT THEY DON'T CARE WHAT I TELL YOU. IT—IT DOESN'T MATTER ANYMORE...THEY ALREADY HAVE ALL THAT THEY WANT FROM ME.
I GAVE THEM HOUDINI.
HE IS THE BRIDGE BETWEEN LIFE AND DEATH, THE MEANS BY WHICH THEY WILL CROSS OVER BACK INTO OUR WORLD.
TOO LATE TO STOP THEM, TOO LATE FOR ALL OF US.
THEN WE HAVE FAILED. THERE TRULY IS NOTHING MORE WE CAN DO.
PERHAPS NOT...
FOR THE MOMENT, THESE ENTITIES STILL DEPEND ON THEIR HUMAN SERVANTS. AND THEY MUST HAVE A LAIR.
TELL ME ONE MORE THING, HOWARD...

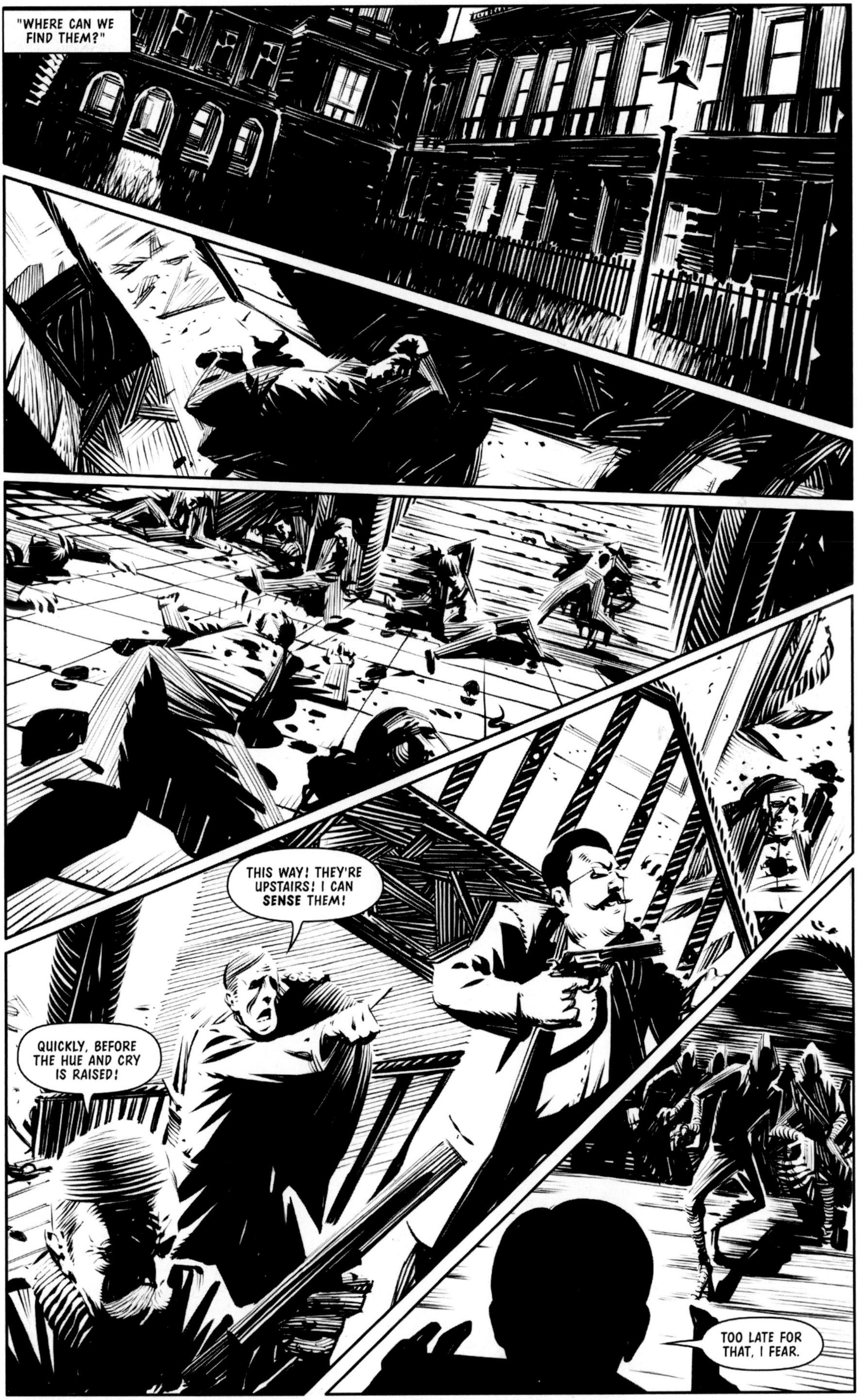
"WHERE CAN WE FIND THEM?"
THIS WAY! THEY'RE UPSTAIRS! I CAN SENSE THEM!
QUICKLY, BEFORE THE HUE AND CRY IS RAISED!
TOO LATE FOR THAT, I FEAR.

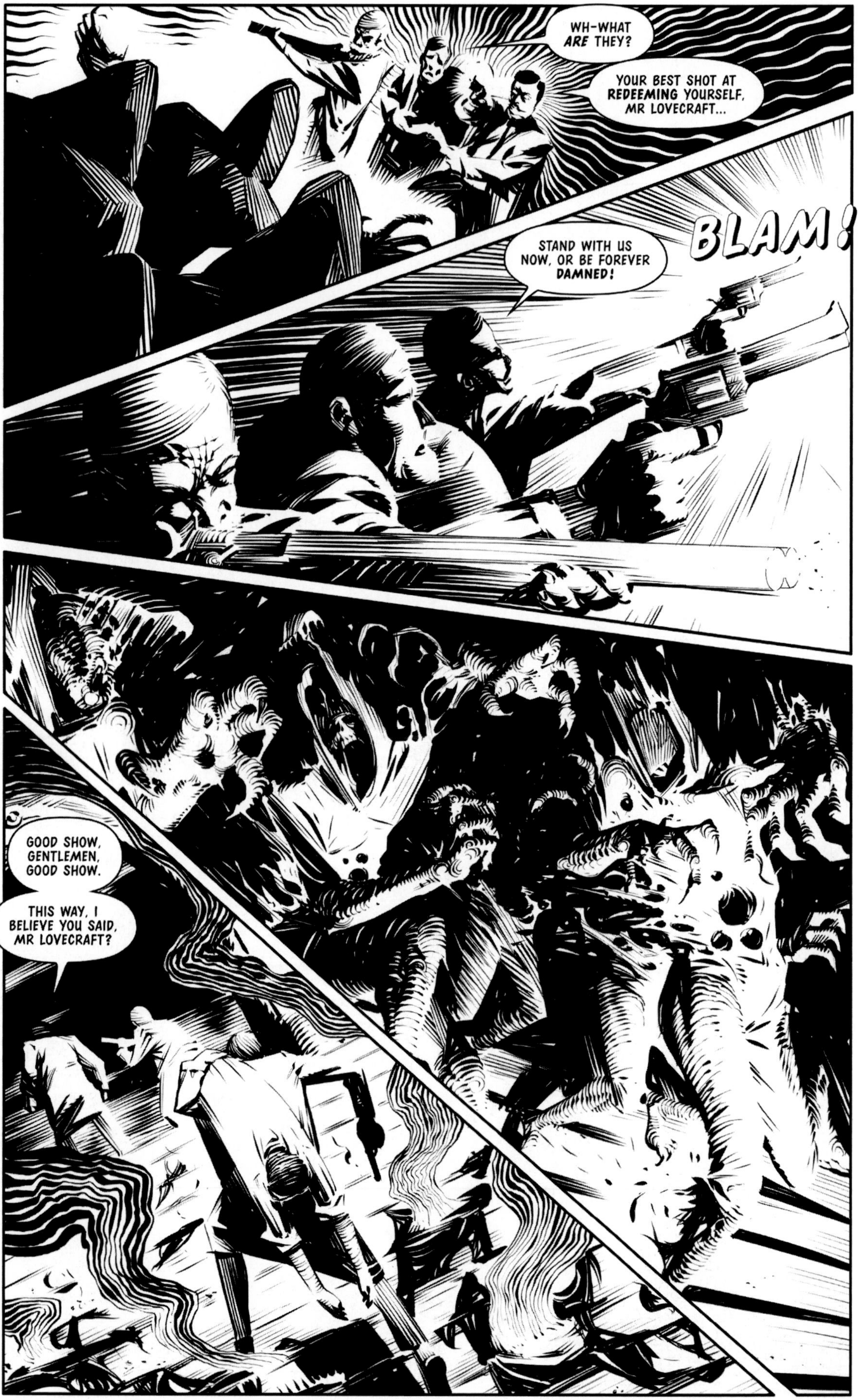
WH-WHAT ARE THEY?
YOUR BEST SHOT AT REDEEMING YOURSELF, MR LOVECRAFT...
BLAM!
STAND WITH US NOW, OR BE FOREVER DAMNED!
GOOD SHOW, GENTLEMEN, GOOD SHOW.
THIS WAY, I BELIEVE YOU SAID, MR LOVECRAFT?

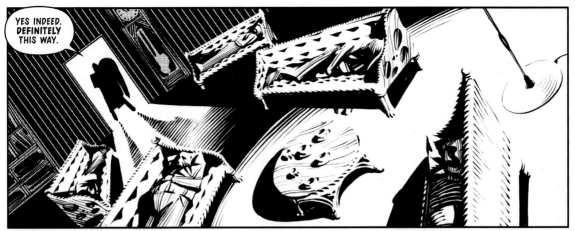

YES INDEED.
DEFINITELY
THIS WAY.

MR LOVECRAFT,
HELP ME BARRICADE
THE DOOR.

SIR ARTHUR,
BEGIN YOUR
PREPARATIONS.

MY GOD...

LOOK AT THEM!
DO WE EVEN
KNOW WHO THEY
ALL ARE?

POLITICIANS AND POTENTATES,
INDUSTRIALISTS AND FINANCIERS,
DEMAGOGUES AND ARISTOCRATS.

THE MOST *DANGEROUS* MEN IN THE
WORLD. THEY ARE THE ENEMY, AND
WE MUST SHOW THEM NO PITY.

WHAT HAVE YOU
THERE, SIR ARTHUR?
ANOTHER ONE OF YOUR
CONCOCTIONS?

NOT QUITE,
MR LOVECRAFT...

POTASSIUM
CYANIDE.

NOW, SHALL
WE BEGIN?

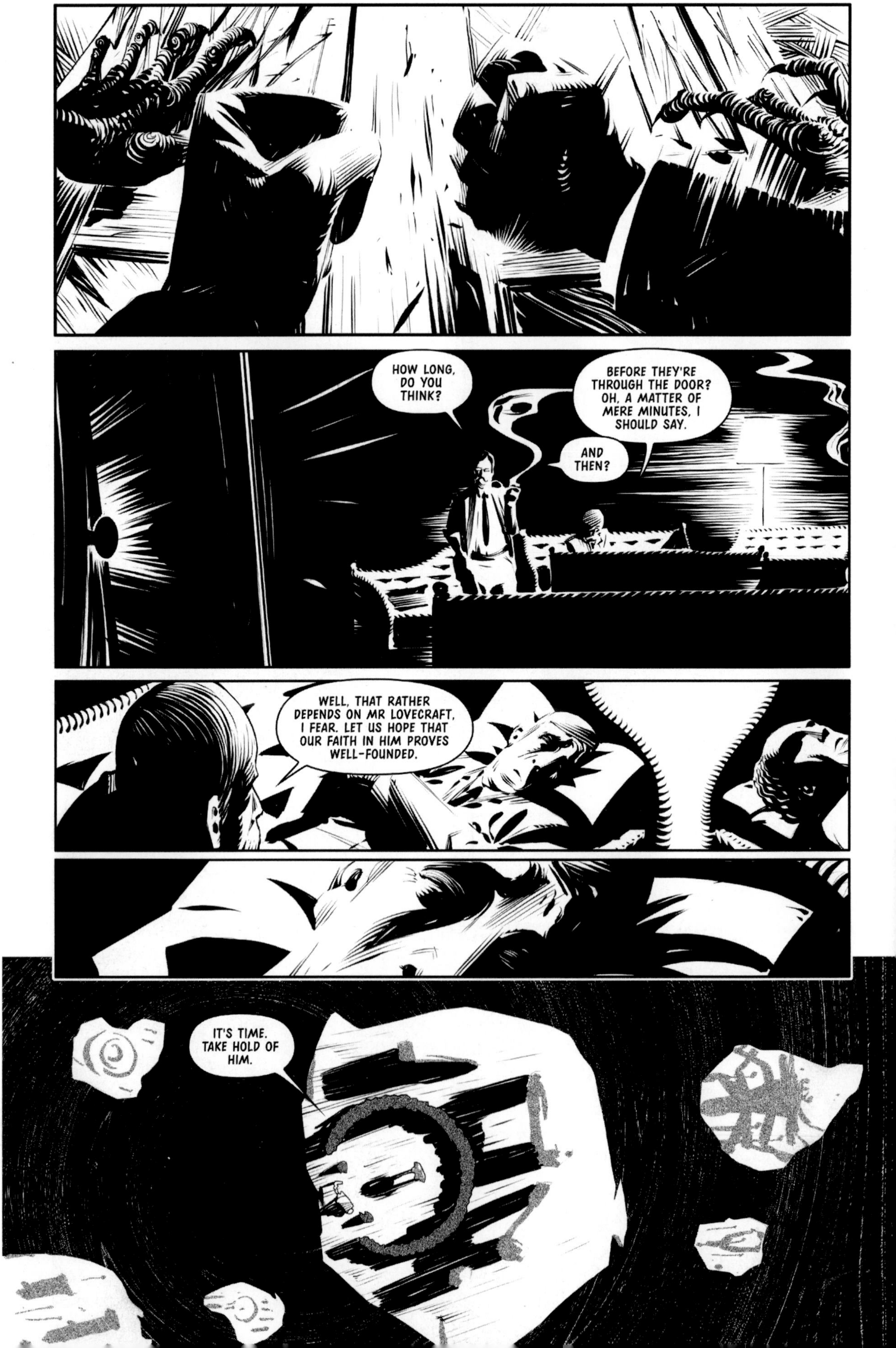
HOW LONG, DO YOU THINK?
BEFORE THEY'RE THROUGH THE DOOR? OH, A MATTER OF MERE MINUTES, I SHOULD SAY.
AND THEN?
WELL, THAT RATHER DEPENDS ON MR LOVECRAFT, I FEAR. LET US HOPE THAT OUR FAITH IN HIM PROVES WELL-FOUNDED.
IT'S TIME. TAKE HOLD OF HIM.

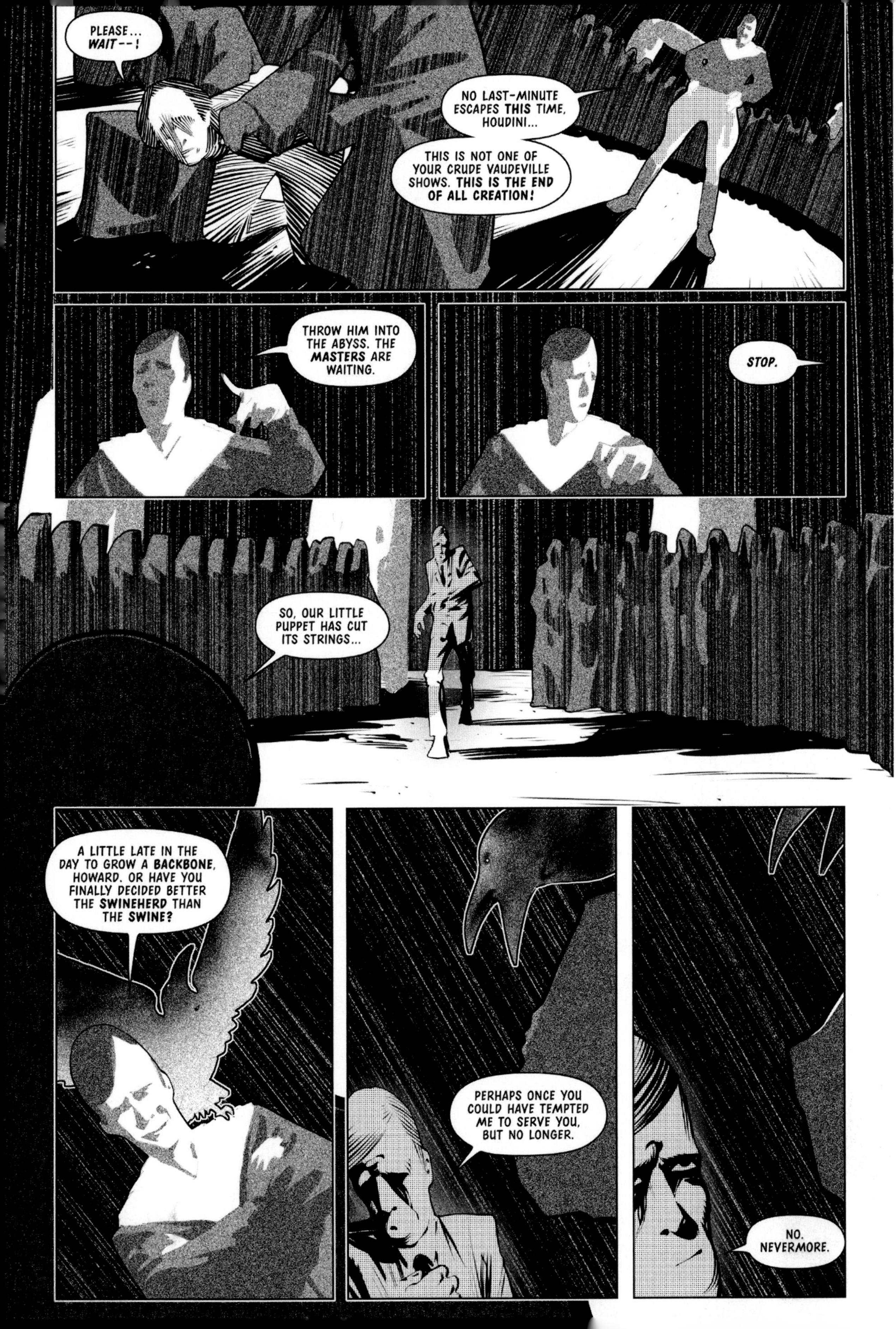
PLEASE... WAIT--!
NO LAST-MINUTE ESCAPES THIS TIME, HOUDINI...
THIS IS NOT ONE OF YOUR CRUDE VAUDEVILLE SHOWS. THIS IS THE END OF ALL CREATION!
THROW HIM INTO THE ABYSS. THE MASTERS ARE WAITING.
STOP.
SO, OUR LITTLE PUPPET HAS CUT ITS STRINGS...
A LITTLE LATE IN THE DAY TO GROW A BACKBONE, HOWARD. OR HAVE YOU FINALLY DECIDED BETTER THE SWINEHERD THAN THE SWINE?
PERHAPS ONCE YOU COULD HAVE TEMPTED ME TO SERVE YOU, BUT NO LONGER.
NO. NEVERMORE.

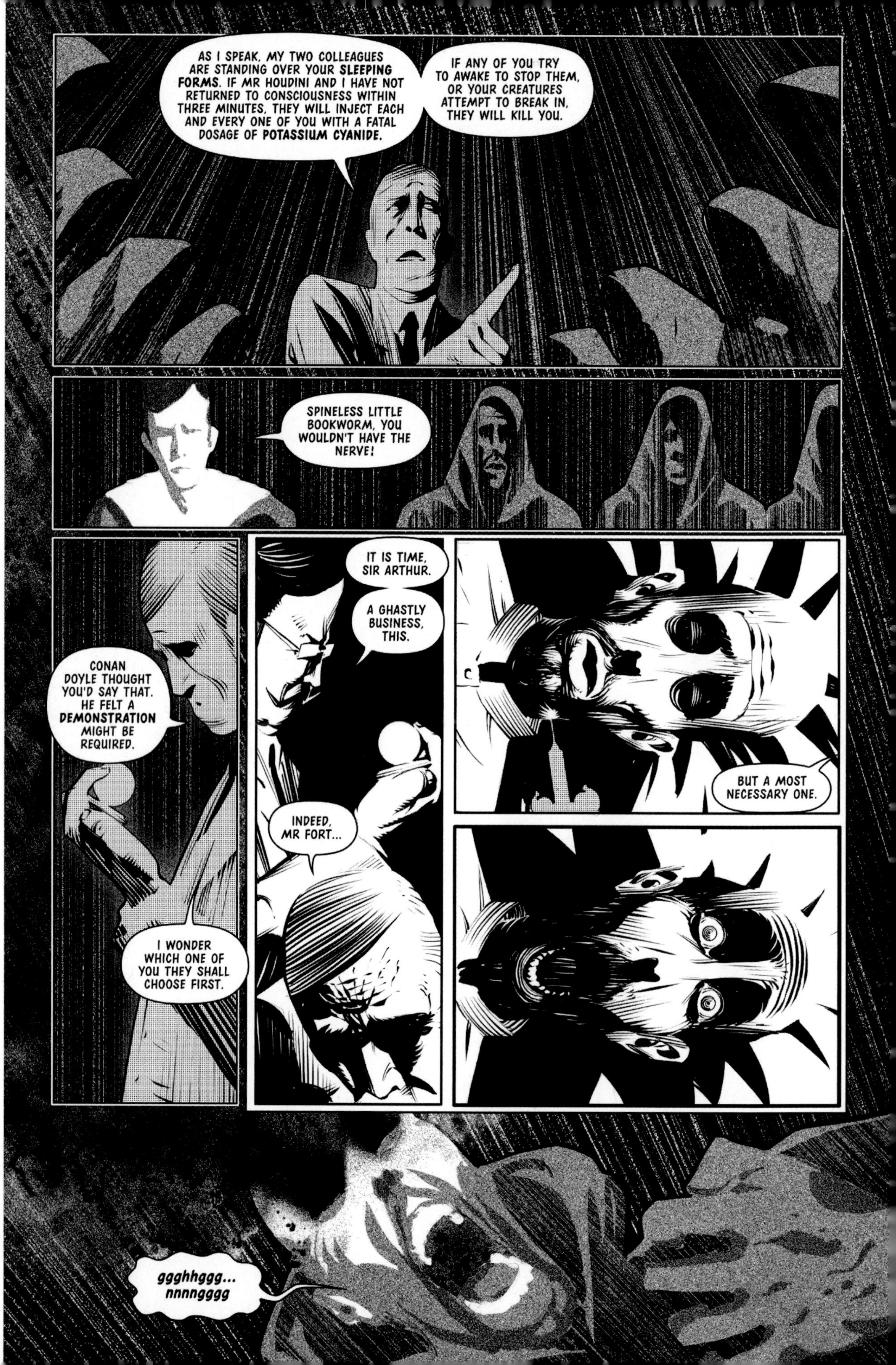

AS I SPEAK, MY TWO COLLEAGUES ARE STANDING OVER YOUR SLEEPING FORMS. IF MR HOUDINI AND I HAVE NOT RETURNED TO CONSCIOUSNESS WITHIN THREE MINUTES, THEY WILL INJECT EACH AND EVERY ONE OF YOU WITH A FATAL DOSAGE OF POTASSIUM CYANIDE.
IF ANY OF YOU TRY TO AWAKE TO STOP THEM, OR YOUR CREATURES ATTEMPT TO BREAK IN, THEY WILL KILL YOU.
SPINELESS LITTLE BOOKWORM, YOU WOULDN'T HAVE THE NERVE!
CONAN DOYLE THOUGHT YOU'D SAY THAT. HE FELT A DEMONSTRATION MIGHT BE REQUIRED.
I WONDER WHICH ONE OF YOU THEY SHALL CHOOSE FIRST.
IT IS TIME, SIR ARTHUR.
A GHASTLY BUSINESS, THIS.
INDEED, MR FORT...
BUT A MOST NECESSARY ONE.
ggghhggg... nnnngggg

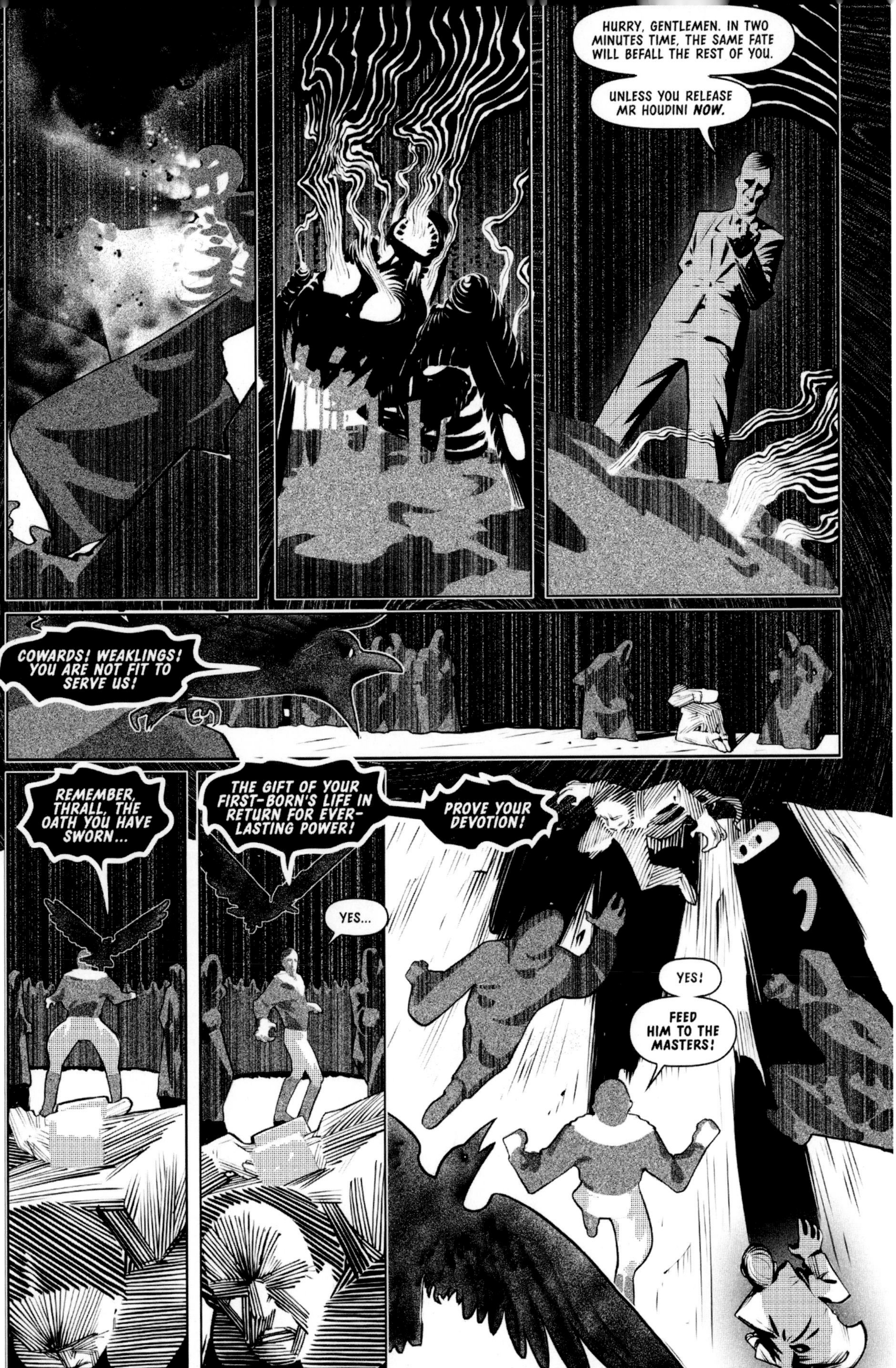
HURRY, GENTLEMEN. IN TWO MINUTES TIME, THE SAME FATE WILL BEFALL THE REST OF YOU.
UNLESS YOU RELEASE MR HOUDINI *NOW*.
COWARDS! WEAKLINGS! YOU ARE NOT FIT TO SERVE US!
REMEMBER, THRALL, THE OATH YOU HAVE SWORN...
THE GIFT OF YOUR FIRST-BORN'S LIFE IN RETURN FOR EVER-LASTING POWER!
YES...
PROVE YOUR DEVOTION!
YES!
FEED HIM TO THE MASTERS!

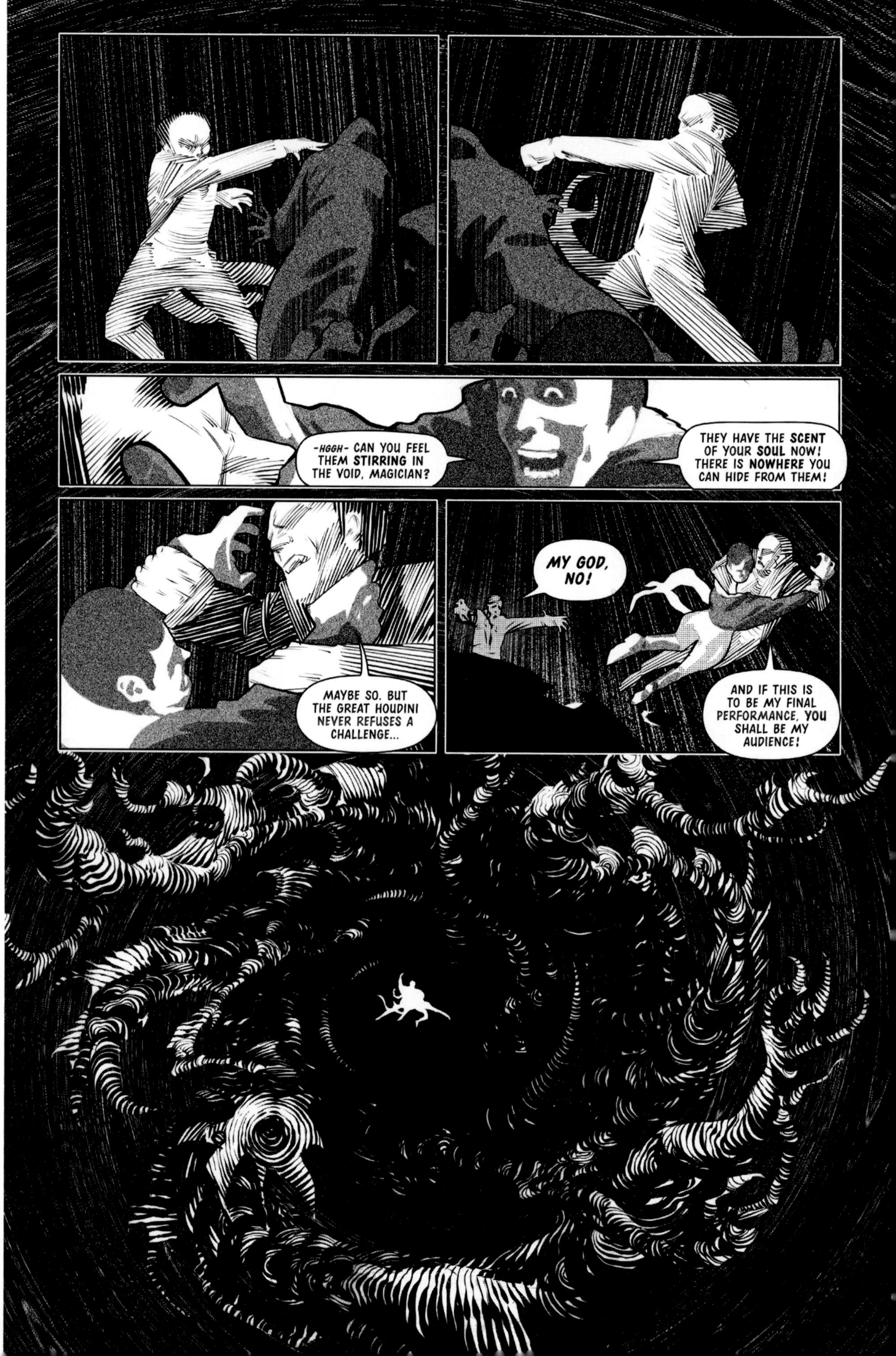

-HGGH- CAN YOU FEEL THEM STIRRING IN THE VOID, MAGICIAN?
THEY HAVE THE SCENT OF YOUR SOUL NOW! THERE IS NOWHERE YOU CAN HIDE FROM THEM!
MAYBE SO. BUT THE GREAT HOUDINI NEVER REFUSES A CHALLENGE...
MY GOD, NO!
AND IF THIS IS TO BE MY FINAL PERFORMANCE, YOU SHALL BE MY AUDIENCE!

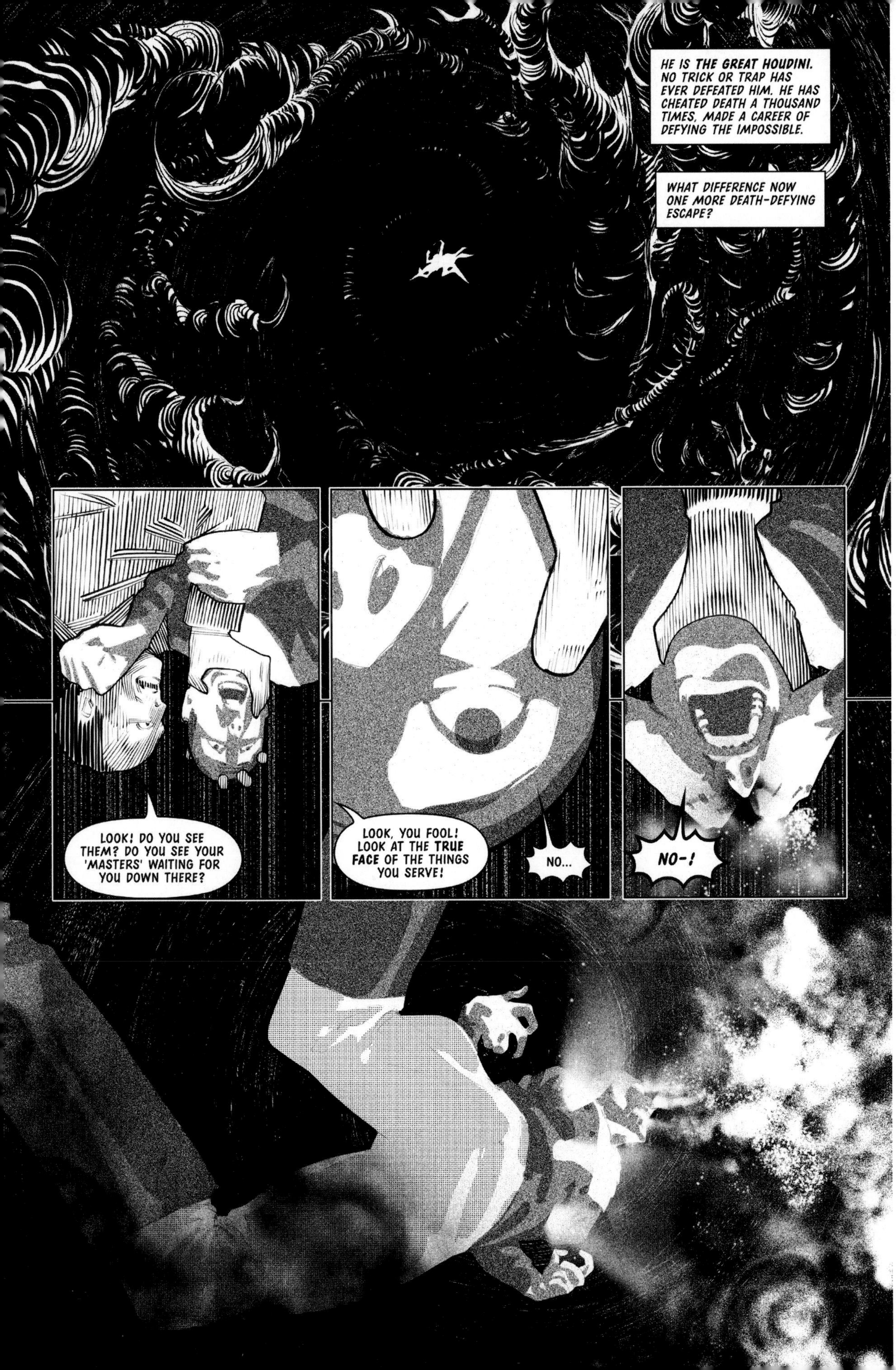
HE IS **THE GREAT HOUDINI.** NO TRICK OR TRAP HAS EVER DEFEATED HIM. HE HAS CHEATED DEATH A THOUSAND TIMES, MADE A CAREER OF DEFYING THE IMPOSSIBLE.
WHAT DIFFERENCE NOW ONE MORE DEATH-DEFYING ESCAPE?
LOOK! DO YOU SEE THEM? DO YOU SEE YOUR 'MASTERS' WAITING FOR YOU DOWN THERE?
LOOK, YOU FOOL! LOOK AT THE **TRUE FACE** OF THE THINGS YOU SERVE!
NO...
NO-!

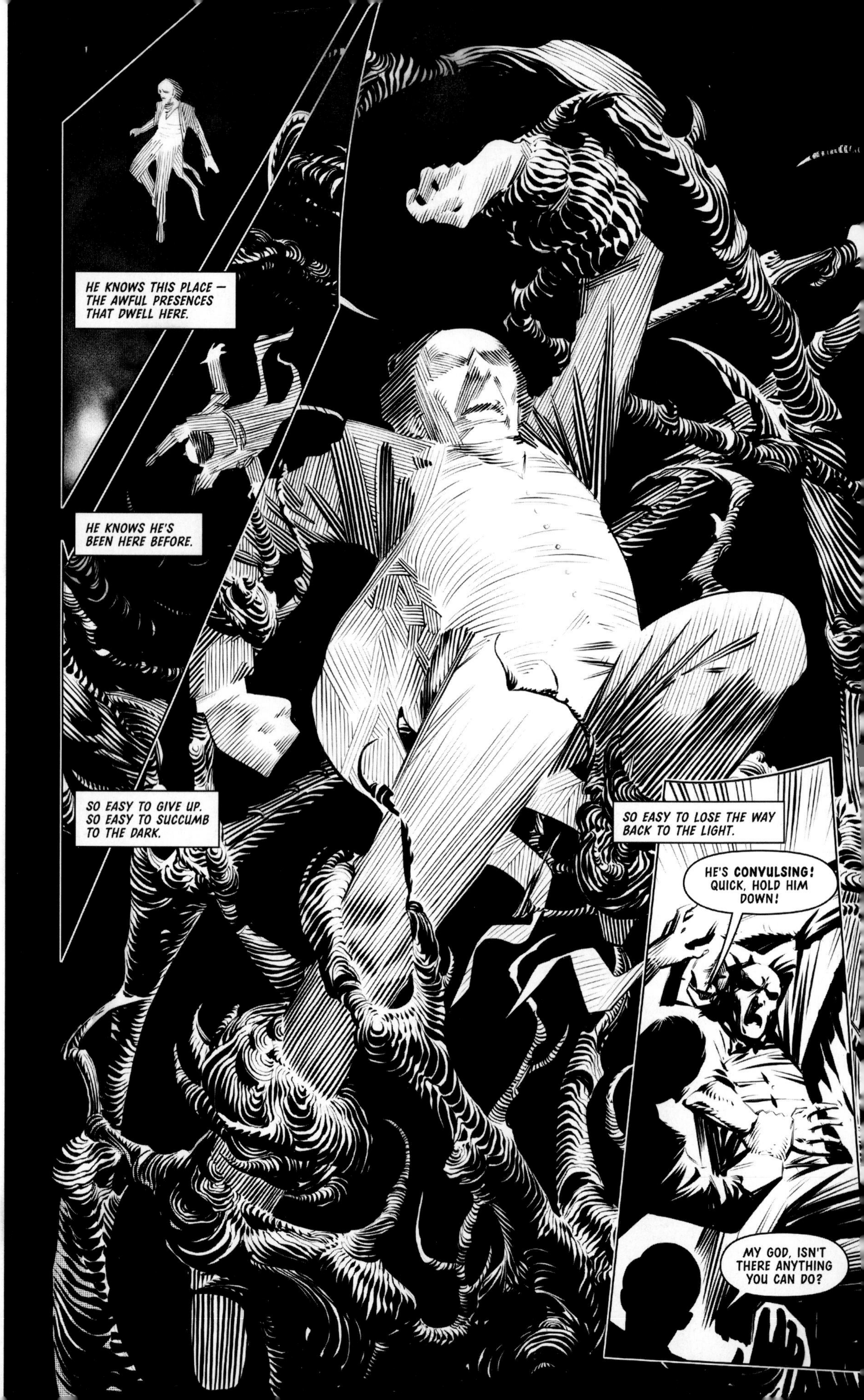

HE KNOWS THIS PLACE — THE AWFUL PRESENCES THAT DWELL HERE.
HE KNOWS HE'S BEEN HERE BEFORE.
SO EASY TO GIVE UP. SO EASY TO SUCCUMB TO THE DARK.
SO EASY TO LOSE THE WAY BACK TO THE LIGHT.
HE'S CONVULSING! QUICK, HOLD HIM DOWN!
MY GOD, ISN'T THERE ANYTHING YOU CAN DO?

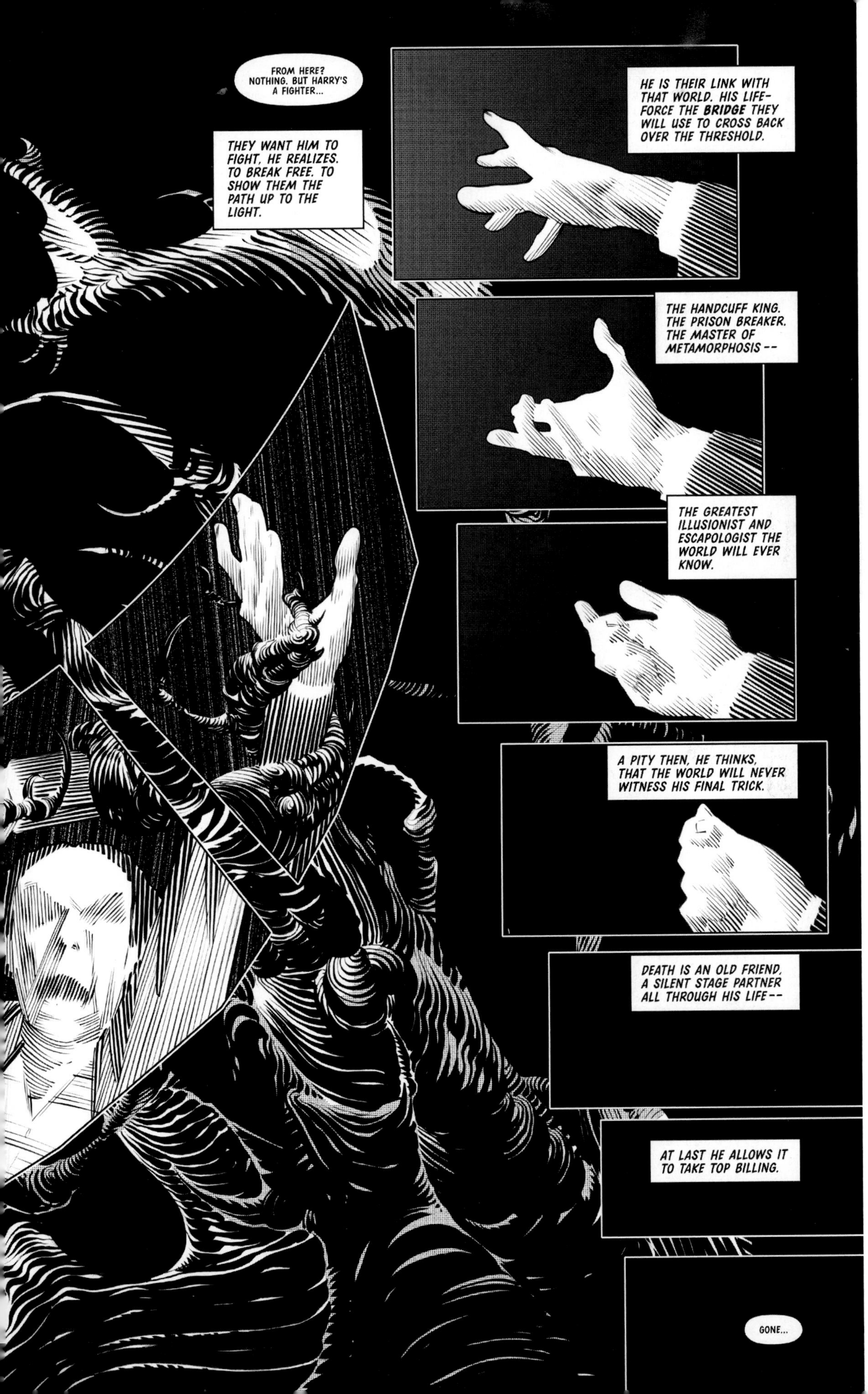
FROM HERE? NOTHING. BUT HARRY'S A FIGHTER...
THEY WANT HIM TO FIGHT, HE REALIZES. TO BREAK FREE. TO SHOW THEM THE PATH UP TO THE LIGHT.
HE IS THEIR LINK WITH THAT WORLD. HIS LIFE-FORCE THE BRIDGE THEY WILL USE TO CROSS BACK OVER THE THRESHOLD.
THE HANDCUFF KING. THE PRISON BREAKER. THE MASTER OF METAMORPHOSIS --
THE GREATEST ILLUSIONIST AND ESCAPOLOGIST THE WORLD WILL EVER KNOW.
A PITY THEN, HE THINKS, THAT THE WORLD WILL NEVER WITNESS HIS FINAL TRICK.
DEATH IS AN OLD FRIEND, A SILENT STAGE PARTNER ALL THROUGH HIS LIFE--
AT LAST HE ALLOWS IT TO TAKE TOP BILLING.
GONE...

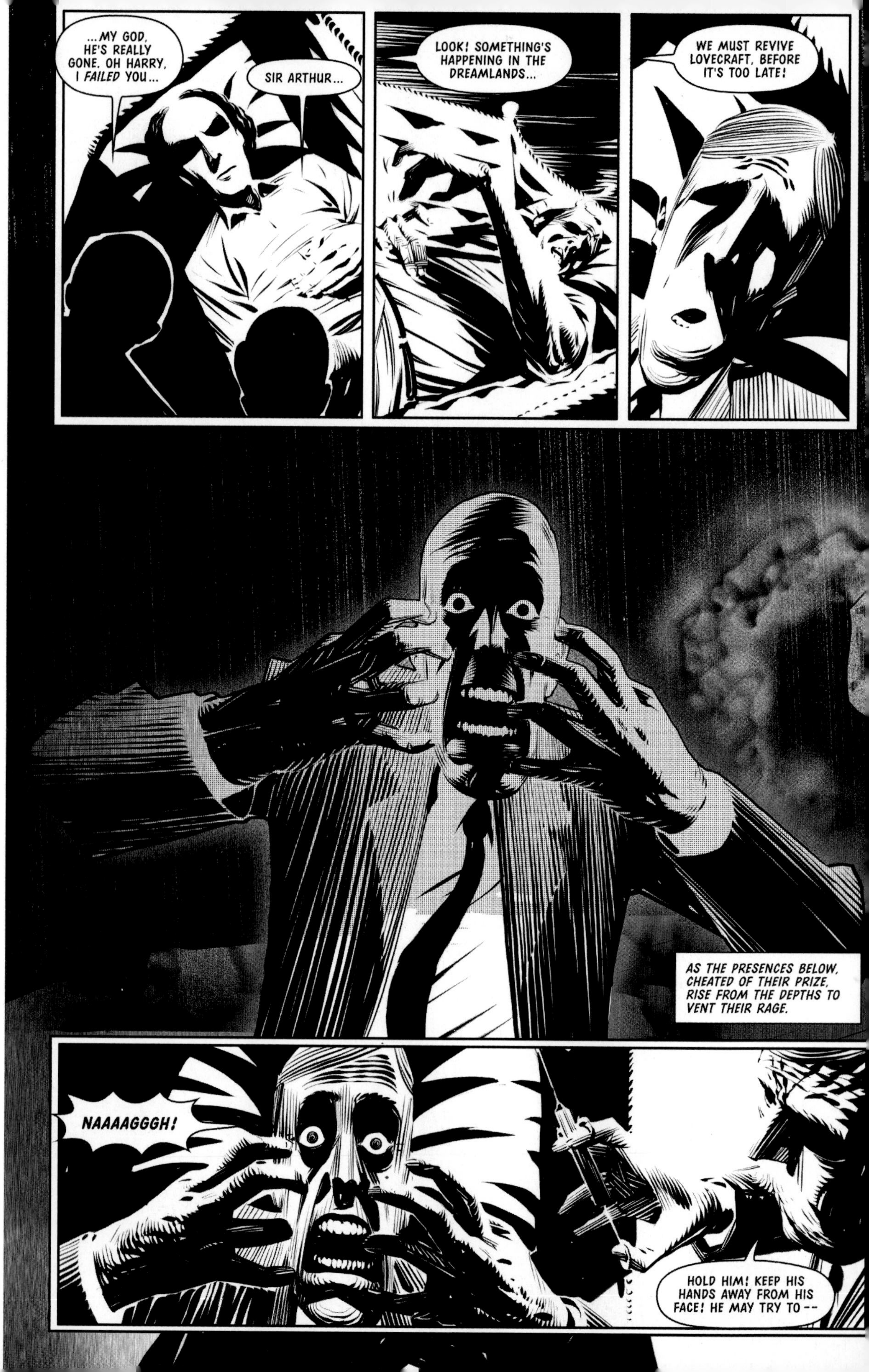
...MY GOD, HE'S REALLY GONE. OH HARRY, I *FAILED* YOU...
SIR ARTHUR...
LOOK! SOMETHING'S HAPPENING IN THE DREAMLANDS...
WE MUST REVIVE LOVECRAFT, BEFORE IT'S TOO LATE!
AS THE PRESENCES BELOW, CHEATED OF THEIR PRIZE, RISE FROM THE DEPTHS TO VENT THEIR RAGE.
NAAAAGGGH!
HOLD HIM! KEEP HIS HANDS AWAY FROM HIS FACE! HE MAY TRY TO --

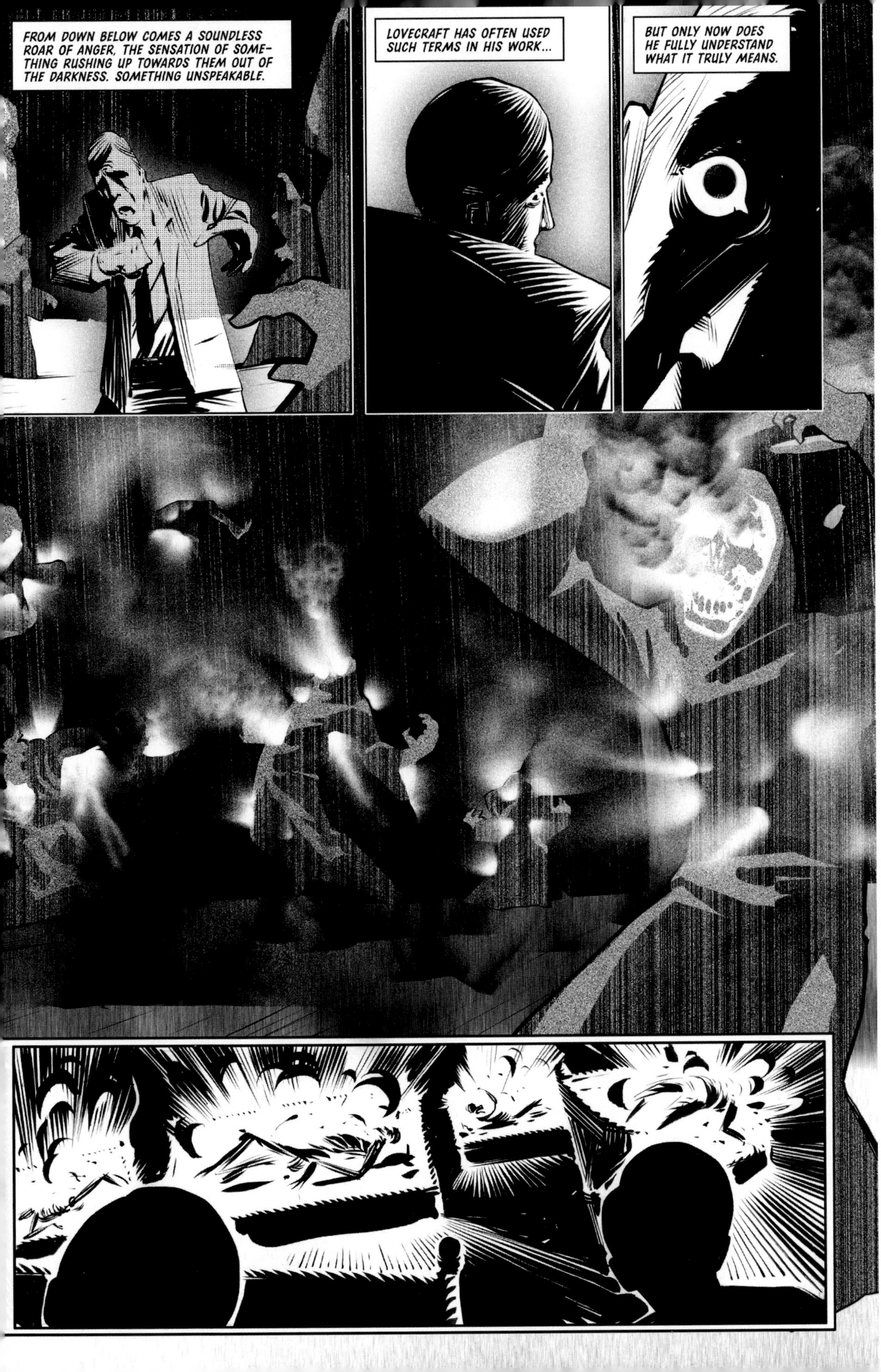
FROM DOWN BELOW COMES A SOUNDLESS ROAR OF ANGER, THE SENSATION OF SOMETHING RUSHING UP TOWARDS THEM OUT OF THE DARKNESS. SOMETHING UNSPEAKABLE.
LOVECRAFT HAS OFTEN USED SUCH TERMS IN HIS WORK...
BUT ONLY NOW DOES HE FULLY UNDERSTAND WHAT IT TRULY MEANS.

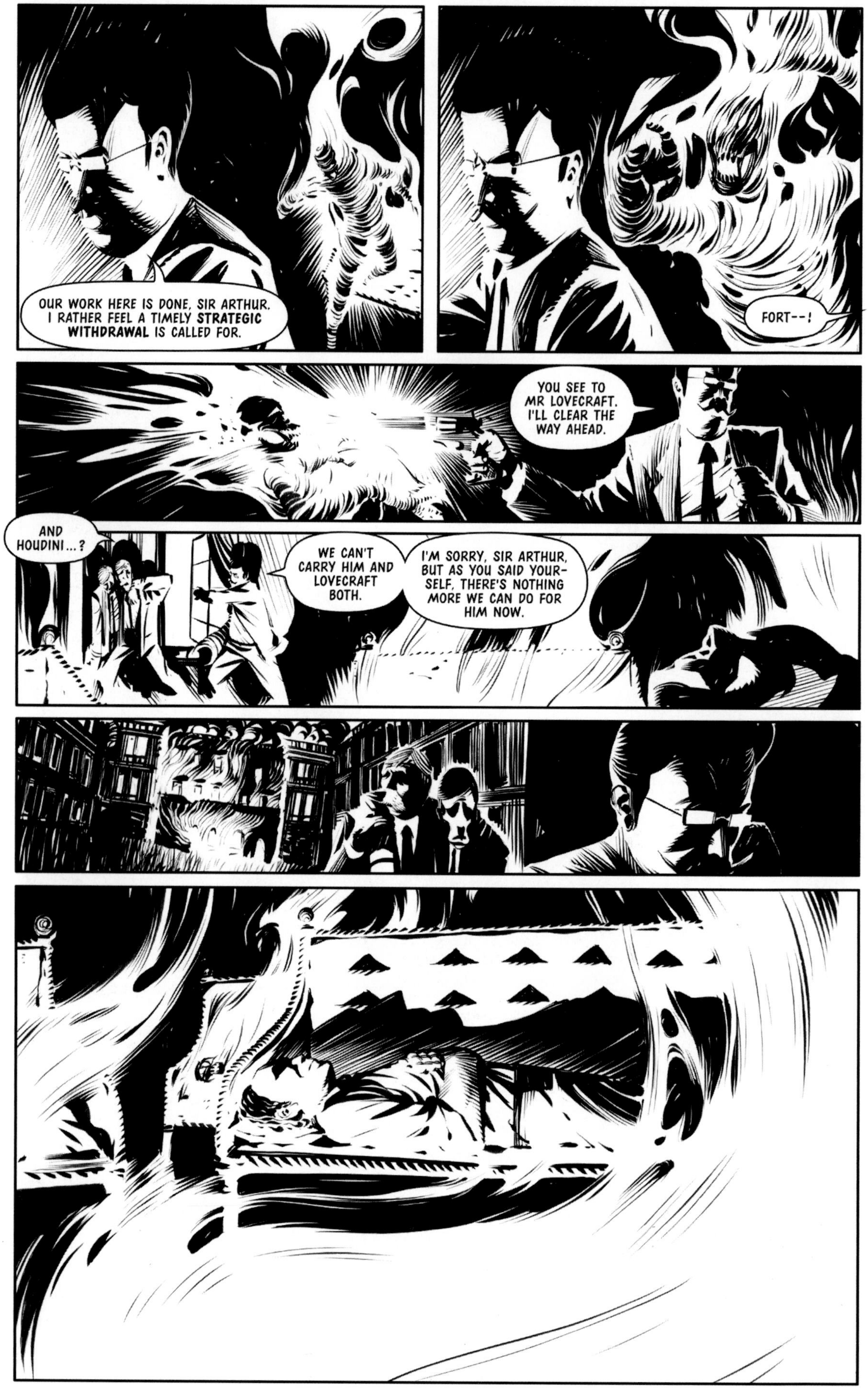
OUR WORK HERE IS DONE, SIR ARTHUR. I RATHER FEEL A TIMELY **STRATEGIC WITHDRAWAL** IS CALLED FOR.
FORT--!
YOU SEE TO MR LOVECRAFT. I'LL CLEAR THE WAY AHEAD.
AND HOUDINI...?
WE CAN'T CARRY HIM AND LOVECRAFT BOTH.
I'M SORRY, SIR ARTHUR, BUT AS YOU SAID YOURSELF, THERE'S NOTHING MORE WE CAN DO FOR HIM NOW.

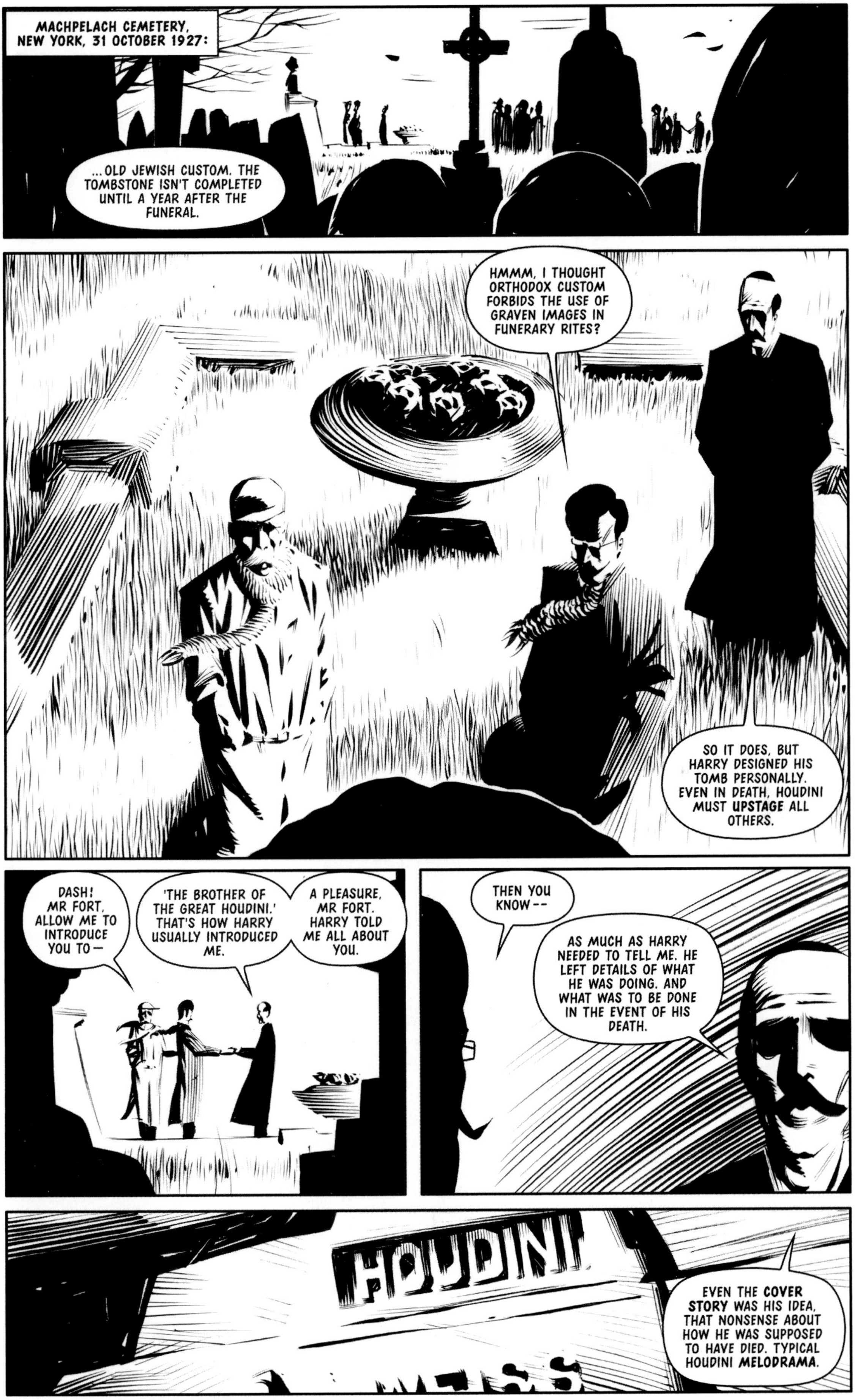
MACHPELACH CEMETERY, NEW YORK, 31 OCTOBER 1927:
...OLD JEWISH CUSTOM. THE TOMBSTONE ISN'T COMPLETED UNTIL A YEAR AFTER THE FUNERAL.
HMMM, I THOUGHT ORTHODOX CUSTOM FORBIDS THE USE OF GRAVEN IMAGES IN FUNERARY RITES?
SO IT DOES, BUT HARRY DESIGNED HIS TOMB PERSONALLY. EVEN IN DEATH, HOUDINI MUST **UPSTAGE** ALL OTHERS.
DASH! MR FORT, ALLOW ME TO INTRODUCE YOU TO—
'THE BROTHER OF THE GREAT HOUDINI.' THAT'S HOW HARRY USUALLY INTRODUCED ME.
A PLEASURE, MR FORT. HARRY TOLD ME ALL ABOUT YOU.
THEN YOU KNOW--
AS MUCH AS HARRY NEEDED TO TELL ME. HE LEFT DETAILS OF WHAT HE WAS DOING. AND WHAT WAS TO BE DONE IN THE EVENT OF HIS DEATH.
HOUDINI
EVEN THE **COVER STORY** WAS HIS IDEA, THAT NONSENSE ABOUT HOW HE WAS SUPPOSED TO HAVE DIED. TYPICAL HOUDINI **MELODRAMA**.

THE WIDOW HOUDINI... I SHOULD GO AND OFFER MY CONDOLENCES

BEST NOT TO, SIR ARTHUR. ROSABELLE STILL DOESN'T UNDERSTAND WHAT *REALLY* HAPPENED THAT NIGHT.

SHE TOOK HIS DEATH HARD. SHE STILL DOES...

HARRY ALWAYS PROMISED THAT HE WOULD SEND WORD BACK TO HER FROM THE OTHER SIDE, SOME PRE-ARRANGED MESSAGE THAT ONLY SHE COULD KNOW.

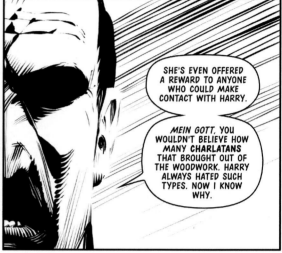

SHE'S EVEN OFFERED A REWARD TO ANYONE WHO COULD MAKE CONTACT WITH HARRY.

MEIN GOTT, YOU WOULDN'T BELIEVE HOW MANY *CHARLATANS* THAT BROUGHT OUT OF THE WOODWORK. HARRY ALWAYS HATED SUCH TYPES. NOW I KNOW WHY.

THEN YOU DON'T BELIEVE SUCH CONTACT IS POSSIBLE?

I BELIEVE THAT IF ANYONE COULD HAVE DONE IT, IT WOULD HAVE BEEN MY BROTHER. AND WE'VE BEEN WAITING A YEAR NOW.

IF ANYTHING OF EHRICH STILL LIVES ON, IT'LL ONLY BE AS PART OF THE *LEGEND* OF THE GREAT HOUDINI.

ANYWAY, THERE IS STILL MUCH TO BE DONE. HARRY'S COLLECTIONS ARE BEING SOLD OFF OR DONATED — THREE TRUCKLOADS ALONE FOR THE **LIBRARY OF CONGRESS.**

AMAZING THAT ONE MAN COULD HAVE ACQUIRED SO MUCH IN ONE LIFE...

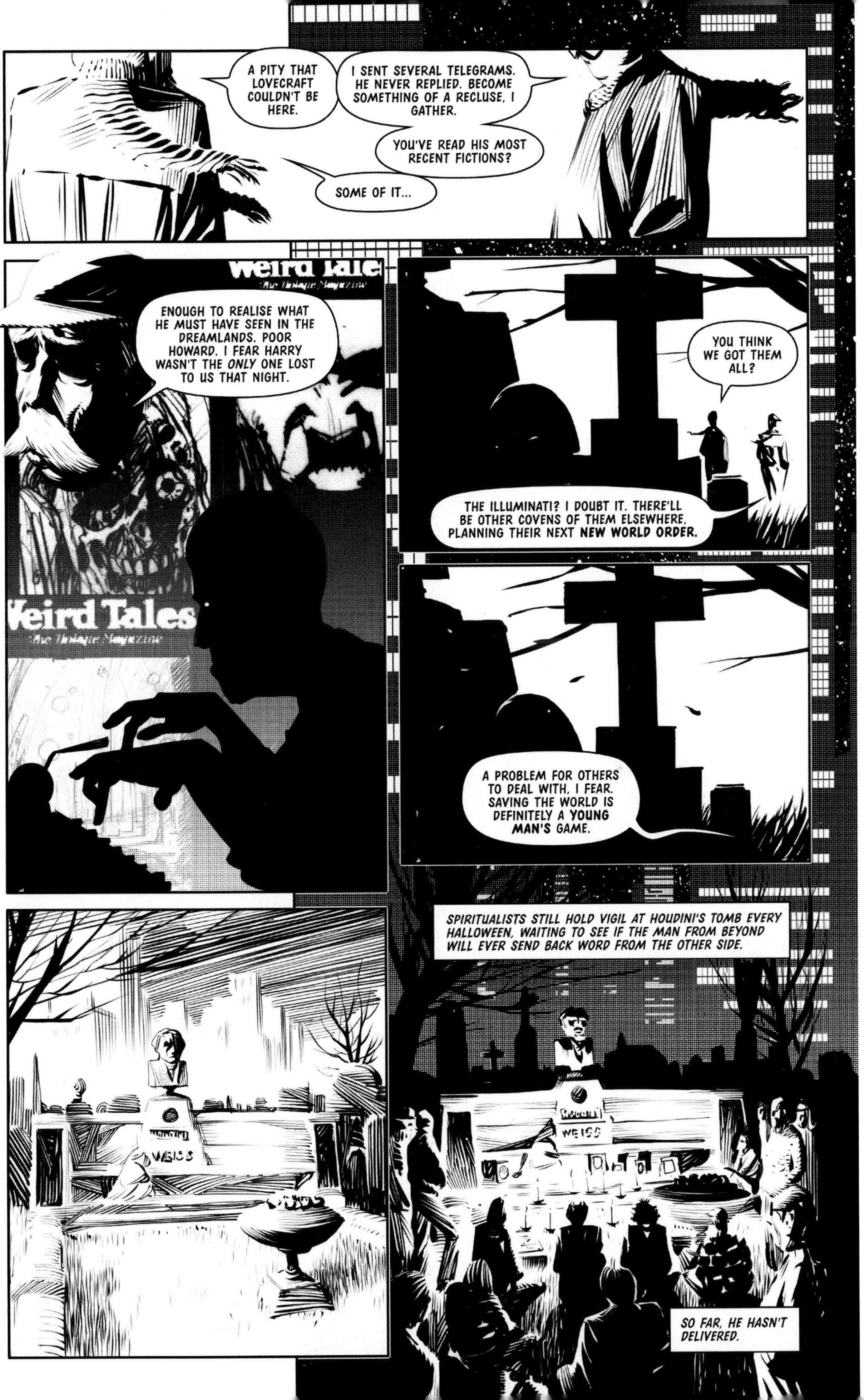
A PITY THAT LOVECRAFT COULDN'T BE HERE.
I SENT SEVERAL TELEGRAMS. HE NEVER REPLIED. BECOME SOMETHING OF A RECLUSE, I GATHER.
YOU'VE READ HIS MOST RECENT FICTIONS?
SOME OF IT...
Weird Tales
ENOUGH TO REALISE WHAT HE MUST HAVE SEEN IN THE DREAMLANDS. POOR HOWARD. I FEAR HARRY WASN'T THE *ONLY* ONE LOST TO US THAT NIGHT.
YOU THINK WE GOT THEM ALL?
THE ILLUMINATI? I DOUBT IT. THERE'LL BE OTHER COVENS OF THEM ELSEWHERE, PLANNING THEIR NEXT **NEW WORLD ORDER.**
A PROBLEM FOR OTHERS TO DEAL WITH, I FEAR. SAVING THE WORLD IS DEFINITELY A **YOUNG MAN'S** GAME.
WEISS
SPIRITUALISTS STILL HOLD VIGIL AT HOUDINI'S TOMB EVERY HALLOWEEN, WAITING TO SEE IF THE MAN FROM BEYOND WILL EVER SEND BACK WORD FROM THE OTHER SIDE.
WEISS
SO FAR, HE HASN'T DELIVERED.

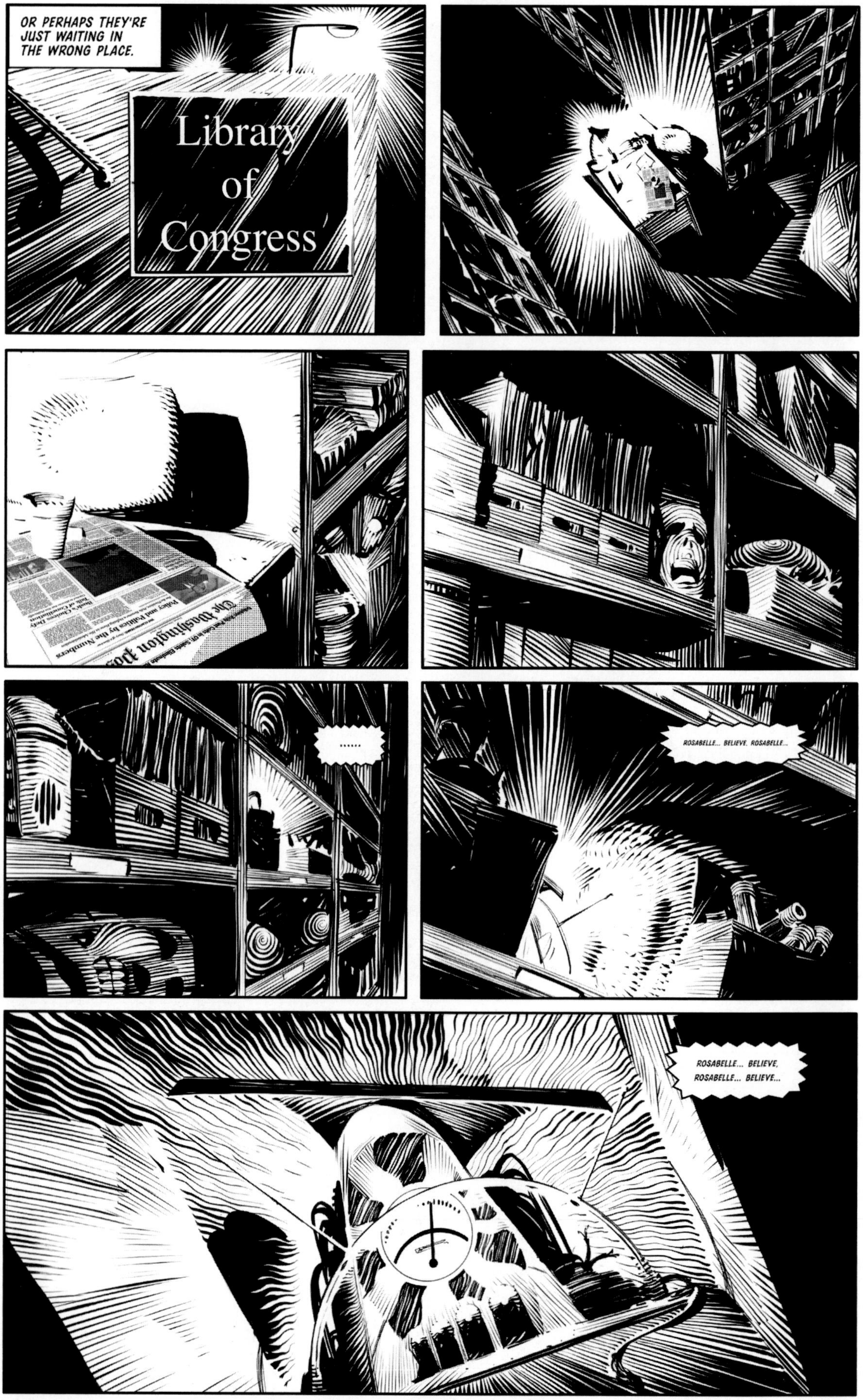
OR PERHAPS THEY'RE JUST WAITING IN THE WRONG PLACE.
Library of Congress
......
ROSABELLE... BELIEVE. ROSABELLE...
ROSABELLE... BELIEVE, ROSABELLE... BELIEVE...

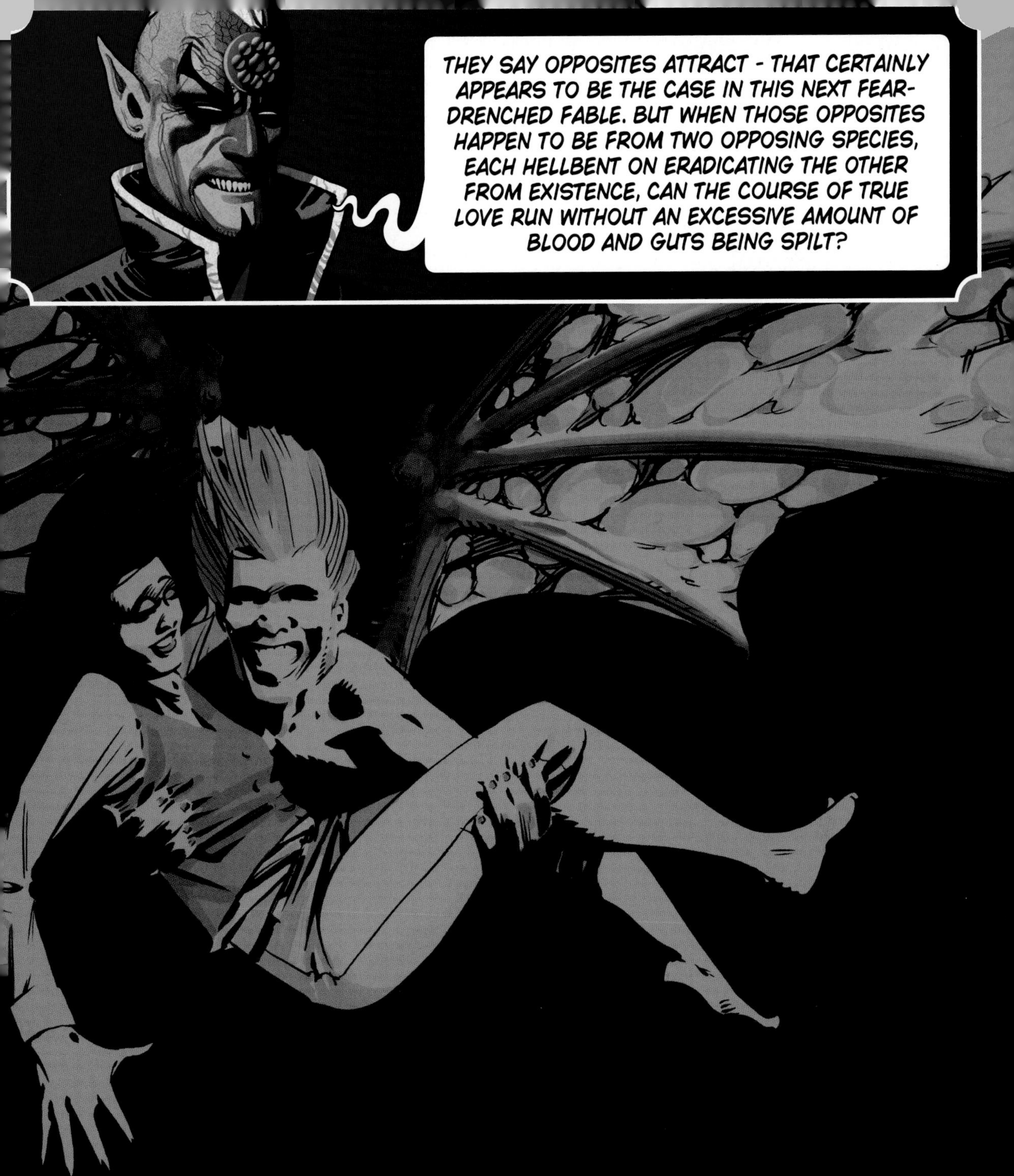
THEY SAY OPPOSITES ATTRACT - THAT CERTAINLY APPEARS TO BE THE CASE IN THIS NEXT FEAR-DRENCHED FABLE. BUT WHEN THOSE OPPOSITES HAPPEN TO BE FROM TWO OPPOSING SPECIES, EACH HELLBENT ON ERADICATING THE OTHER FROM EXISTENCE, CAN THE COURSE OF TRUE LOVE RUN WITHOUT AN EXCESSIVE AMOUNT OF BLOOD AND GUTS BEING SPILT?

A LOVE LIKE BLOOD

Script: John Smith
Art: Frazer Irving
Letters: Annie Parkhouse

Originally published in *2000 AD* Progs 1243-1249

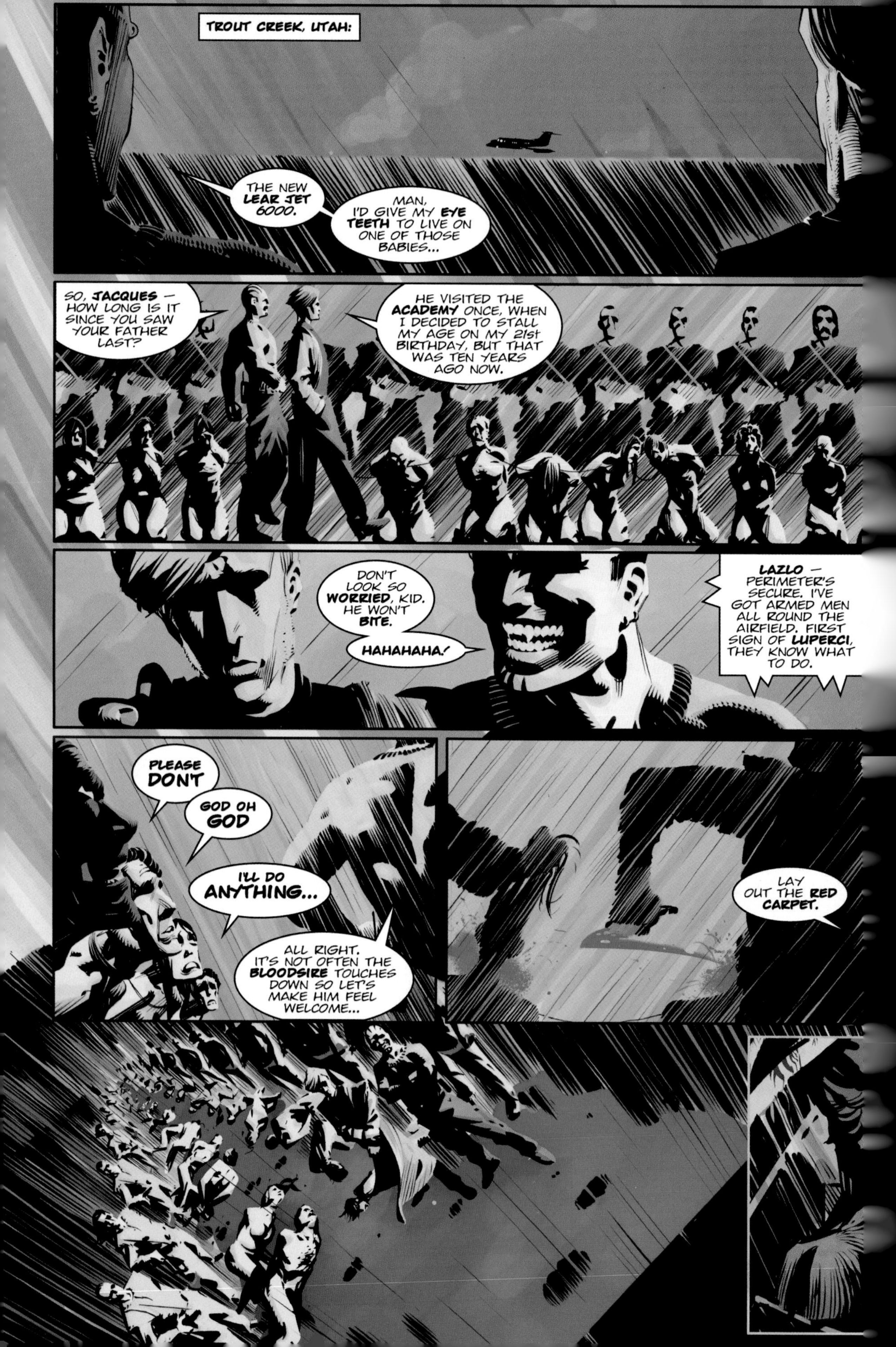
TROUT CREEK, UTAH:
THE NEW LEAR JET 6000.
MAN, I'D GIVE MY EYE TEETH TO LIVE ON ONE OF THOSE BABIES...
SO, JACQUES — HOW LONG IS IT SINCE YOU SAW YOUR FATHER LAST?
HE VISITED THE ACADEMY ONCE, WHEN I DECIDED TO STALL MY AGE ON MY 21st BIRTHDAY, BUT THAT WAS TEN YEARS AGO NOW.
DON'T LOOK SO WORRIED, KID. HE WON'T BITE.
HAHAHAHA!
LAZLO — PERIMETER'S SECURE. I'VE GOT ARMED MEN ALL ROUND THE AIRFIELD. FIRST SIGN OF LUPERCI, THEY KNOW WHAT TO DO.
PLEASE DON'T
GOD OH GOD
I'LL DO ANYTHING...
ALL RIGHT. IT'S NOT OFTEN THE BLOODSIRE TOUCHES DOWN SO LET'S MAKE HIM FEEL WELCOME...
LAY OUT THE RED CARPET.

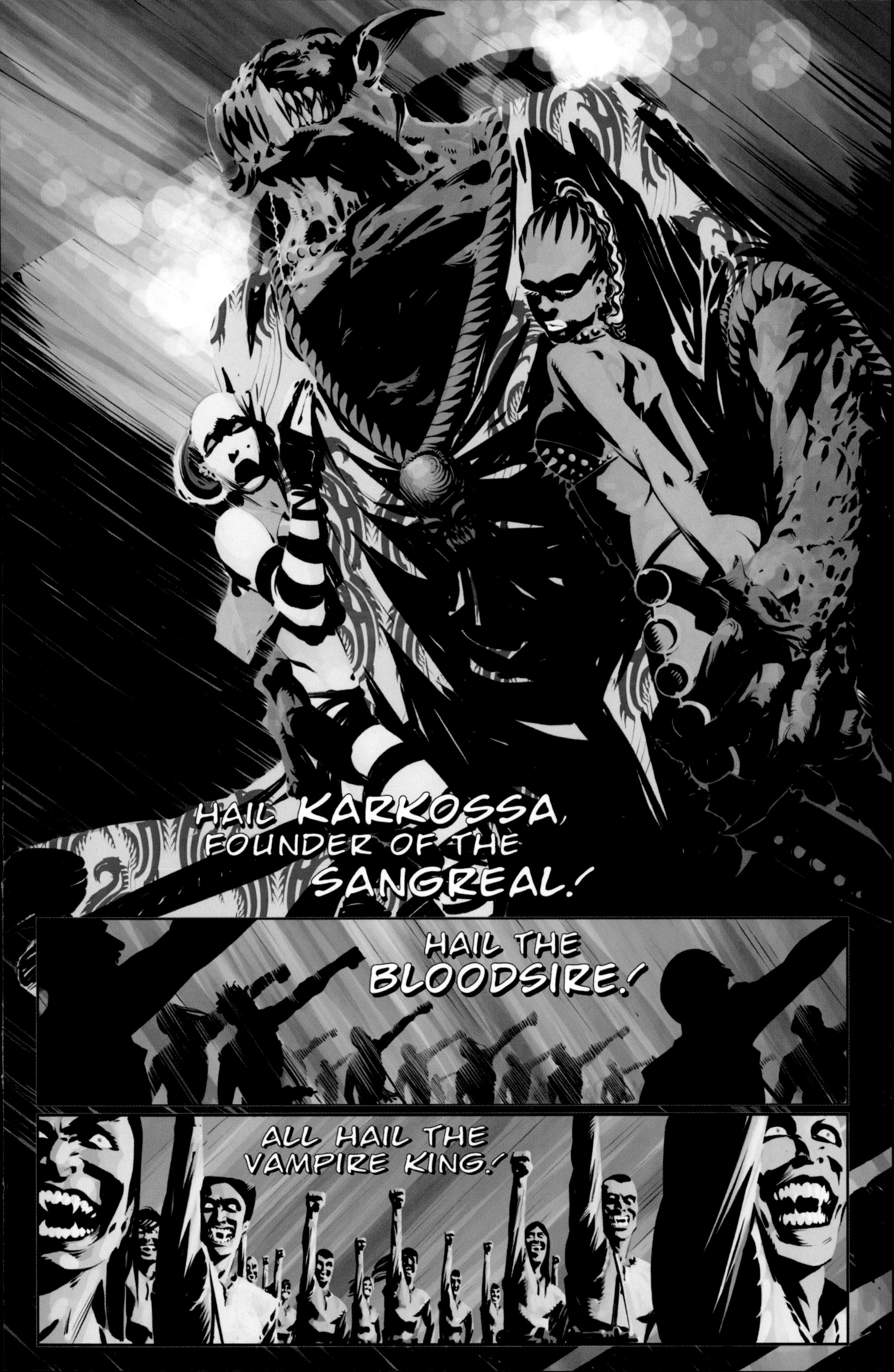
HAIL KARKOSSA, FOUNDER OF THE SANGREAL!
HAIL THE BLOODSIRE!
ALL HAIL THE VAMPIRE KING!

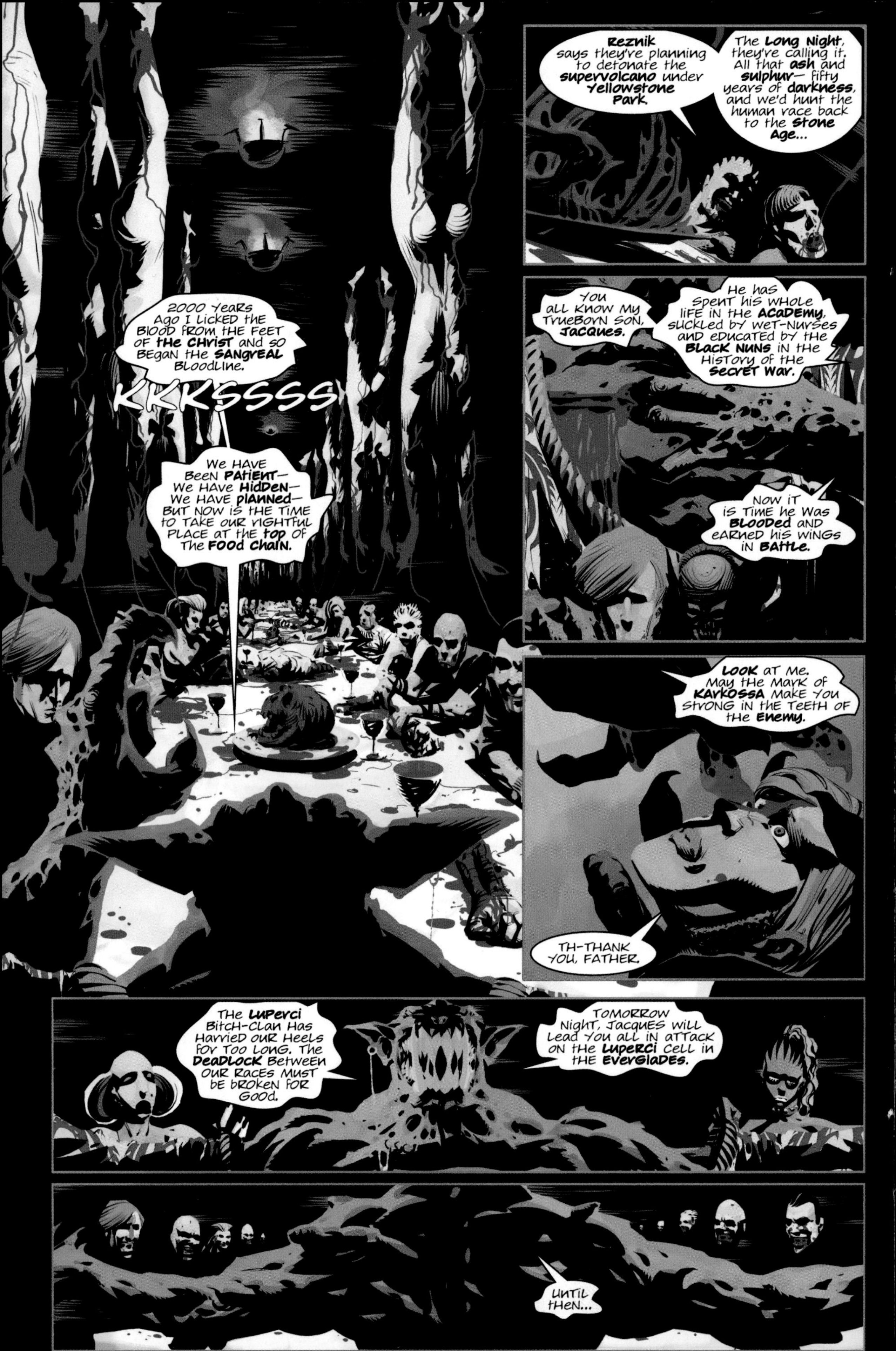
2000 YEARS AGO I LICKED THE BLOOD FROM THE FEET OF THE CHRIST AND SO BEGAN THE SANGREAL BLOODLINE.
KKKSSSS
WE HAVE BEEN PATIENT— WE HAVE HIDDEN— WE HAVE PLANNED— BUT NOW IS THE TIME TO TAKE OUR RIGHTFUL PLACE AT THE TOP OF THE FOOD CHAIN.
Reznik says they're planning to detonate the supervolcano under Yellowstone Park.
The Long Night, they're calling it. All that ash and sulphur— fifty years of darkness, and we'd hunt the human race back to the Stone Age...
YOU ALL KNOW MY TRUEBORN SON, JACQUES.
HE HAS SPENT HIS WHOLE LIFE IN THE ACADEMY, SUCKLED BY WET-NURSES AND EDUCATED BY THE BLACK NUNS IN THE HISTORY OF THE SECRET WAR.
NOW IT IS TIME HE WAS BLOODED AND EARNED HIS WINGS IN BATTLE.
LOOK AT ME. MAY THE MARK OF KARKOSSA MAKE YOU STRONG IN THE TEETH OF THE ENEMY.
TH-THANK YOU, FATHER.
THE LUPERCI BITCH-CLAN HAS HARRIED OUR HEELS FOR TOO LONG. THE DEADLOCK BETWEEN OUR RACES MUST BE BROKEN FOR GOOD.
TOMORROW NIGHT, JACQUES WILL LEAD YOU ALL IN ATTACK ON THE LUPERCI CELL IN THE EVERGLADES.
UNTIL THEN...

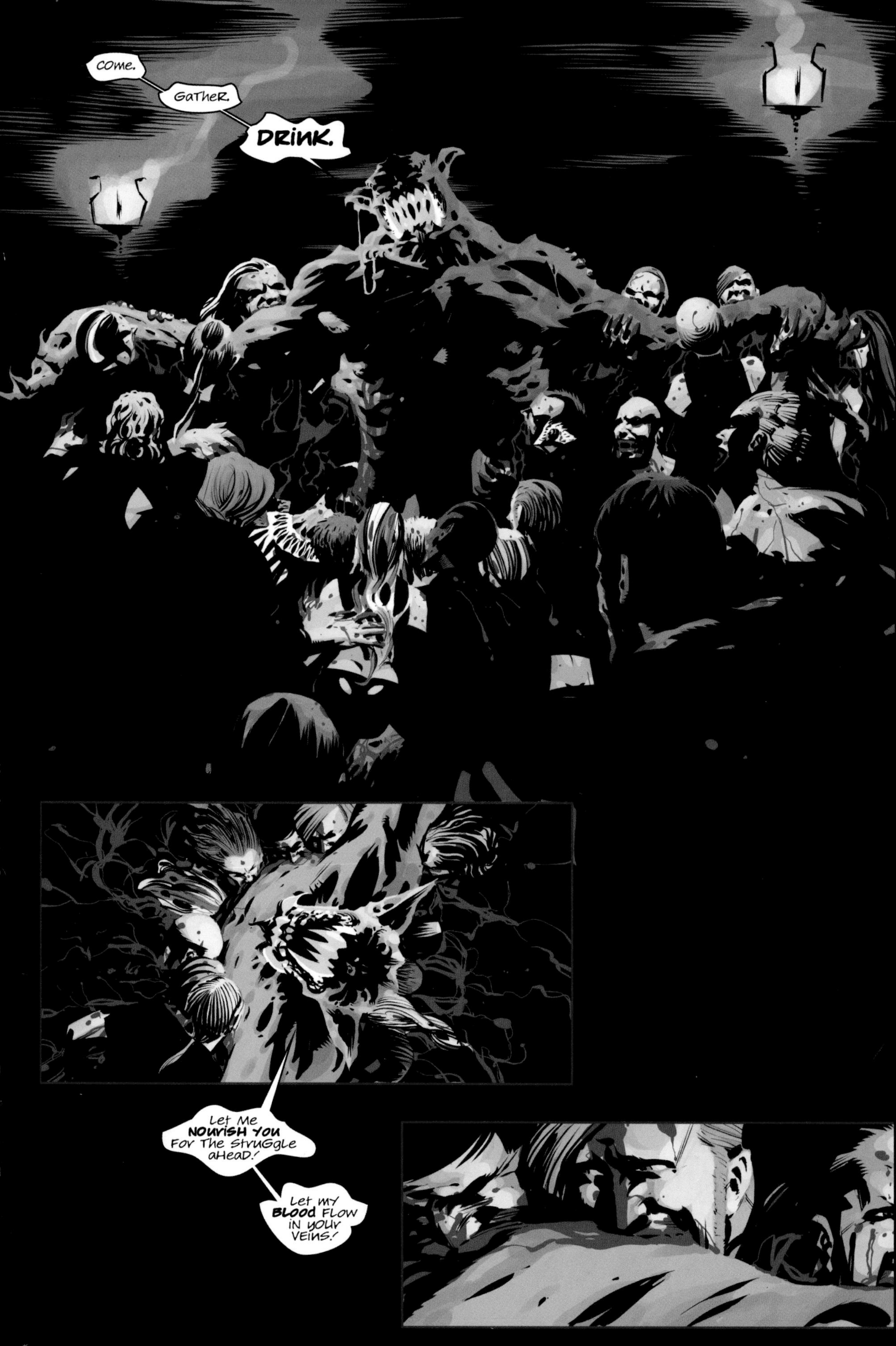
Come.
Gather.
DRINK.
Let Me NOURISH YOU For The Struggle aheaD!
Let my BLOOD Flow in your Veins!

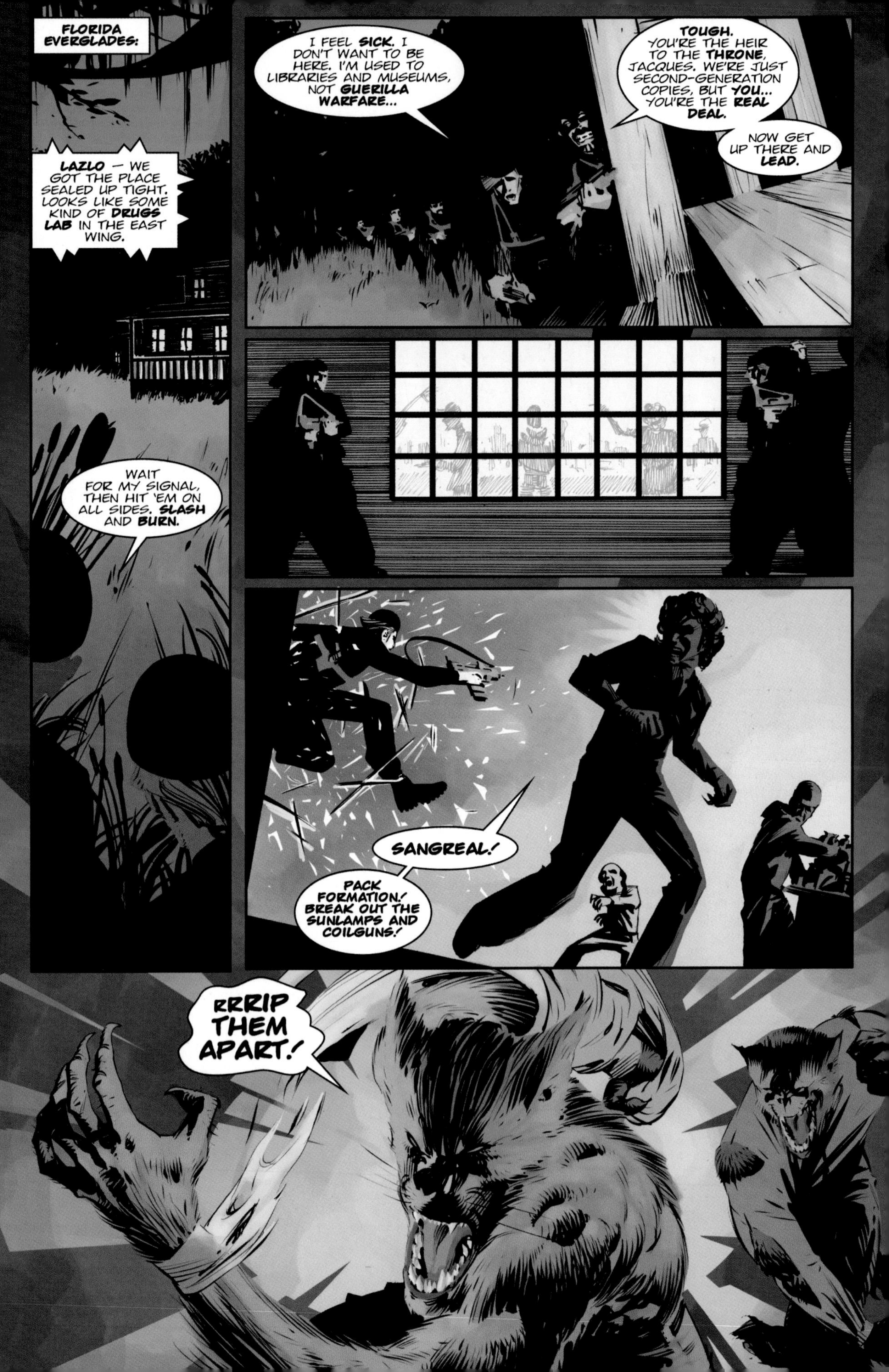
FLORIDA EVERGLADES:
I FEEL SICK. I DON'T WANT TO BE HERE. I'M USED TO LIBRARIES AND MUSEUMS, NOT GUERILLA WARFARE...
TOUGH. YOU'RE THE HEIR TO THE THRONE, JACQUES. WE'RE JUST SECOND-GENERATION COPIES, BUT YOU... YOU'RE THE REAL DEAL.
NOW GET UP THERE AND LEAD.
LAZLO — WE GOT THE PLACE SEALED UP TIGHT. LOOKS LIKE SOME KIND OF DRUGS LAB IN THE EAST WING.
WAIT FOR MY SIGNAL, THEN HIT 'EM ON ALL SIDES. SLASH AND BURN.
SANGREAL!
PACK FORMATION! BREAK OUT THE SUNLAMPS AND COILGUNS!
rRRIP THEM APART!

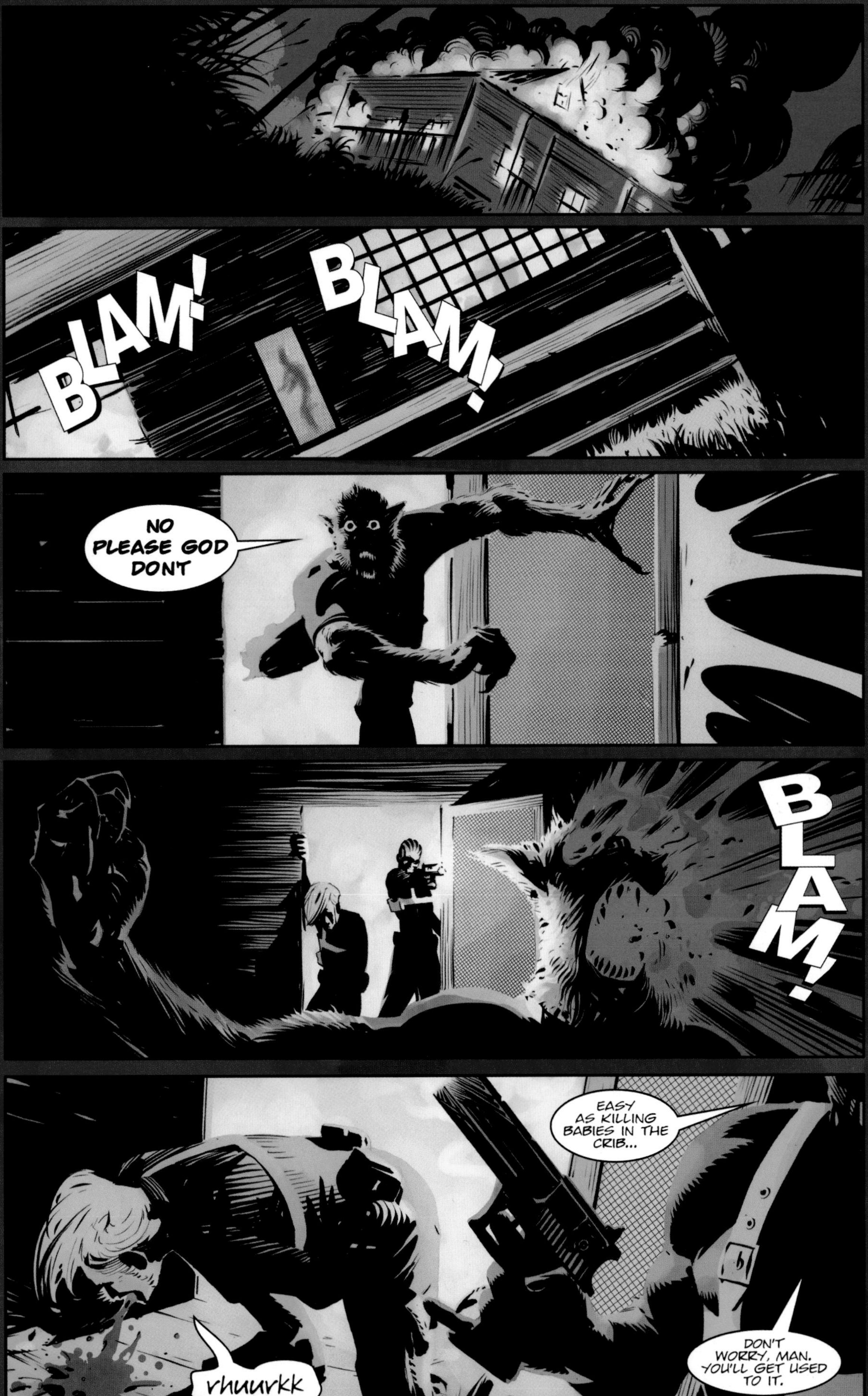
BLAM!
BLAM!
NO PLEASE GOD DON'T
BLAM!
EASY AS KILLING BABIES IN THE CRIB...
rhuurkk
DON'T WORRY, MAN. YOU'LL GET USED TO IT.

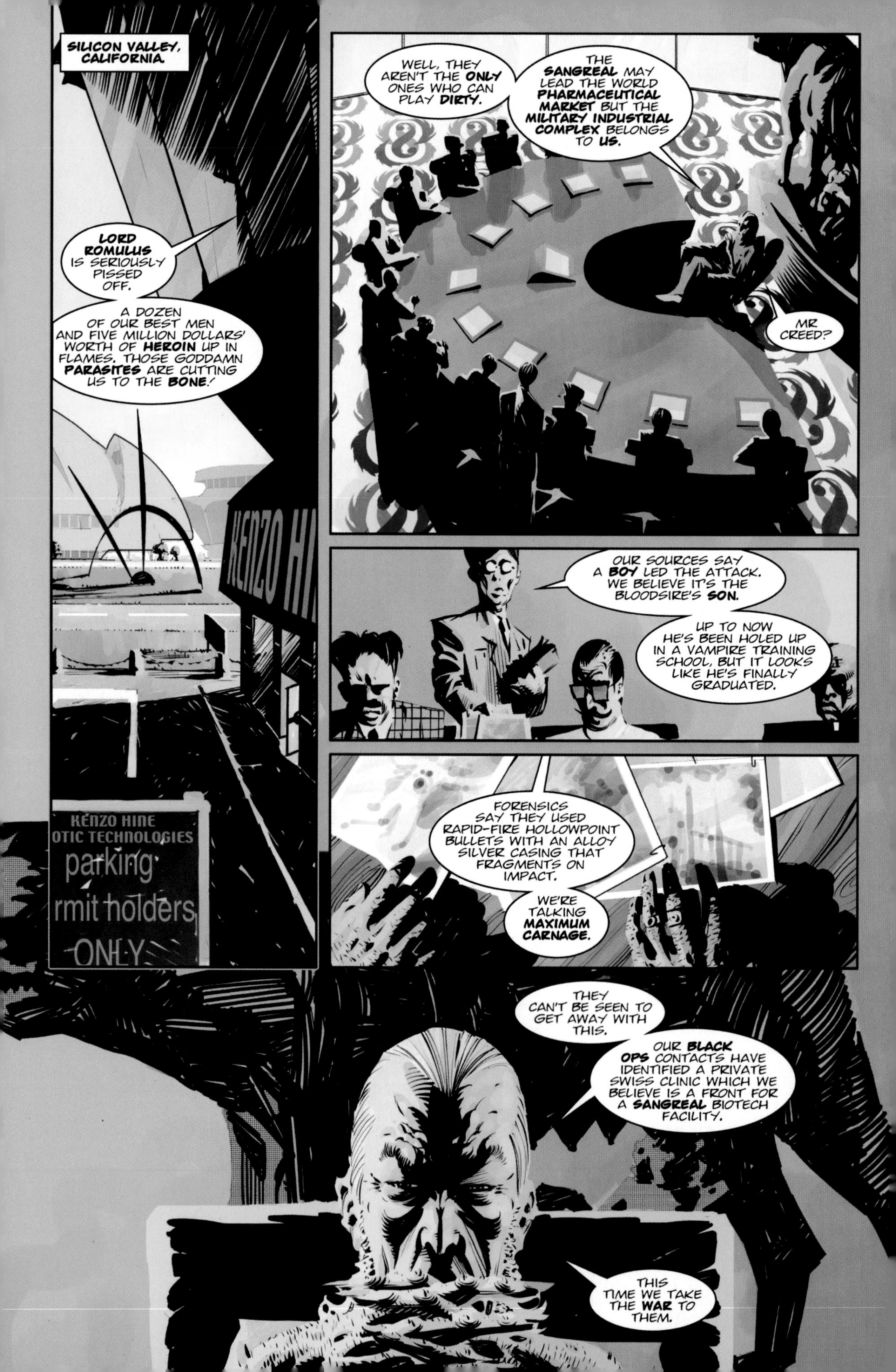
SILICON VALLEY, CALIFORNIA.
LORD ROMULUS IS SERIOUSLY PISSED OFF.
A DOZEN OF OUR BEST MEN AND FIVE MILLION DOLLARS' WORTH OF HEROIN UP IN FLAMES. THOSE GODDAMN PARASITES ARE CUTTING US TO THE BONE!
KENZO HI
KENZO HINE
OTIC TECHNOLOGIES
parking
rmit holders
ONLY
WELL, THEY AREN'T THE ONLY ONES WHO CAN PLAY DIRTY.
THE SANGREAL MAY LEAD THE WORLD PHARMACEUTICAL MARKET BUT THE MILITARY INDUSTRIAL COMPLEX BELONGS TO US.
MR CREED?
OUR SOURCES SAY A BOY LED THE ATTACK. WE BELIEVE IT'S THE BLOODSIRE'S SON.
UP TO NOW HE'S BEEN HOLED UP IN A VAMPIRE TRAINING SCHOOL, BUT IT LOOKS LIKE HE'S FINALLY GRADUATED.
FORENSICS SAY THEY USED RAPID-FIRE HOLLOWPOINT BULLETS WITH AN ALLOY SILVER CASING THAT FRAGMENTS ON IMPACT.
WE'RE TALKING MAXIMUM CARNAGE.
THEY CAN'T BE SEEN TO GET AWAY WITH THIS.
OUR BLACK OPS CONTACTS HAVE IDENTIFIED A PRIVATE SWISS CLINIC WHICH WE BELIEVE IS A FRONT FOR A SANGREAL BIOTECH FACILITY.
THIS TIME WE TAKE THE WAR TO THEM.

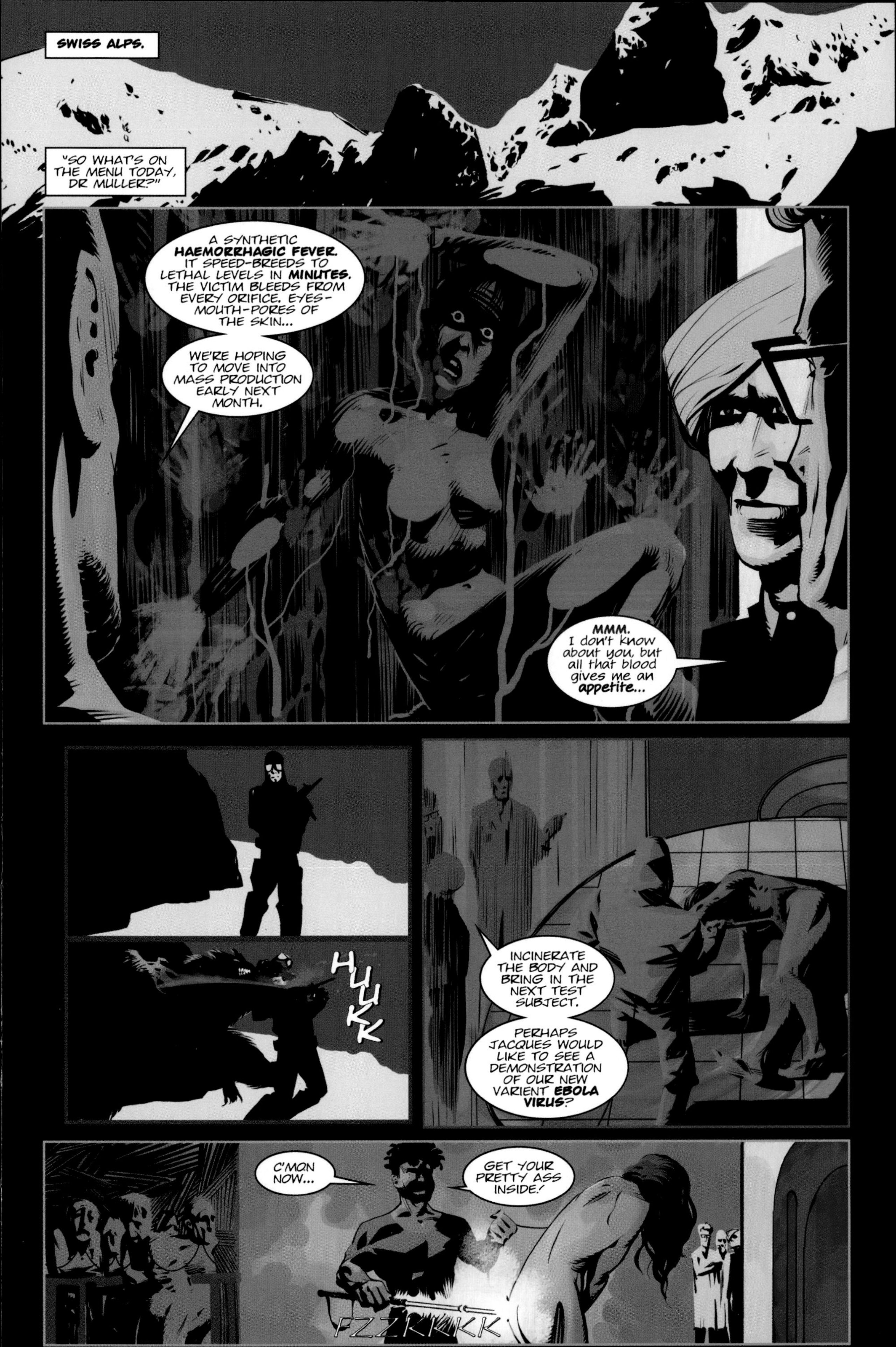

SWISS ALPS.
"SO WHAT'S ON THE MENU TODAY, DR MULLER?"
A SYNTHETIC HAEMORRHAGIC FEVER. IT SPEED-BREEDS TO LETHAL LEVELS IN MINUTES. THE VICTIM BLEEDS FROM EVERY ORIFICE. EYES-MOUTH-PORES OF THE SKIN...
WE'RE HOPING TO MOVE INTO MASS PRODUCTION EARLY NEXT MONTH.
MMM. I don't know about you, but all that blood gives me an appetite...
HUUKK
INCINERATE THE BODY AND BRING IN THE NEXT TEST SUBJECT.
PERHAPS JACQUES WOULD LIKE TO SEE A DEMONSTRATION OF OUR NEW VARIENT EBOLA VIRUS?
C'MON NOW...
GET YOUR PRETTY ASS INSIDE!
FZZRKKKK

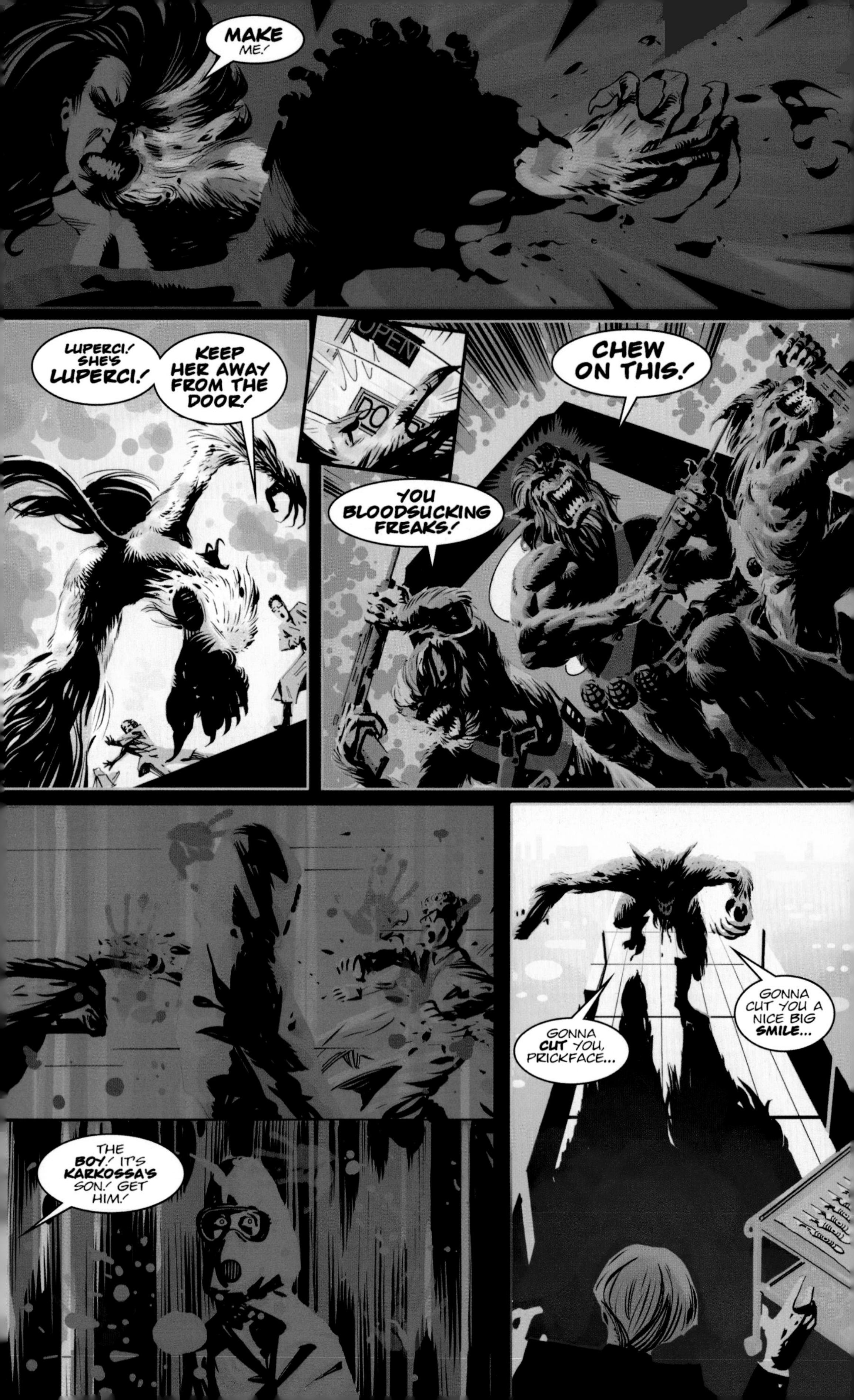
MAKE ME!
LUPERCI! SHE'S LUPERCI!
KEEP HER AWAY FROM THE DOOR!
OPEN
CHEW ON THIS!
YOU BLOODSUCKING FREAKS!
THE BOY! IT'S KARKOSSA'S SON! GET HIM!
GONNA CUT YOU, PRICKFACE...
GONNA CUT YOU A NICE BIG SMILE...

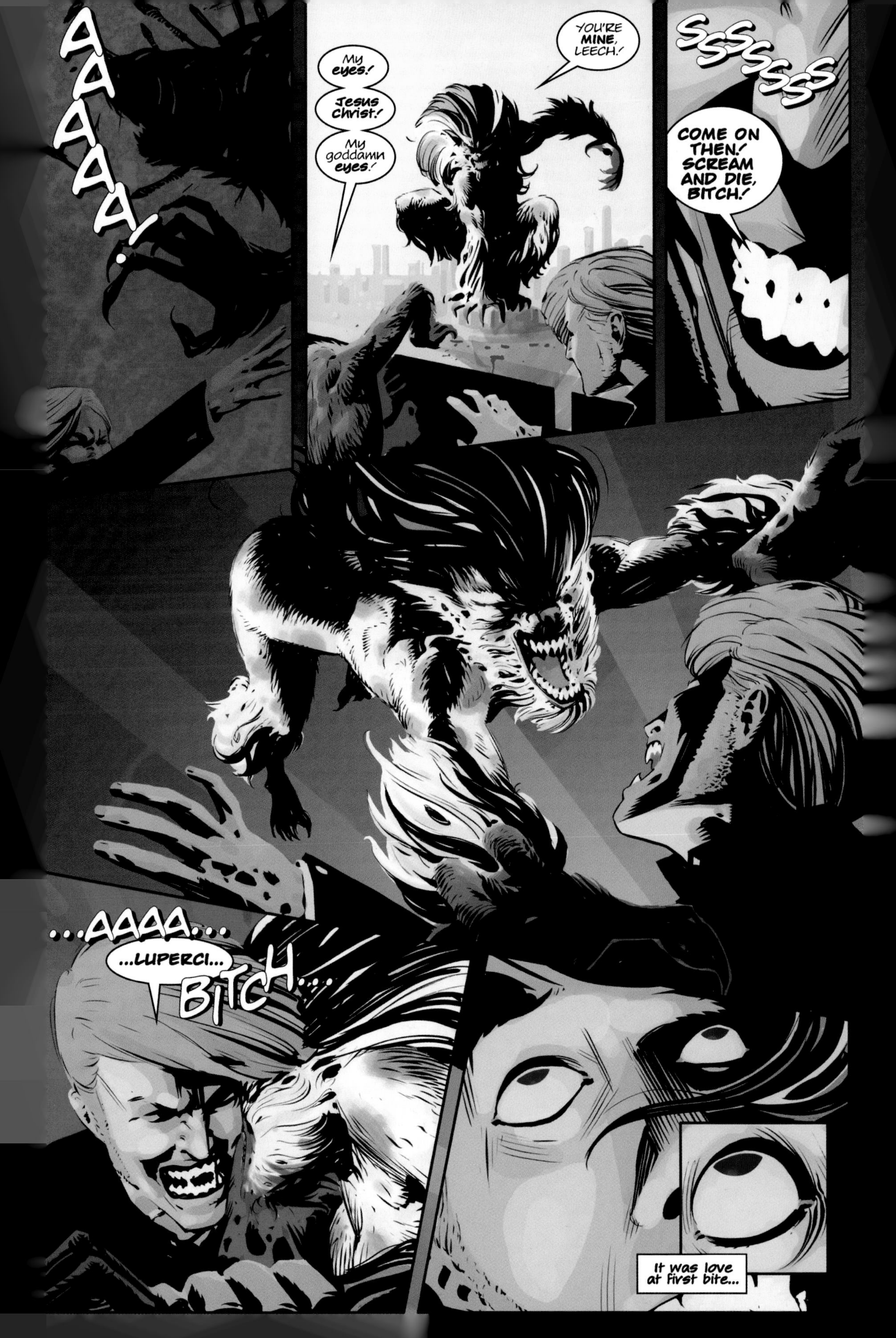
AAAAAA!
My eyes!
Jesus Christ!
My goddamn eyes!
YOU'RE MINE, LEECH!
SSSSSSSS
COME ON THEN! SCREAM AND DIE, BITCH!
...AAAA...
...LUPERCI...
BITCH...
It was love at first bite...

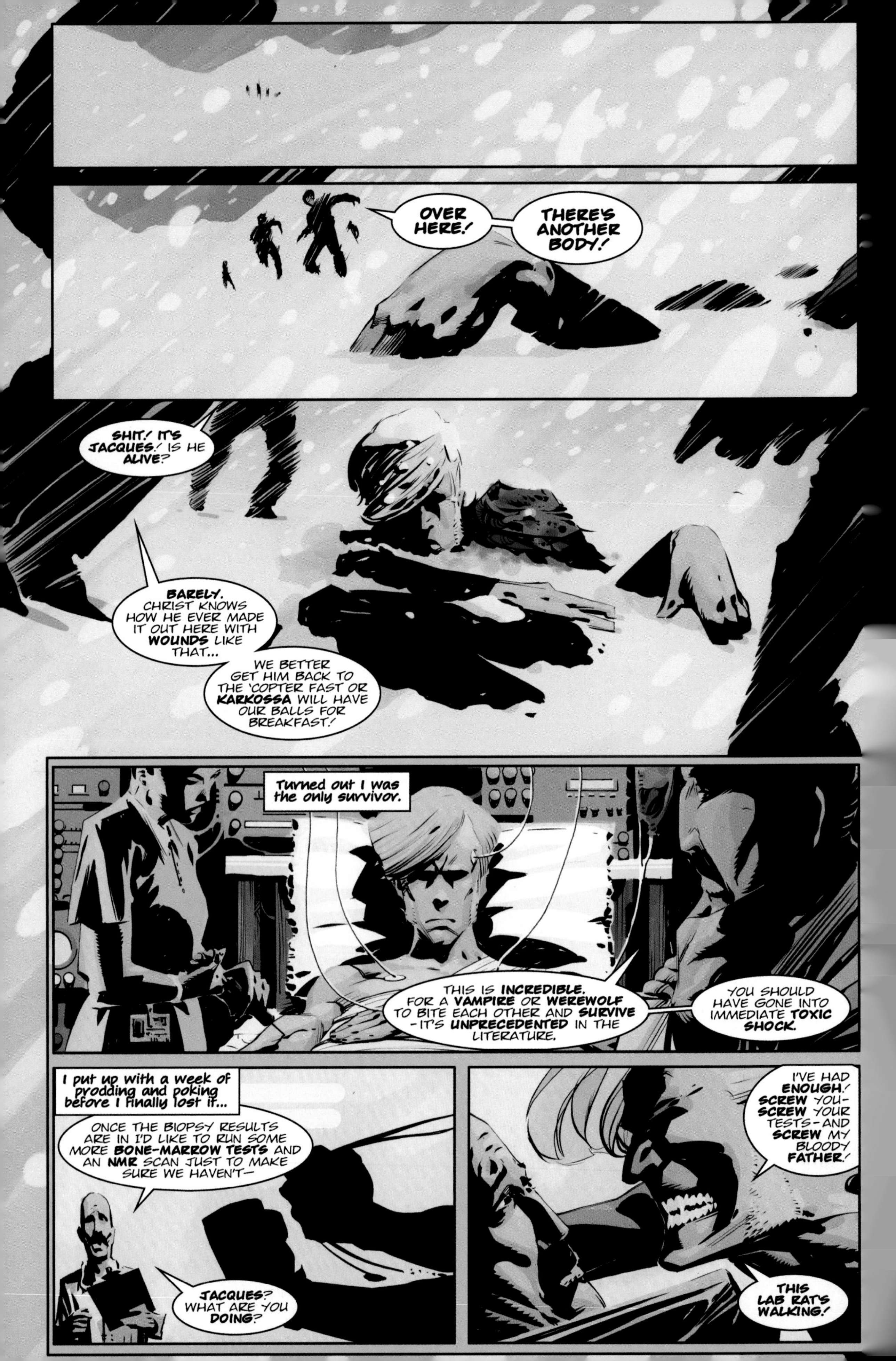
OVER HERE!
THERE'S ANOTHER BODY!
SHIT! IT'S JACQUES! IS HE ALIVE?
BARELY. CHRIST KNOWS HOW HE EVER MADE IT OUT HERE WITH WOUNDS LIKE THAT...
WE BETTER GET HIM BACK TO THE 'COPTER FAST OR KARKOSSA WILL HAVE OUR BALLS FOR BREAKFAST!
Turned out I was the only survivor.
THIS IS INCREDIBLE. FOR A VAMPIRE OR WEREWOLF TO BITE EACH OTHER AND SURVIVE –IT'S UNPRECEDENTED IN THE LITERATURE.
YOU SHOULD HAVE GONE INTO IMMEDIATE TOXIC SHOCK.
I put up with a week of prodding and poking before I finally lost it...
ONCE THE BIOPSY RESULTS ARE IN I'D LIKE TO RUN SOME MORE BONE-MARROW TESTS AND AN NMR SCAN JUST TO MAKE SURE WE HAVEN'T—
JACQUES? WHAT ARE YOU DOING?
I'VE HAD ENOUGH! SCREW YOU– SCREW YOUR TESTS–AND SCREW MY BLOODY FATHER!
THIS LAB RAT'S WALKING!

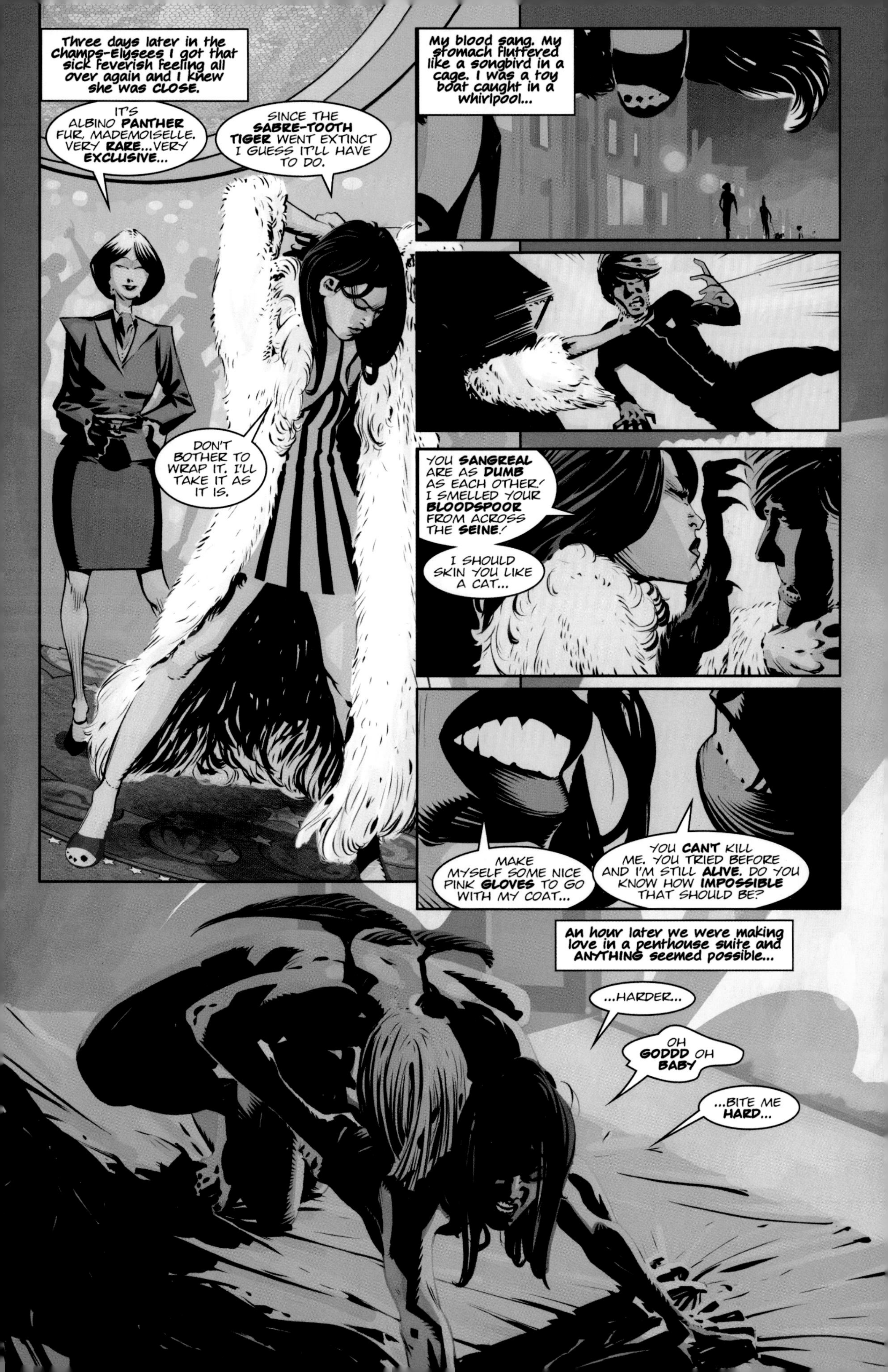
Three days later in the Champs-Elysees I got that sick feverish feeling all over again and I knew she was CLOSE.
IT'S ALBINO PANTHER FUR, MADEMOISELLE. VERY RARE...VERY EXCLUSIVE...
SINCE THE SABRE-TOOTH TIGER WENT EXTINCT I GUESS IT'LL HAVE TO DO.
DON'T BOTHER TO WRAP IT. I'LL TAKE IT AS IT IS.
My blood sang. My stomach fluttered like a songbird in a cage. I was a toy boat caught in a whirlpool...
YOU SANGREAL ARE AS DUMB AS EACH OTHER! I SMELLED YOUR BLOODSPOOR FROM ACROSS THE SEINE!
I SHOULD SKIN YOU LIKE A CAT...
MAKE MYSELF SOME NICE PINK GLOVES TO GO WITH MY COAT...
YOU CAN'T KILL ME. YOU TRIED BEFORE AND I'M STILL ALIVE. DO YOU KNOW HOW IMPOSSIBLE THAT SHOULD BE?
An hour later we were making love in a penthouse suite and ANYTHING seemed possible...
...HARDER...
OH GODDD OH BABY
...BITE ME HARD...

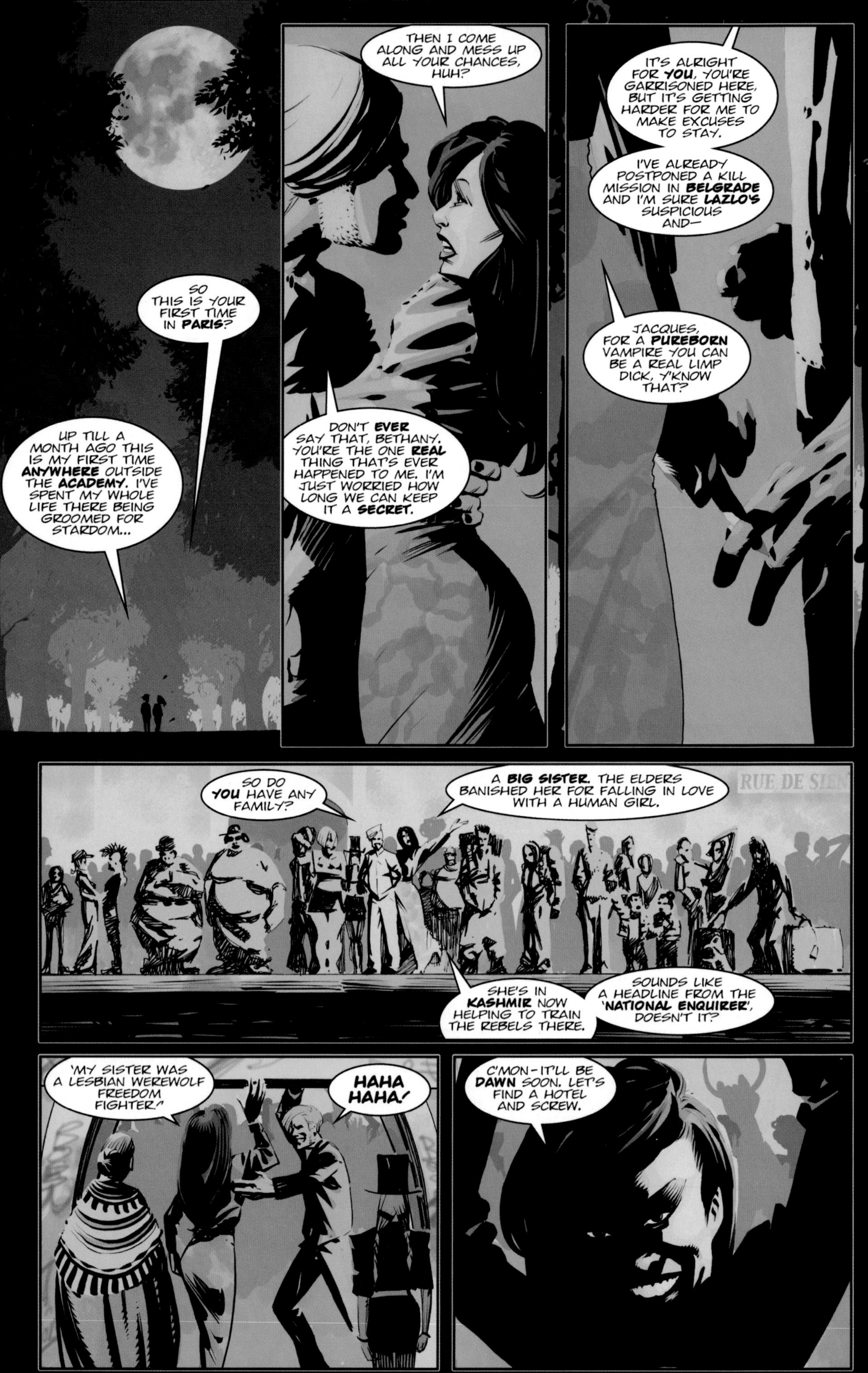
SO THIS IS YOUR FIRST TIME IN PARIS?
UP TILL A MONTH AGO THIS IS MY FIRST TIME ANYWHERE OUTSIDE THE ACADEMY. I'VE SPENT MY WHOLE LIFE THERE BEING GROOMED FOR STARDOM...
THEN I COME ALONG AND MESS UP ALL YOUR CHANCES, HUH?
DON'T EVER SAY THAT, BETHANY. YOU'RE THE ONE REAL THING THAT'S EVER HAPPENED TO ME. I'M JUST WORRIED HOW LONG WE CAN KEEP IT A SECRET.
IT'S ALRIGHT FOR YOU, YOU'RE GARRISONED HERE, BUT IT'S GETTING HARDER FOR ME TO MAKE EXCUSES TO STAY.
I'VE ALREADY POSTPONED A KILL MISSION IN BELGRADE AND I'M SURE LAZLO'S SUSPICIOUS AND—
JACQUES, FOR A PUREBORN VAMPIRE YOU CAN BE A REAL LIMP DICK, Y'KNOW THAT?
RUE DE SIEN
SO DO YOU HAVE ANY FAMILY?
A BIG SISTER. THE ELDERS BANISHED HER FOR FALLING IN LOVE WITH A HUMAN GIRL.
SHE'S IN KASHMIR NOW HELPING TO TRAIN THE REBELS THERE.
SOUNDS LIKE A HEADLINE FROM THE 'NATIONAL ENQUIRER', DOESN'T IT?
'MY SISTER WAS A LESBIAN WEREWOLF FREEDOM FIGHTER.'
HAHA HAHA!
C'MON-IT'LL BE DAWN SOON. LET'S FIND A HOTEL AND SCREW.

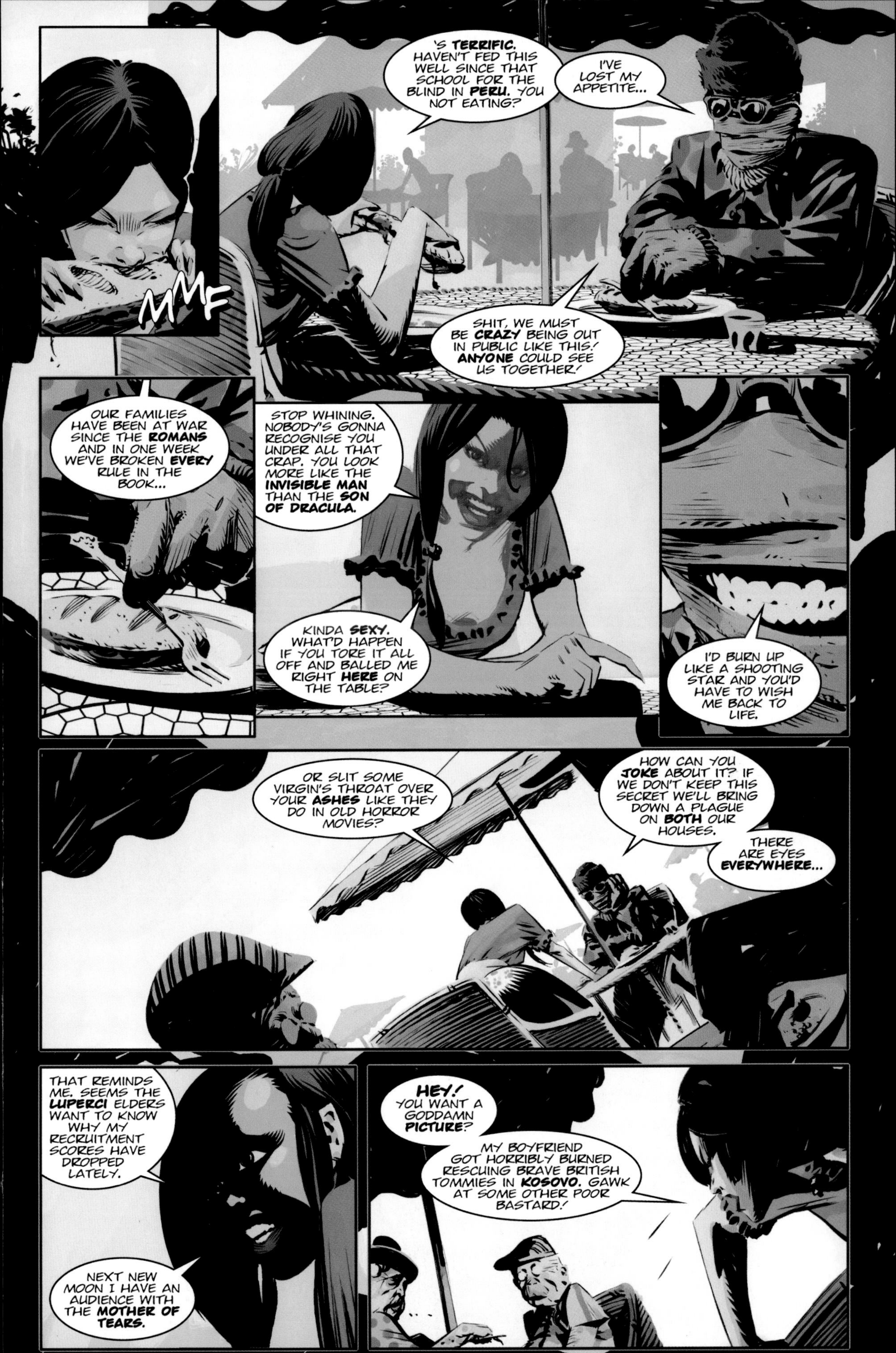
MMF
'S TERRIFIC. HAVEN'T FED THIS WELL SINCE THAT SCHOOL FOR THE BLIND IN PERU. YOU NOT EATING?
I'VE LOST MY APPETITE...
SHIT, WE MUST BE CRAZY BEING OUT IN PUBLIC LIKE THIS! ANYONE COULD SEE US TOGETHER!
OUR FAMILIES HAVE BEEN AT WAR SINCE THE ROMANS AND IN ONE WEEK WE'VE BROKEN EVERY RULE IN THE BOOK...
STOP WHINING. NOBODY'S GONNA RECOGNISE YOU UNDER ALL THAT CRAP. YOU LOOK MORE LIKE THE INVISIBLE MAN THAN THE SON OF DRACULA.
KINDA SEXY. WHAT'D HAPPEN IF YOU TORE IT ALL OFF AND BALLED ME RIGHT HERE ON THE TABLE?
I'D BURN UP LIKE A SHOOTING STAR AND YOU'D HAVE TO WISH ME BACK TO LIFE.
OR SLIT SOME VIRGIN'S THROAT OVER YOUR ASHES LIKE THEY DO IN OLD HORROR MOVIES?
HOW CAN YOU JOKE ABOUT IT? IF WE DON'T KEEP THIS SECRET WE'LL BRING DOWN A PLAGUE ON BOTH OUR HOUSES.
THERE ARE EYES EVERYWHERE...
THAT REMINDS ME. SEEMS THE LUPERCI ELDERS WANT TO KNOW WHY MY RECRUITMENT SCORES HAVE DROPPED LATELY.
NEXT NEW MOON I HAVE AN AUDIENCE WITH THE MOTHER OF TEARS.
HEY! YOU WANT A GODDAMN PICTURE?
MY BOYFRIEND GOT HORRIBLY BURNED RESCUING BRAVE BRITISH TOMMIES IN KOSOVO. GAWK AT SOME OTHER POOR BASTARD!
...

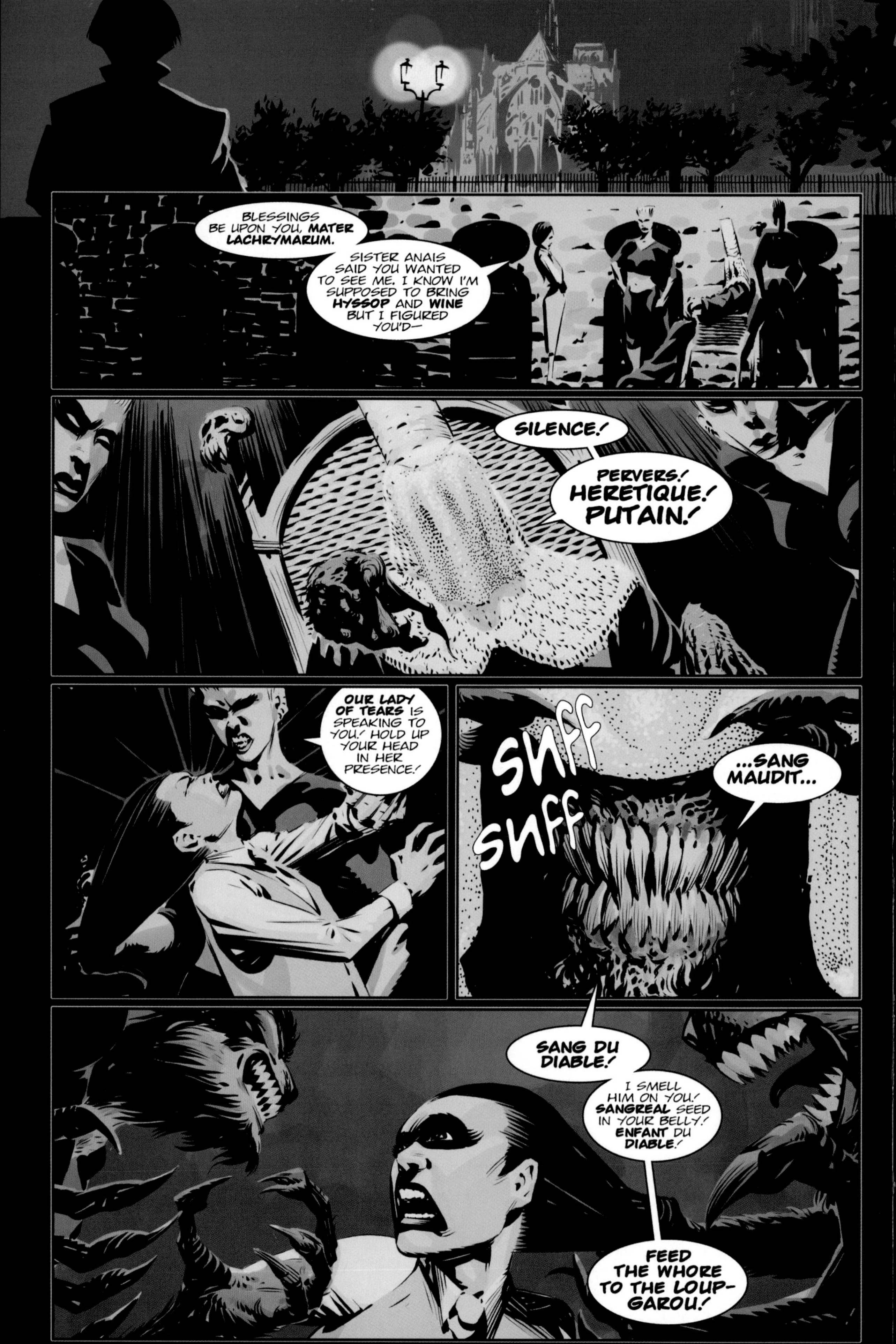
BLESSINGS BE UPON YOU, MATER LACHRYMARUM.
SISTER ANAIS SAID YOU WANTED TO SEE ME. I KNOW I'M SUPPOSED TO BRING HYSSOP AND WINE BUT I FIGURED YOU'D—
SILENCE!
PERVERS! HERETIQUE! PUTAIN!
OUR LADY OF TEARS IS SPEAKING TO YOU! HOLD UP YOUR HEAD IN HER PRESENCE!
SNFF SNFF
...SANG MAUDIT...
SANG DU DIABLE!
I SMELL HIM ON YOU! SANGREAL SEED IN YOUR BELLY! ENFANT DU DIABLE!
FEED THE WHORE TO THE LOUP-GAROU!

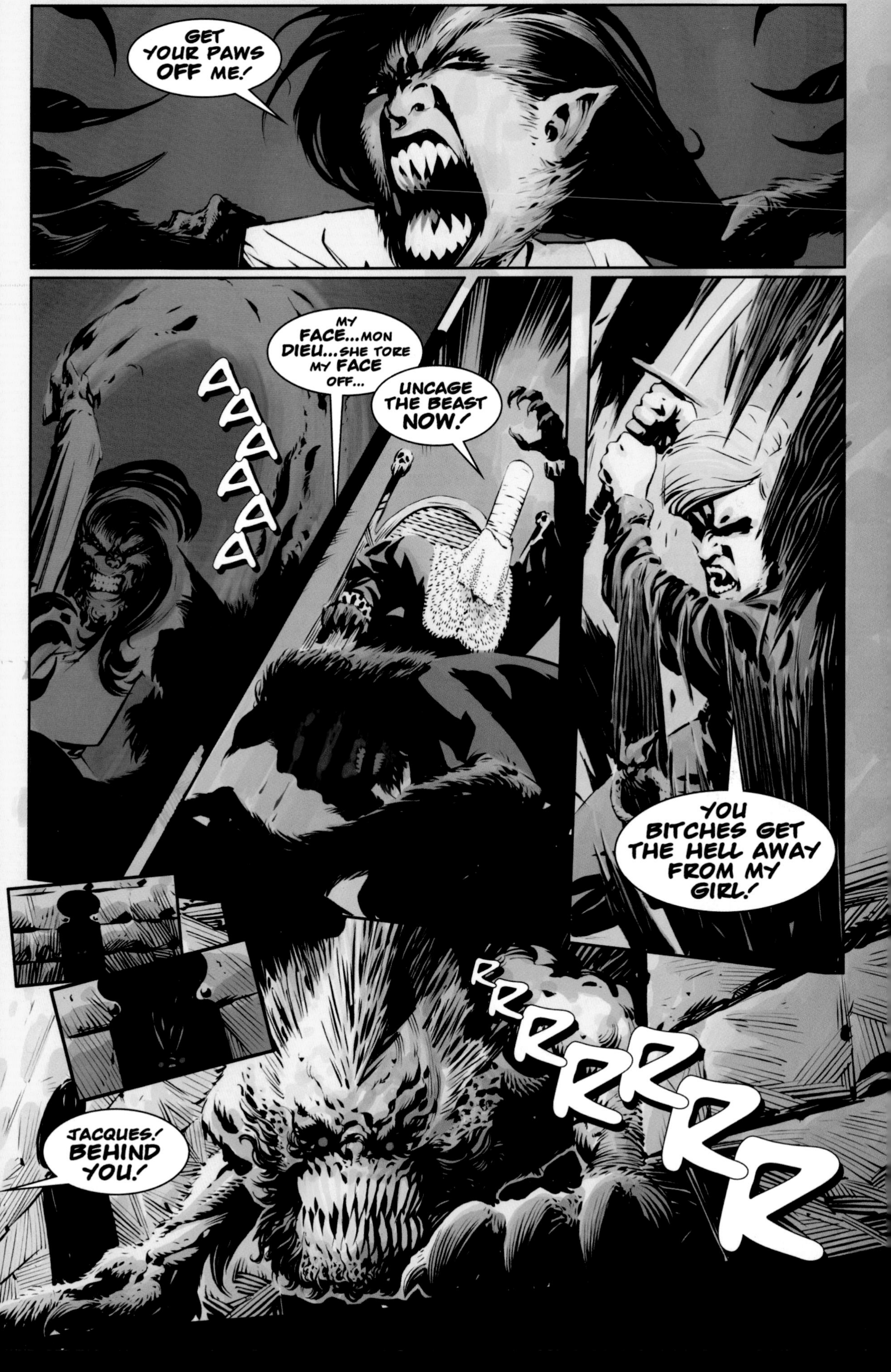
GET YOUR PAWS OFF ME!
AAAAAA
MY FACE...MON DIEU...SHE TORE MY FACE OFF...
UNCAGE THE BEAST NOW!
YOU BITCHES GET THE HELL AWAY FROM MY GIRL!
RRRRRRRR
JACQUES! BEHIND YOU!

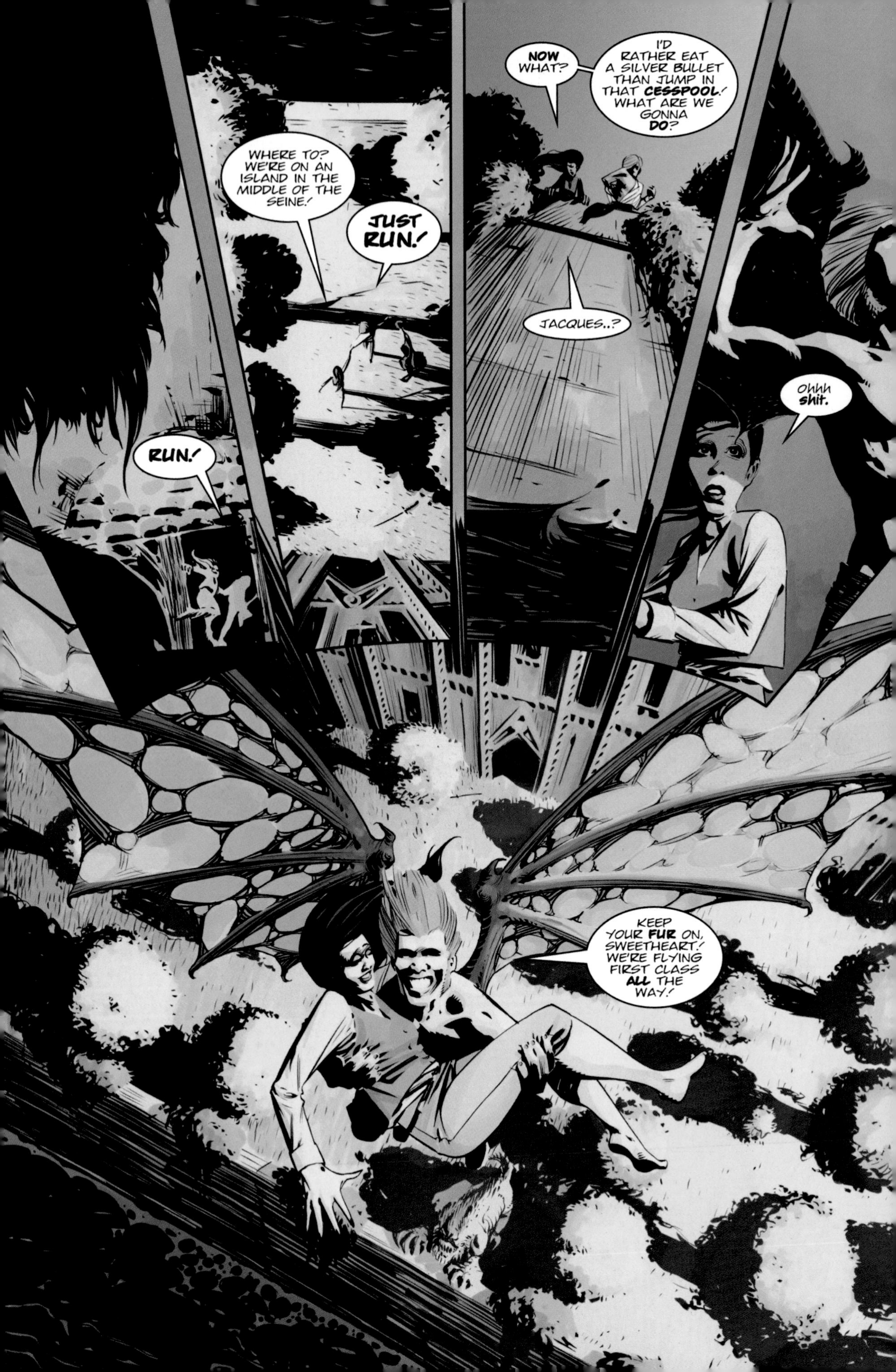
RUN!
WHERE TO? WE'RE ON AN ISLAND IN THE MIDDLE OF THE SEINE!
JUST RUN!
NOW WHAT?
I'D RATHER EAT A SILVER BULLET THAN JUMP IN THAT CESSPOOL! WHAT ARE WE GONNA DO?
JACQUES..?
Ohhh shit.
KEEP YOUR FUR ON, SWEETHEART! WE'RE FLYING FIRST CLASS ALL THE WAY!

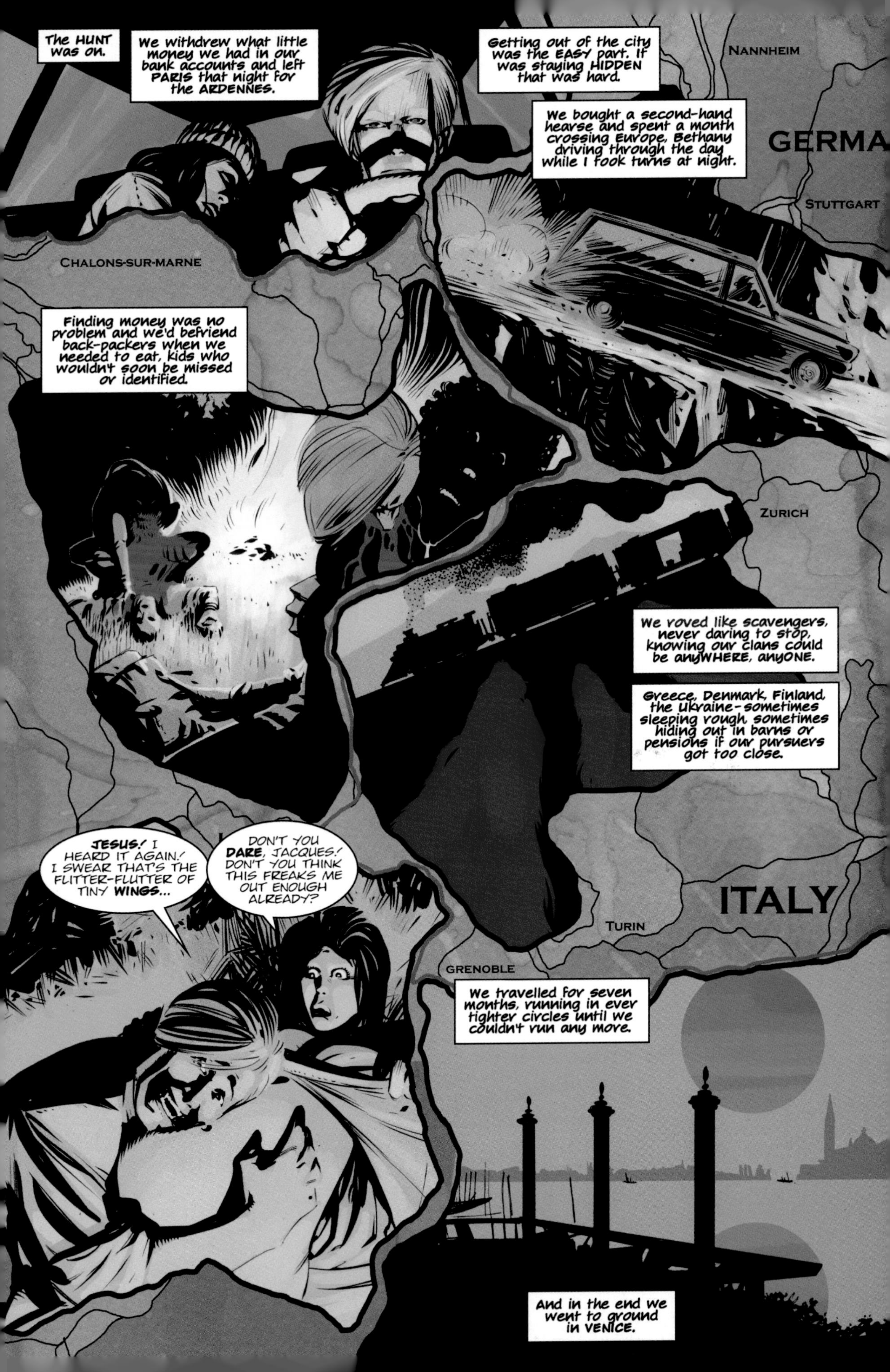

The HUNT was on.
We withdrew what little money we had in our bank accounts and left PARIS that night for the ARDENNES.
Getting out of the city was the EASY part. It was staying HIDDEN that was hard.
NANNHEIM
We bought a second-hand hearse and spent a month crossing Europe, Bethany driving through the day while I took turns at night.
GERMA
STUTTGART
CHALONS-SUR-MARNE
Finding money was no problem and we'd befriend back-packers when we needed to eat, kids who wouldn't soon be missed or identified.
ZURICH
We roved like scavengers, never daring to stop, knowing our clans could be anyWHERE, anyONE.
Greece, Denmark, Finland, the Ukraine - sometimes sleeping rough, sometimes hiding out in barns or pensions if our pursuers got too close.
JESUS! I HEARD IT AGAIN! I SWEAR THAT'S THE FLITTER-FLUTTER OF TINY WINGS...
DON'T YOU DARE, JACQUES! DON'T YOU THINK THIS FREAKS ME OUT ENOUGH ALREADY?
ITALY
TURIN
GRENOBLE
We travelled for seven months, running in ever tighter circles until we couldn't run any more.
And in the end we went to ground in VENICE.

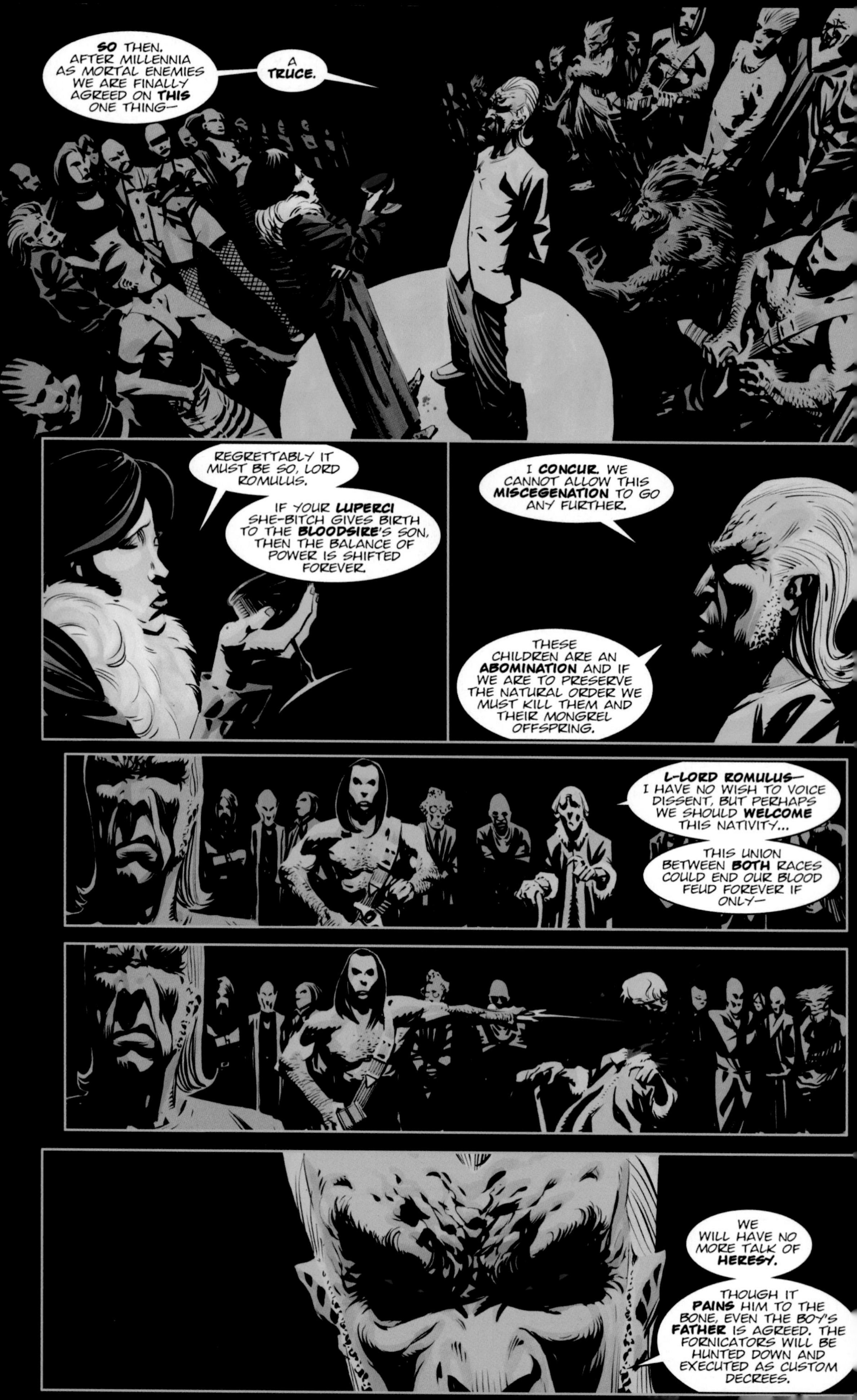
SO THEN. AFTER MILLENNIA AS MORTAL ENEMIES WE ARE FINALLY AGREED ON THIS ONE THING—
A TRUCE.
REGRETTABLY IT MUST BE SO, LORD ROMULUS.
IF YOUR LUPERCI SHE-BITCH GIVES BIRTH TO THE BLOODSIRE'S SON, THEN THE BALANCE OF POWER IS SHIFTED FOREVER.
I CONCUR. WE CANNOT ALLOW THIS MISCEGENATION TO GO ANY FURTHER.
THESE CHILDREN ARE AN ABOMINATION AND IF WE ARE TO PRESERVE THE NATURAL ORDER WE MUST KILL THEM AND THEIR MONGREL OFFSPRING.
L-LORD ROMULUS— I HAVE NO WISH TO VOICE DISSENT, BUT PERHAPS WE SHOULD WELCOME THIS NATIVITY...
THIS UNION BETWEEN BOTH RACES COULD END OUR BLOOD FEUD FOREVER IF ONLY—
WE WILL HAVE NO MORE TALK OF HERESY.
THOUGH IT PAINS HIM TO THE BONE, EVEN THE BOY'S FATHER IS AGREED. THE FORNICATORS WILL BE HUNTED DOWN AND EXECUTED AS CUSTOM DECREES.

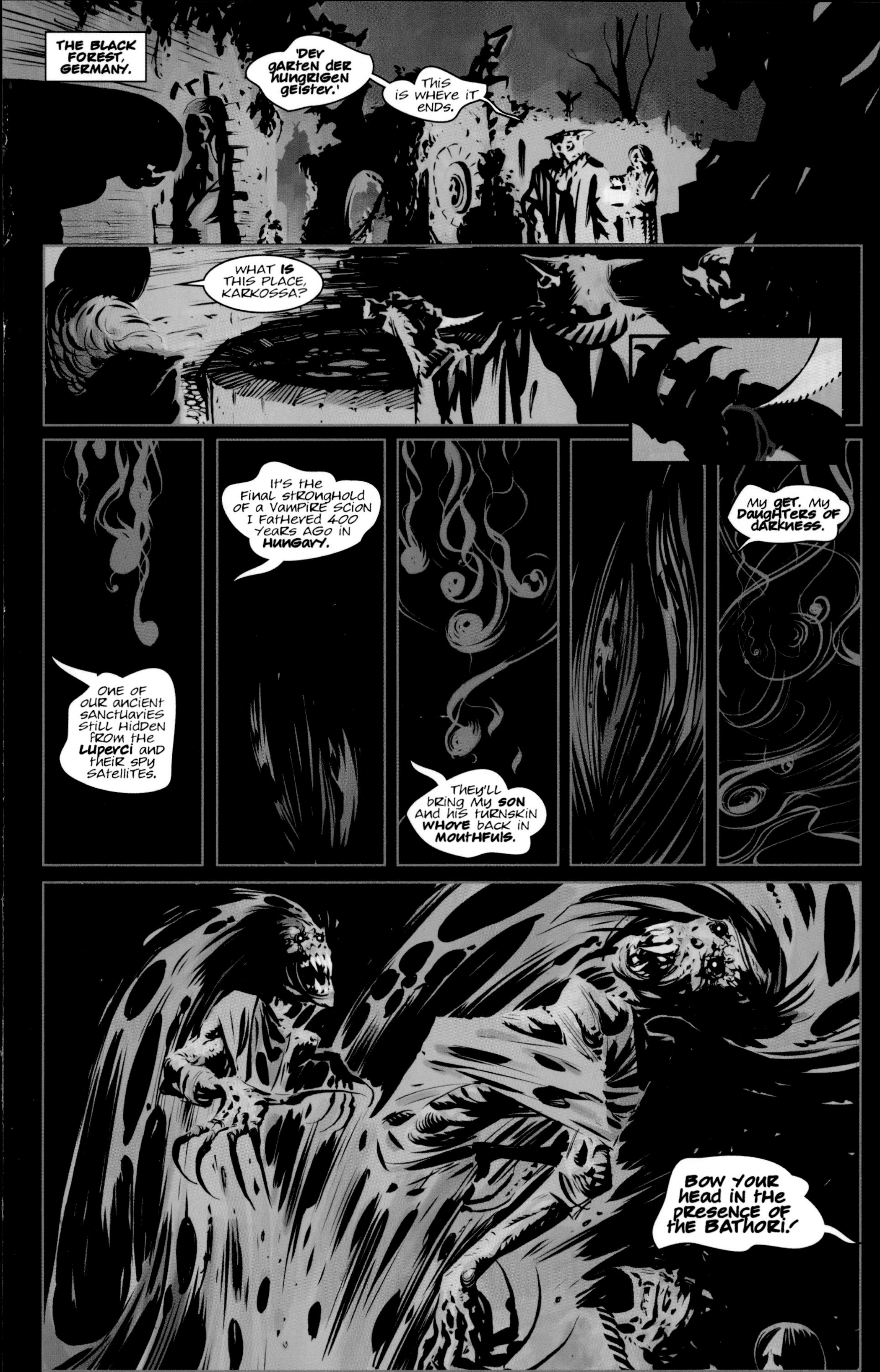
THE BLACK FOREST, GERMANY.
'Der garten der hungrigen geister.'
This is where it ends.
WHAT IS THIS PLACE, KARKOSSA?
One of our ancient sanctuaries still hidden from the Luperci and their spy satellites.
It's the final stronghold of a vampire scion I fathered 400 years ago in Hungary.
They'll bring my son and his turnskin whore back in mouthfuls.
My get. My daughters of darkness.
Bow your head in the presence of the Bathori!

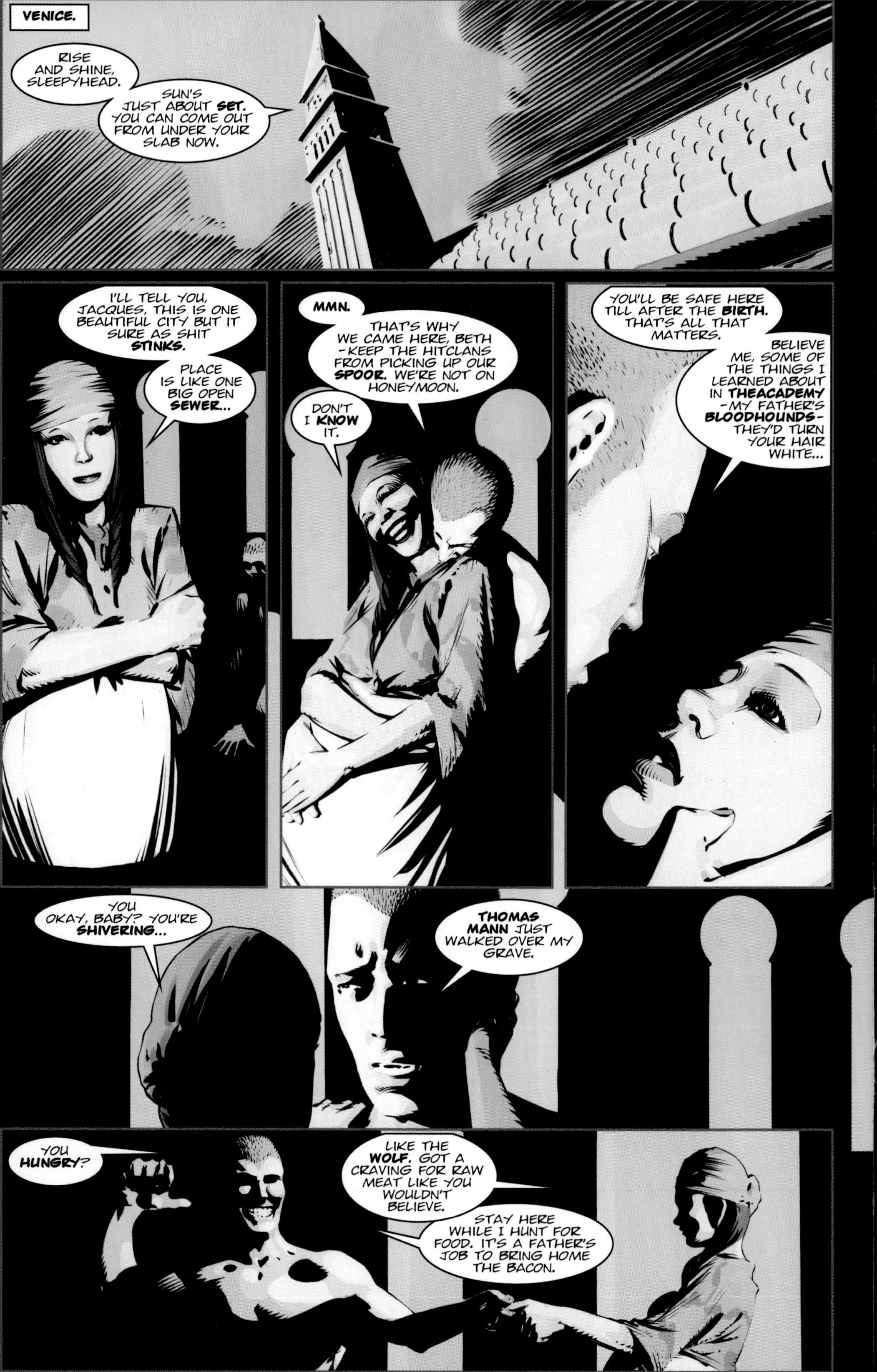
VENICE.
RISE AND SHINE, SLEEPYHEAD.
SUN'S JUST ABOUT SET. YOU CAN COME OUT FROM UNDER YOUR SLAB NOW.
I'LL TELL YOU, JACQUES, THIS IS ONE BEAUTIFUL CITY BUT IT SURE AS SHIT STINKS.
PLACE IS LIKE ONE BIG OPEN SEWER...
MMN.
THAT'S WHY WE CAME HERE, BETH -KEEP THE HITCLANS FROM PICKING UP OUR SPOOR. WE'RE NOT ON HONEYMOON.
DON'T I KNOW IT.
YOU'LL BE SAFE HERE TILL AFTER THE BIRTH. THAT'S ALL THAT MATTERS.
BELIEVE ME, SOME OF THE THINGS I LEARNED ABOUT IN THEACADEMY -MY FATHER'S BLOODHOUNDS- THEY'D TURN YOUR HAIR WHITE...
YOU OKAY, BABY? YOU'RE SHIVERING...
THOMAS MANN JUST WALKED OVER MY GRAVE.
YOU HUNGRY?
LIKE THE WOLF. GOT A CRAVING FOR RAW MEAT LIKE YOU WOULDN'T BELIEVE.
STAY HERE WHILE I HUNT FOR FOOD. IT'S A FATHER'S JOB TO BRING HOME THE BACON.

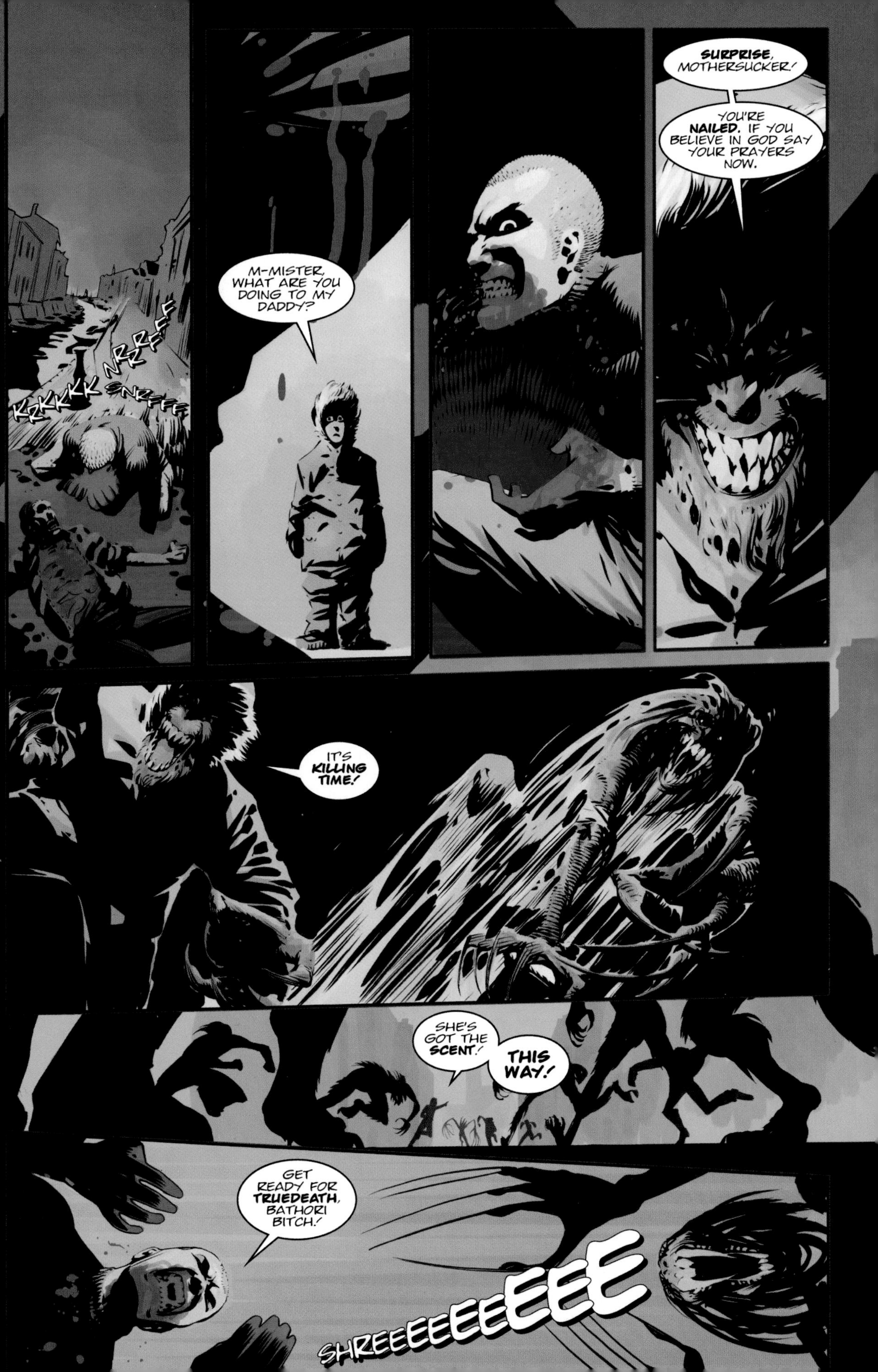
KRKKKK
SNRFFF
NRRRFF
M-MISTER, WHAT ARE YOU DOING TO MY DADDY?
SURPRISE, MOTHERSUCKER!
YOU'RE NAILED. IF YOU BELIEVE IN GOD SAY YOUR PRAYERS NOW.
IT'S KILLING TIME!
SHE'S GOT THE SCENT!
THIS WAY!
GET READY FOR TRUEDEATH, BATHORI BITCH!
SHREEEEEEEEEEE

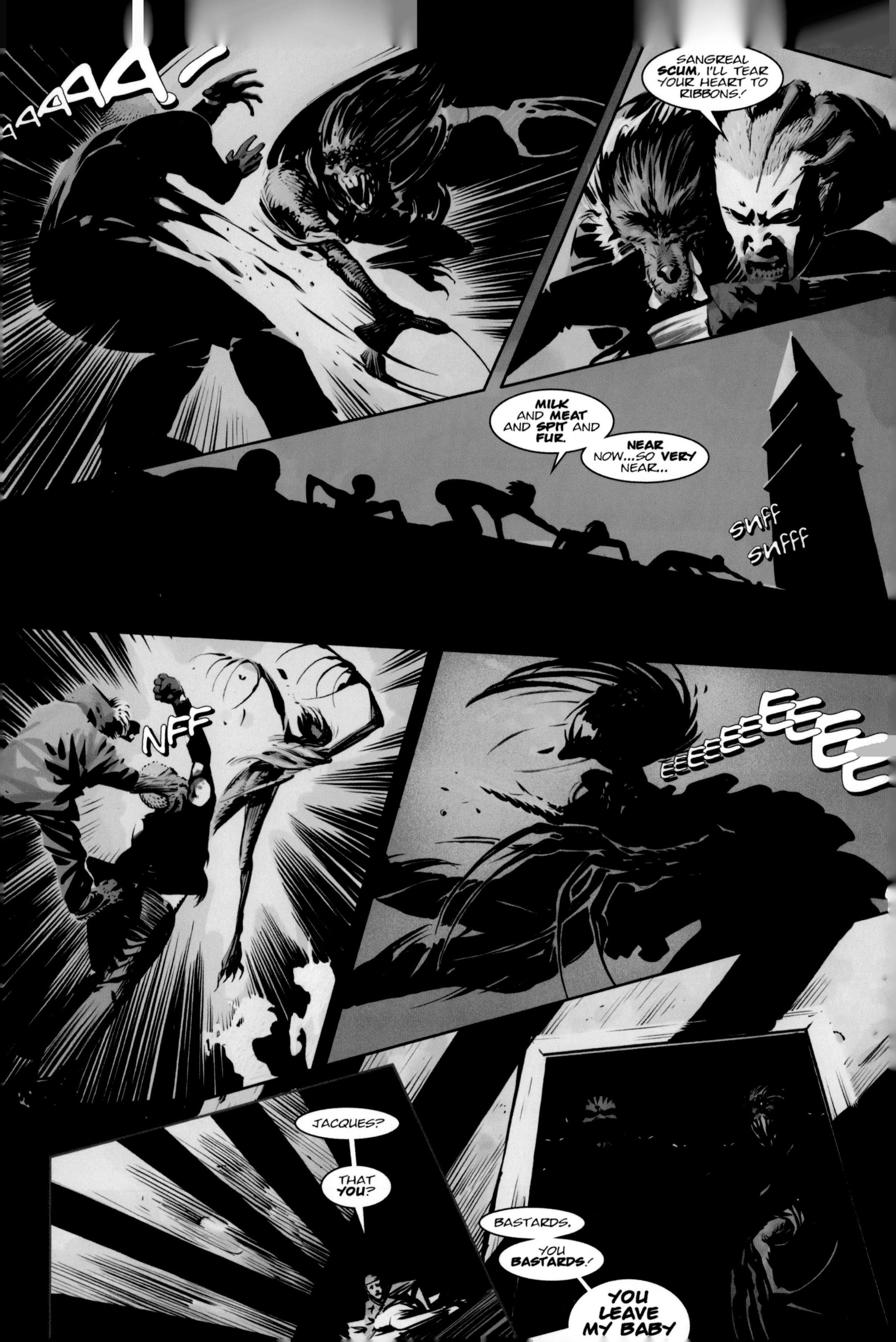

AAAAAAPP!!
SANGREAL SCUM, I'LL TEAR YOUR HEART TO RIBBONS!
MILK AND MEAT AND SPIT AND FUR.
NEAR NOW...SO VERY NEAR...
SNFF SNFFF
NFF
EEEEEEEEEEEEEUU
JACQUES?
THAT YOU?
BASTARDS.
YOU BASTARDS!
YOU LEAVE MY BABY

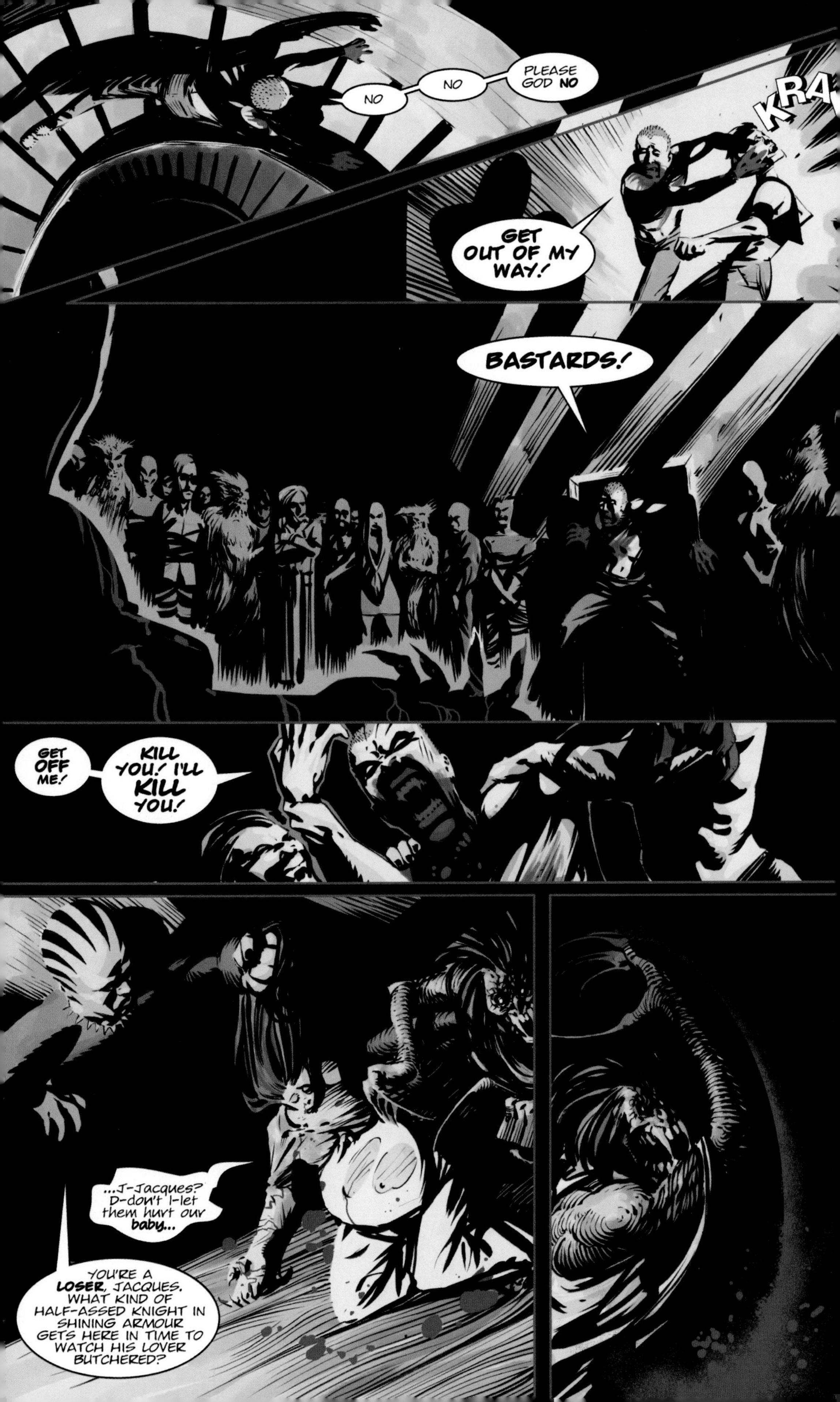
NO
NO
PLEASE GOD NO
KRA
GET OUT OF MY WAY!
BASTARDS!
GET OFF ME!
KILL YOU! I'LL KILL YOU!
...J-Jacques? D-don't l-let them hurt our baby...
YOU'RE A LOSER, JACQUES. WHAT KIND OF HALF-ASSED KNIGHT IN SHINING ARMOUR GETS HERE IN TIME TO WATCH HIS LOVER BUTCHERED?

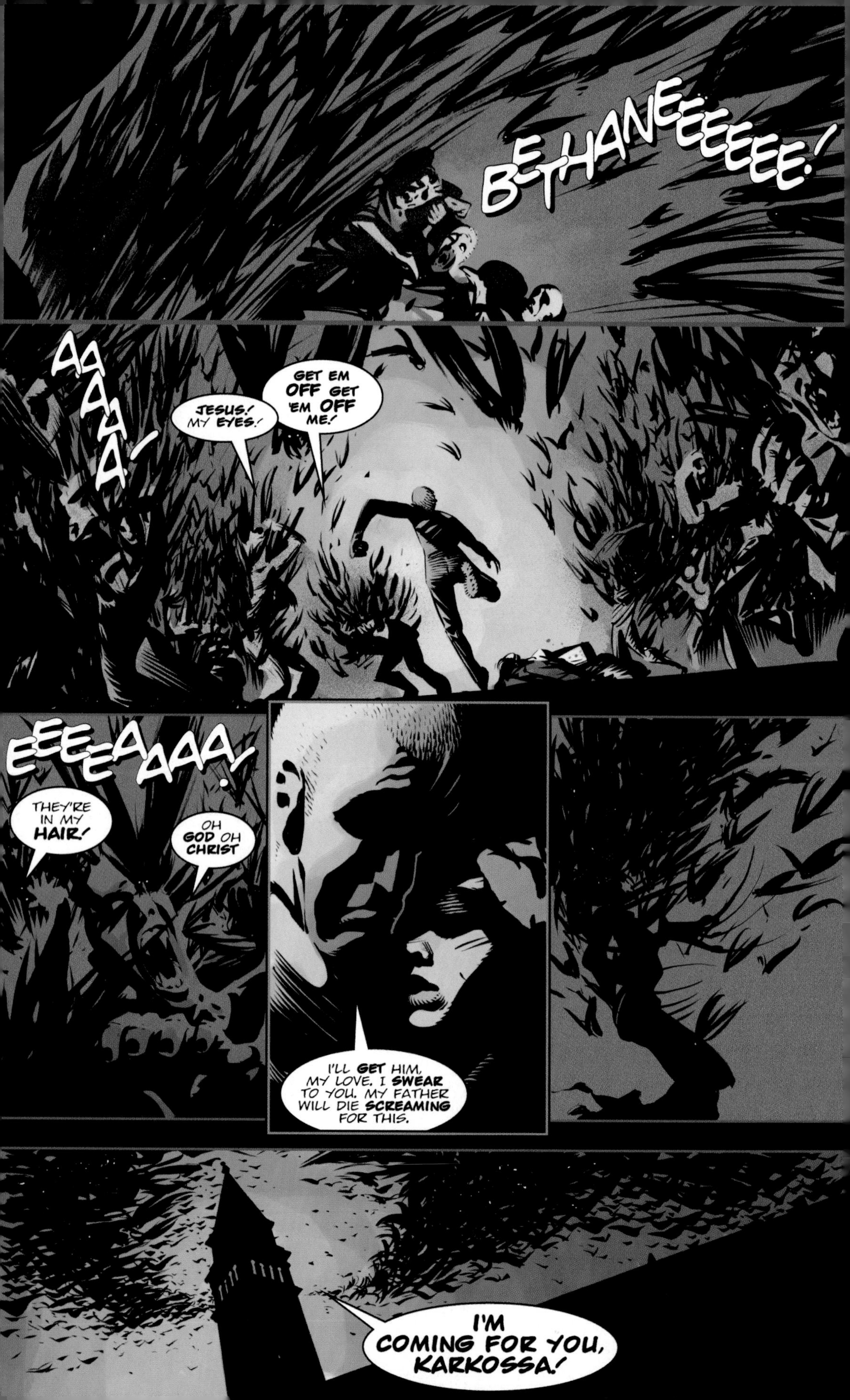
BETHANEEEEEEE!
AAAAAA!
JESUS! MY EYES!
GET EM OFF GET 'EM OFF ME!
EEEEAAAA!
THEY'RE IN MY HAIR!
OH GOD OH CHRIST
I'LL GET HIM, MY LOVE. I SWEAR TO YOU. MY FATHER WILL DIE SCREAMING FOR THIS.
I'M COMING FOR YOU, KARKOSSA!

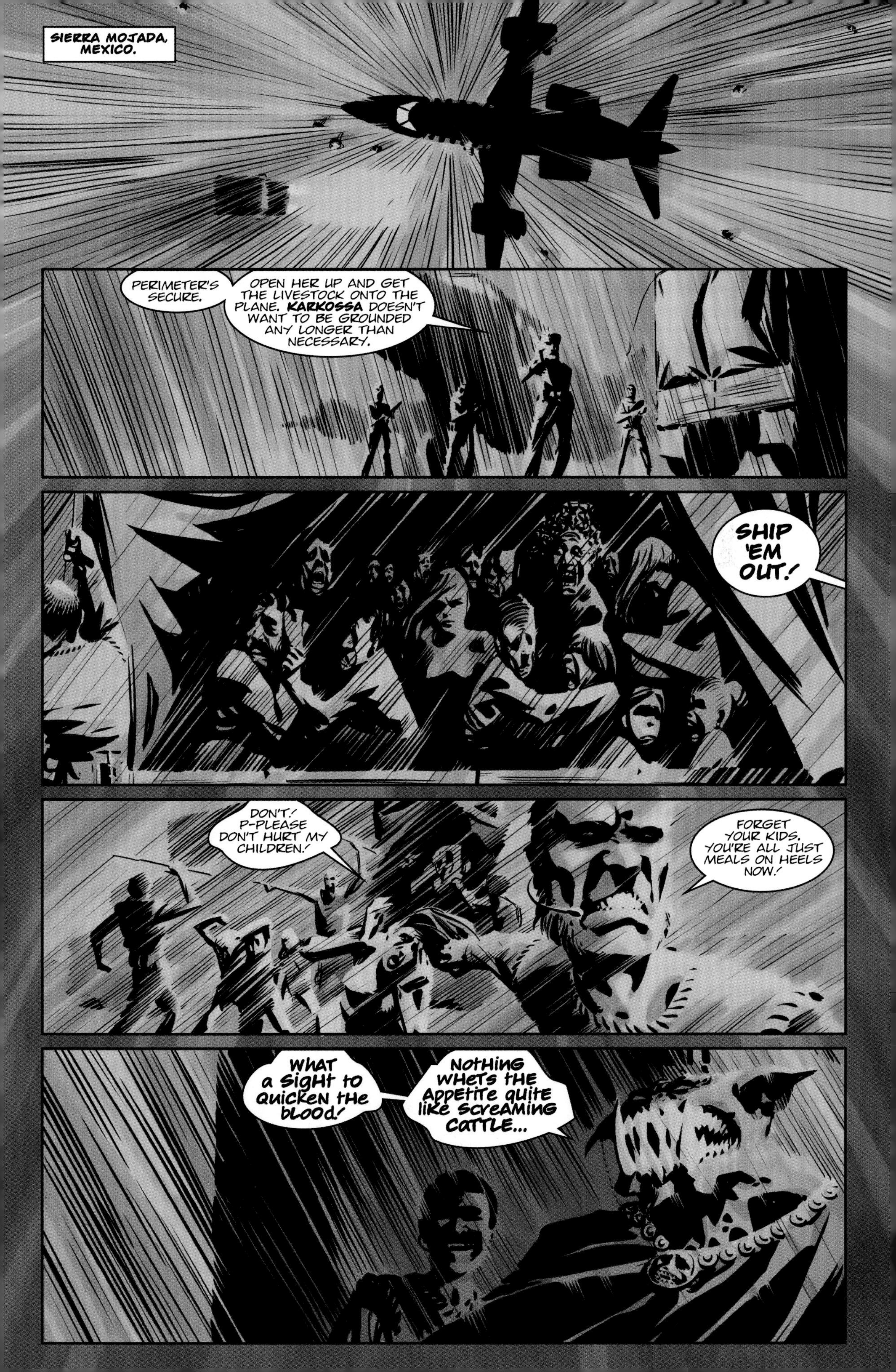
SIERRA MOJADA, MEXICO.
PERIMETER'S SECURE.
OPEN HER UP AND GET THE LIVESTOCK ONTO THE PLANE. KARKOSSA DOESN'T WANT TO BE GROUNDED ANY LONGER THAN NECESSARY.
SHIP 'EM OUT!
DON'T! P-PLEASE DON'T HURT MY CHILDREN!
FORGET YOUR KIDS. YOU'RE ALL JUST MEALS ON HEELS NOW!
WHAT A SIGHT TO QUICKEN THE BLOOD!
NOTHING WHETS THE APPETITE QUITE LIKE SCREAMING CATTLE...

SHIFT YOUR CARCASSES! MOVE IT!

FZZZZZKTT

WHAT **IS** THIS PLACE? W-WHAT ARE THEY GOING TO **DO** TO US? J-JESUS CHRIST **ALMIGHTY**...

SAVE YOUR BREATH FOR SOMEONE WHO GIVES A SHIT.

JUST DON'T EXPECT A **RETURN** TICKET...

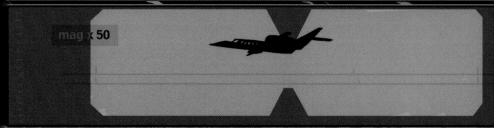

mag x 50

wd: 350
ht: 50/75
S.A.H: 1005

YOU'RE IN FOR A BIG **SURPRISE**, DADDIO.

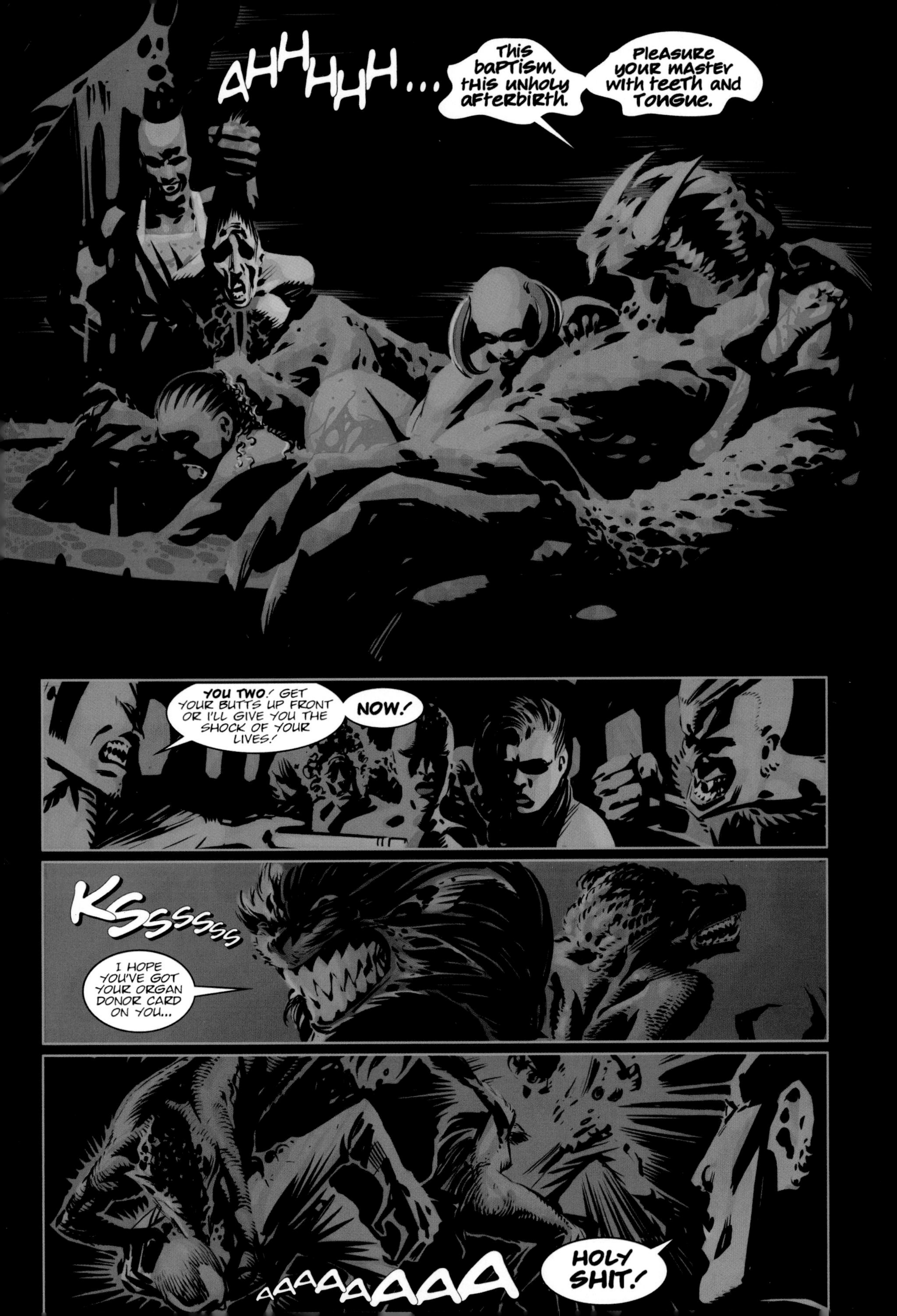
AHHHHHH...
This baptism, this unholy afterbirth.
Pleasure your master with teeth and tongue.
YOU TWO! GET YOUR BUTTS UP FRONT OR I'LL GIVE YOU THE SHOCK OF YOUR LIVES!
NOW!
KSSSSSSS
I HOPE YOU'VE GOT YOUR ORGAN DONOR CARD ON YOU...
AAAAAAAAA
HOLY SHIT!

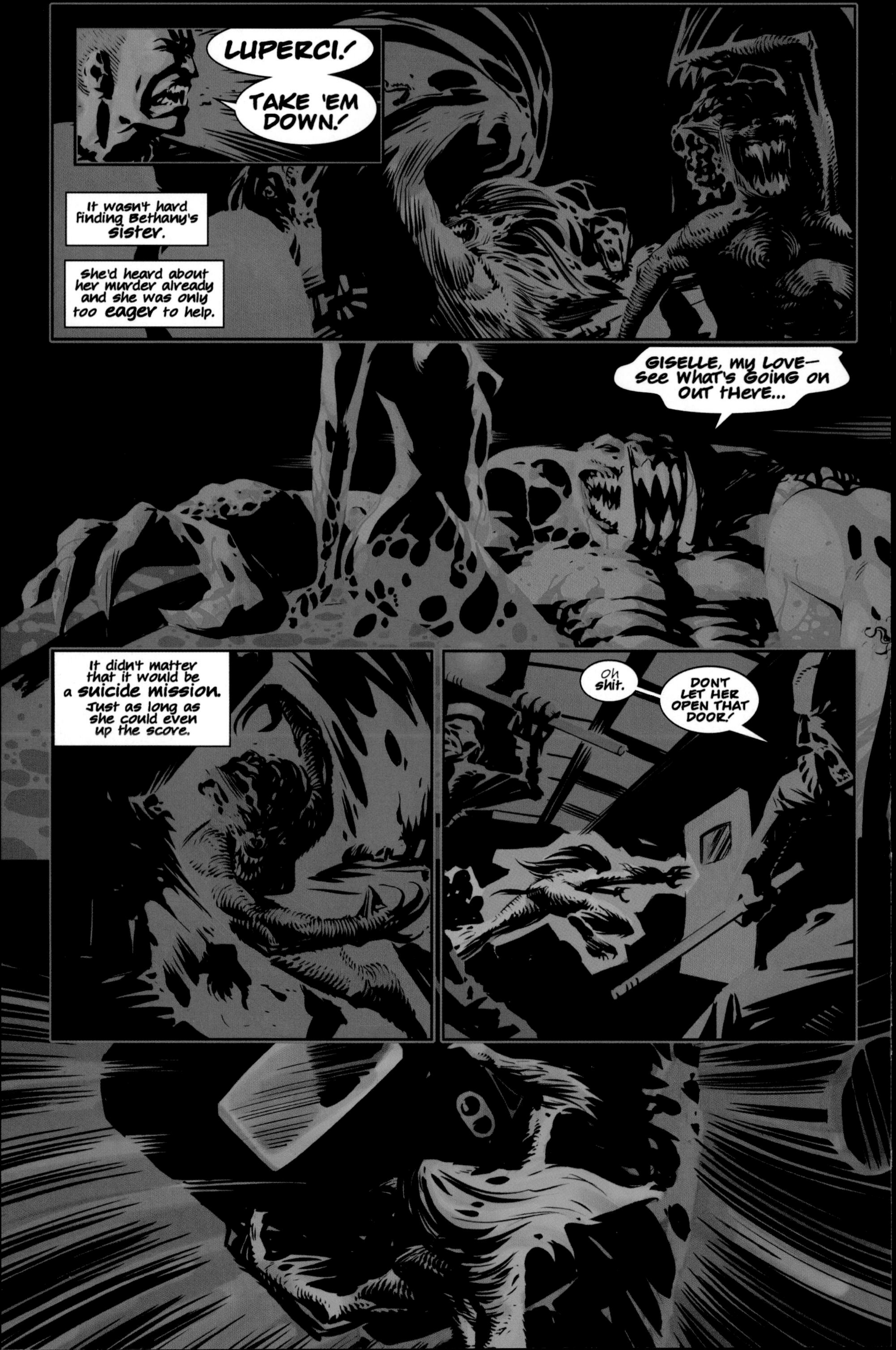
LUPERCI!
TAKE 'EM DOWN!
It wasn't hard finding Bethany's sister.
She'd heard about her murder already and she was only too eager to help.
GISELLE, MY LOVE— SEE WHAT'S GOING ON OUT THERE...
It didn't matter that it would be a suicide mission. Just as long as she could even up the score.
Oh shit.
DON'T LET HER OPEN THAT DOOR!

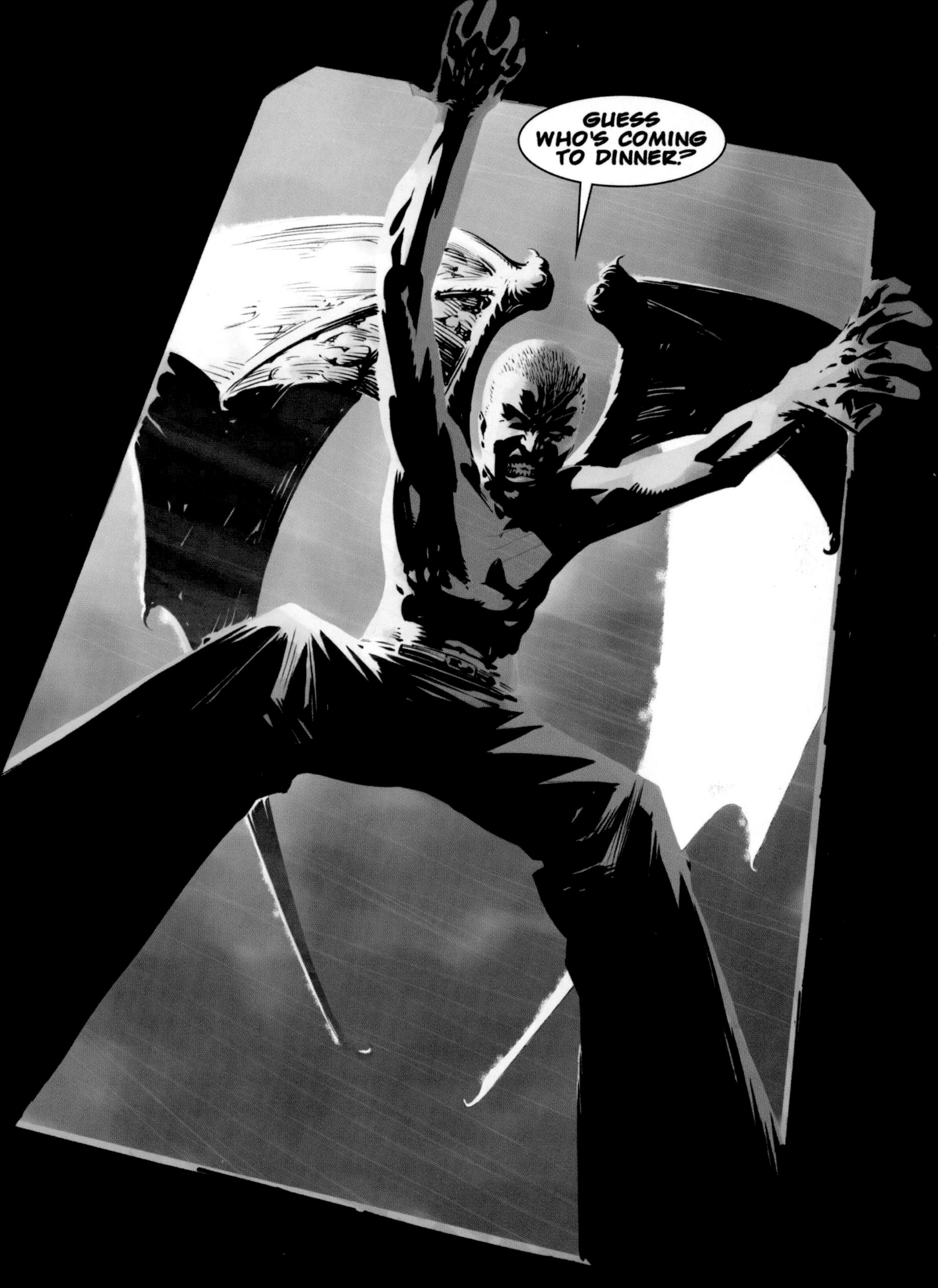
GUESS WHO'S COMING TO DINNER?

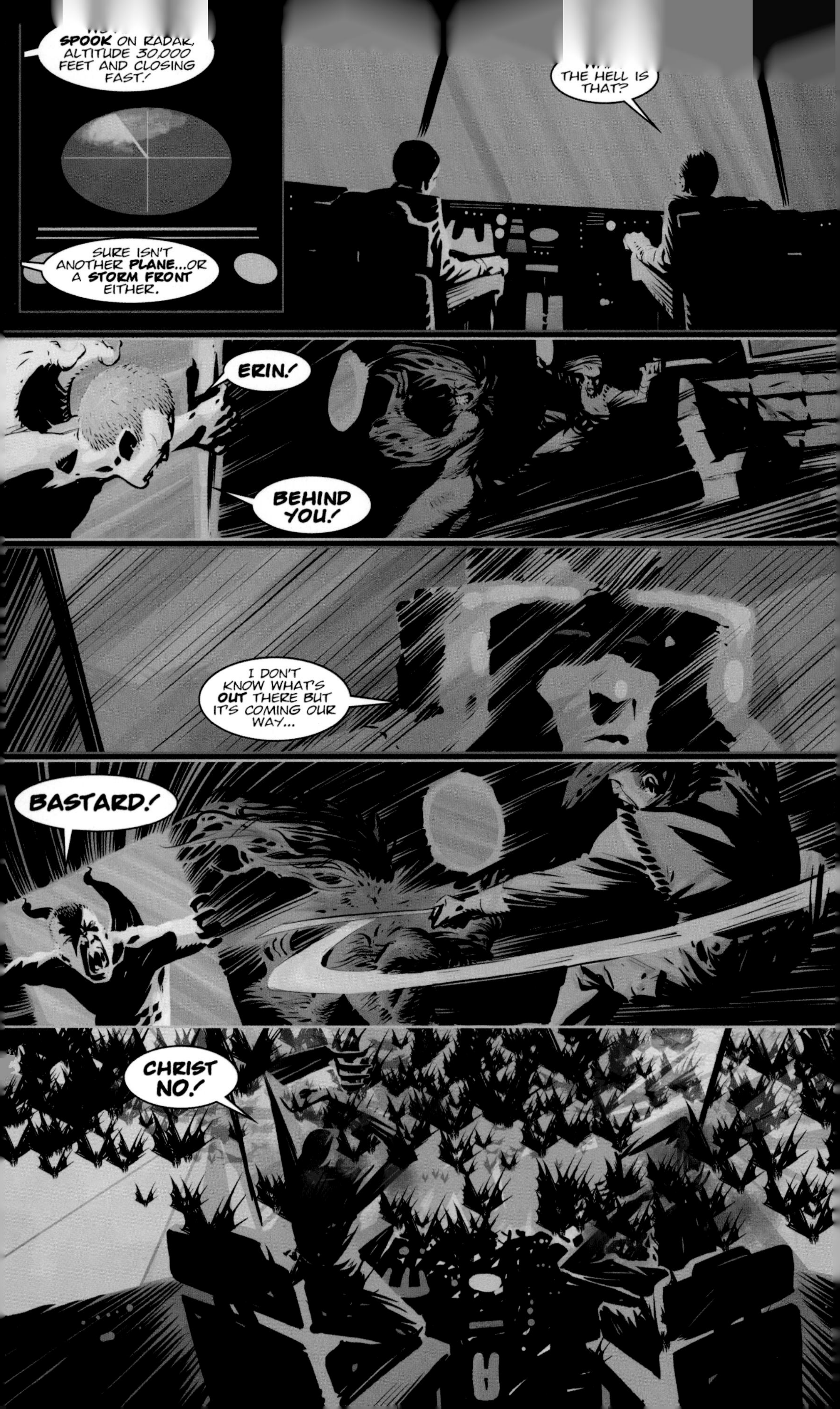
SPOOK ON RADAR, ALTITUDE 30,000 FEET AND CLOSING FAST!
THE HELL IS THAT?
SURE ISN'T ANOTHER PLANE...OR A STORM FRONT EITHER.
ERIN!
BEHIND YOU!
I DON'T KNOW WHAT'S OUT THERE BUT IT'S COMING OUR WAY...
BASTARD!
CHRIST NO!

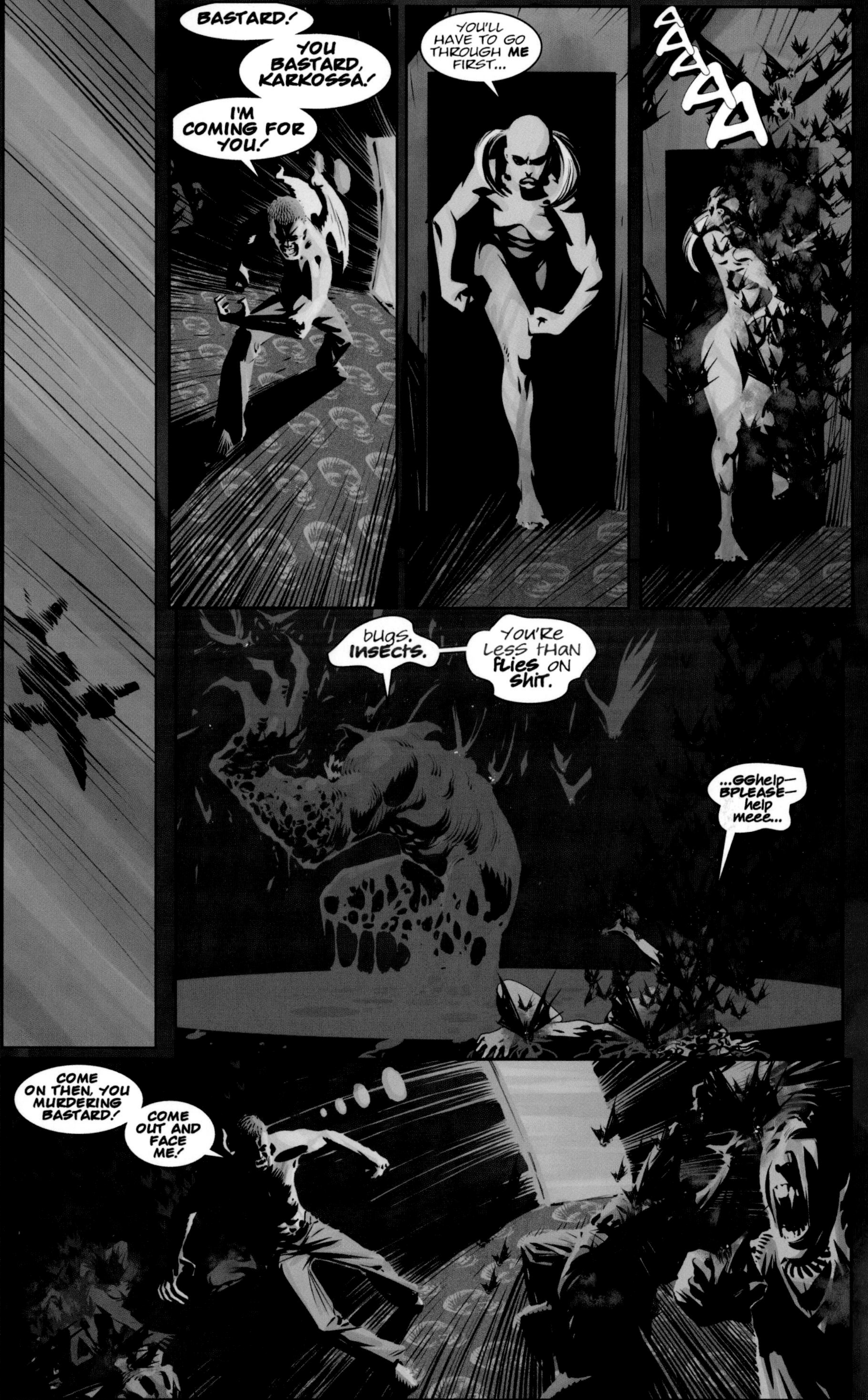
BASTARD!
YOU BASTARD, KARKOSSA!
I'M COMING FOR YOU!
YOU'LL HAVE TO GO THROUGH ME FIRST...
AAAAA
bugs. INSECTS.
YOU'RE LESS THAN FLIES ON SHIT.
...GGhelp—BPLEASE—help meee...
COME ON THEN, YOU MURDERING BASTARD!
COME OUT AND FACE ME!

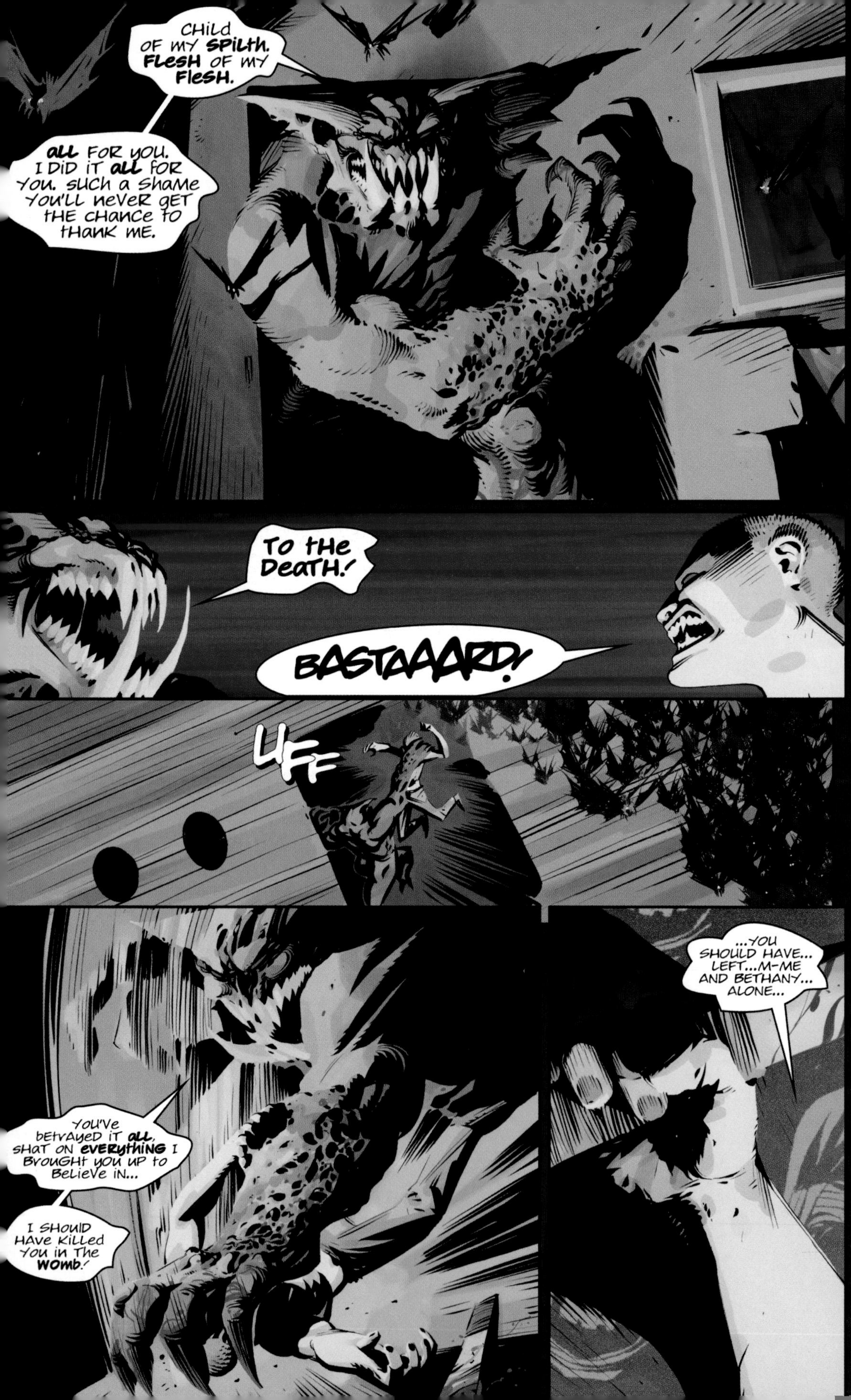
CHILD OF MY SPILTH. FLESH OF MY FLESH.
ALL FOR YOU. I DID IT ALL FOR YOU. SUCH A SHAME YOU'LL NEVER GET THE CHANCE TO THANK ME.
TO THE DEATH!
BASTAAARD!
UFF
YOU'VE BETRAYED IT ALL, SHAT ON EVERYTHING I BROUGHT YOU UP TO BELIEVE IN...
I SHOULD HAVE KILLED YOU IN THE WOMB!
...YOU SHOULD HAVE... LEFT...M-ME AND BETHANY... ALONE...

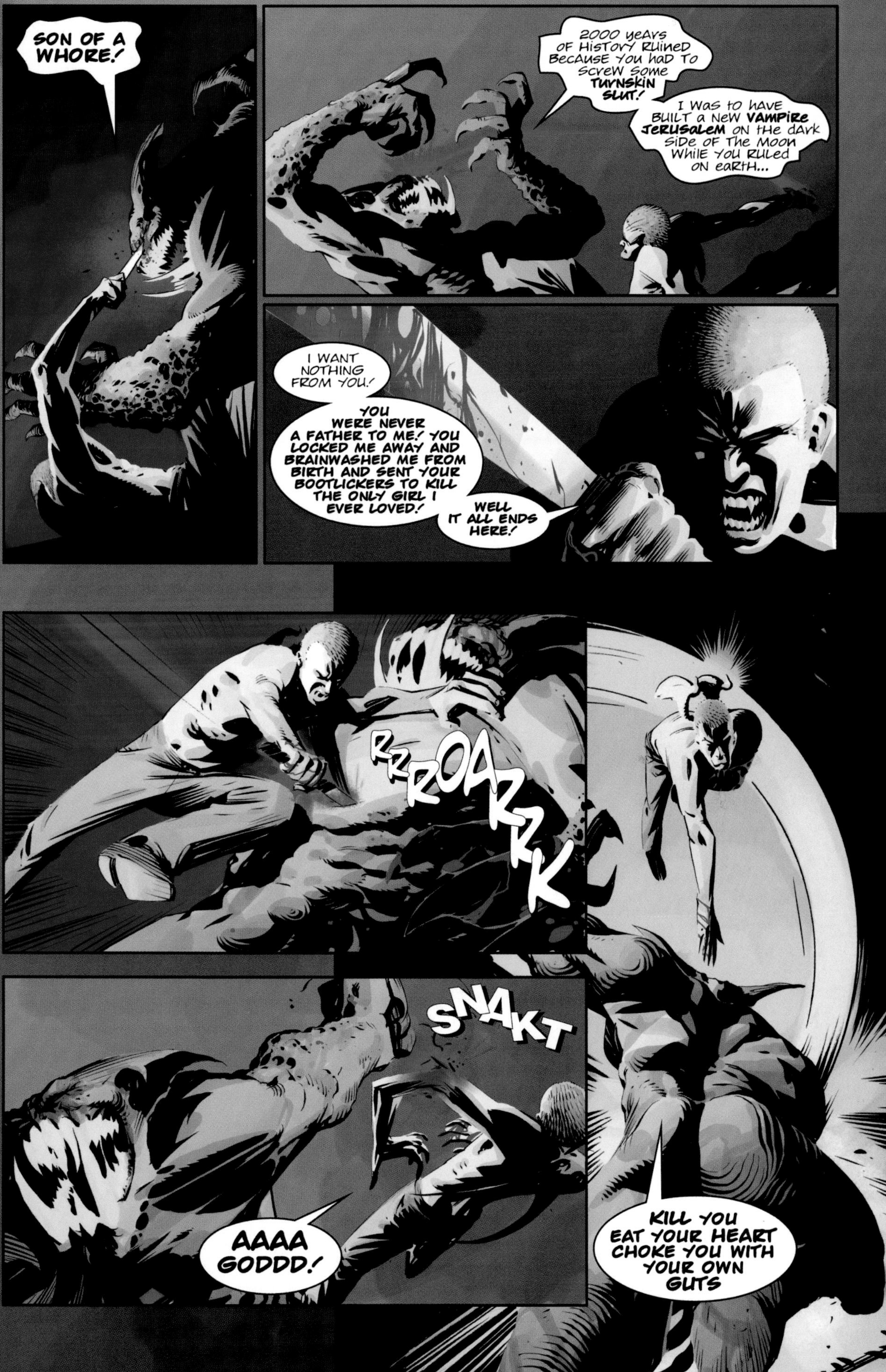
SON OF A WHORE!
2000 YEARS OF HISTORY RUINED BECAUSE YOU HAD TO SCREW SOME TURNSKIN SLUT!
I WAS TO HAVE BUILT A NEW VAMPIRE JERUSALEM ON THE DARK SIDE OF THE MOON WHILE YOU RULED ON EARTH...
I WANT NOTHING FROM YOU!
YOU WERE NEVER A FATHER TO ME! YOU LOCKED ME AWAY AND BRAINWASHED ME FROM BIRTH AND SENT YOUR BOOTLICKERS TO KILL THE ONLY GIRL I EVER LOVED!
WELL IT ALL ENDS HERE!
RRROARRRK
SNAKT
AAAA GODDD!
KILL YOU EAT YOUR HEART CHOKE YOU WITH YOUR OWN GUTS

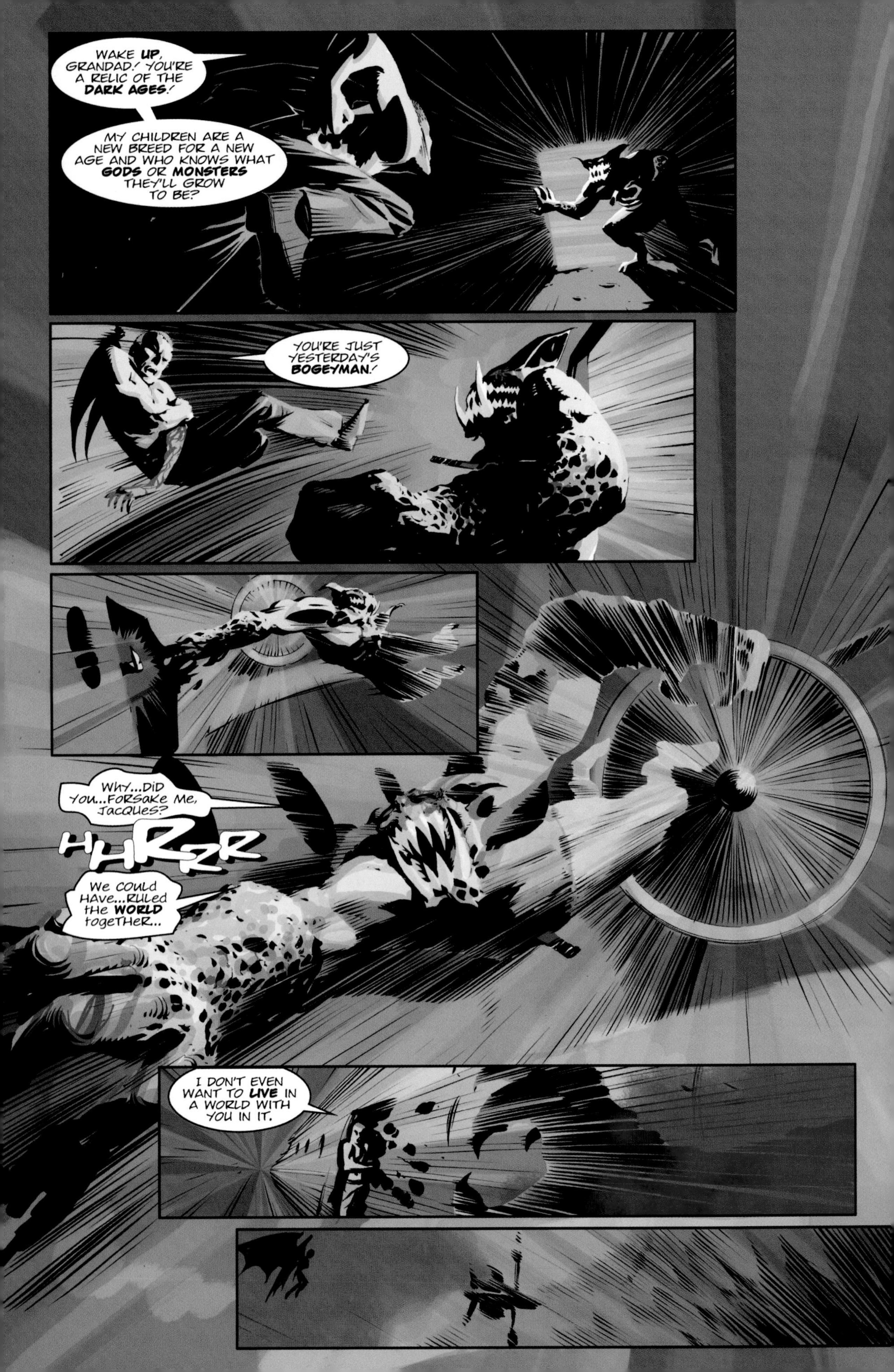
WAKE **UP**, GRANDAD! YOU'RE A RELIC OF THE **DARK AGES**!
MY CHILDREN ARE A NEW BREED FOR A NEW AGE AND WHO KNOWS WHAT **GODS** OR **MONSTERS** THEY'LL GROW TO BE?
YOU'RE JUST YESTERDAY'S **BOGEYMAN**!
Why...DID You...FORSake Me, JacQues?
HHRRR
We COULD HAVE...RULED the **WORLD** together...
I DON'T EVEN WANT TO **LIVE** IN A WORLD WITH YOU IN IT.

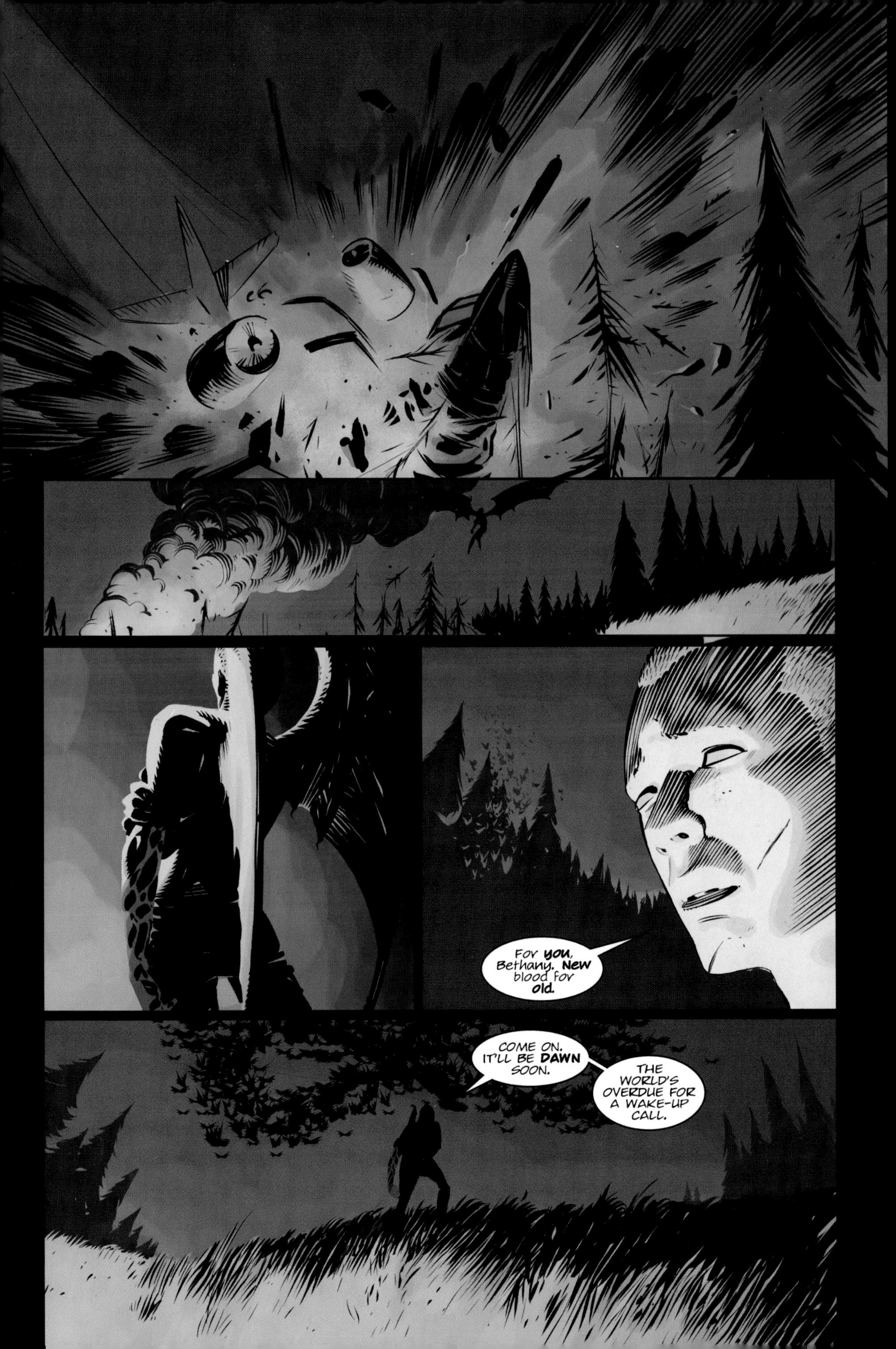
For you, Bethany. New blood for old.
COME ON. IT'LL BE DAWN SOON.
THE WORLD'S OVERDUE FOR A WAKE-UP CALL.

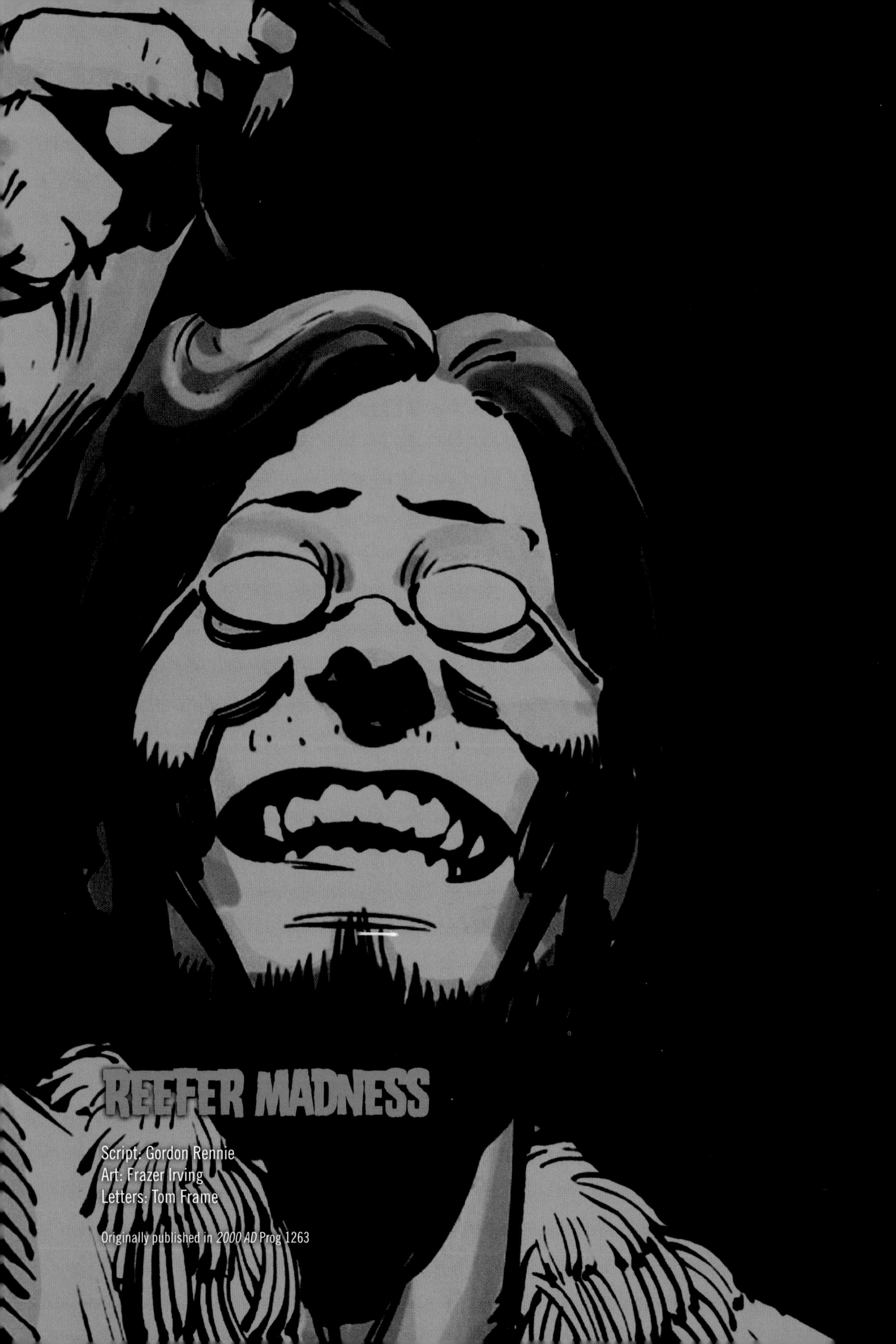

REEFER MADNESS

Script: Gordon Rennie
Art: Frazer Irving
Letters: Tom Frame

Originally published in *2000 AD* Prog 1263

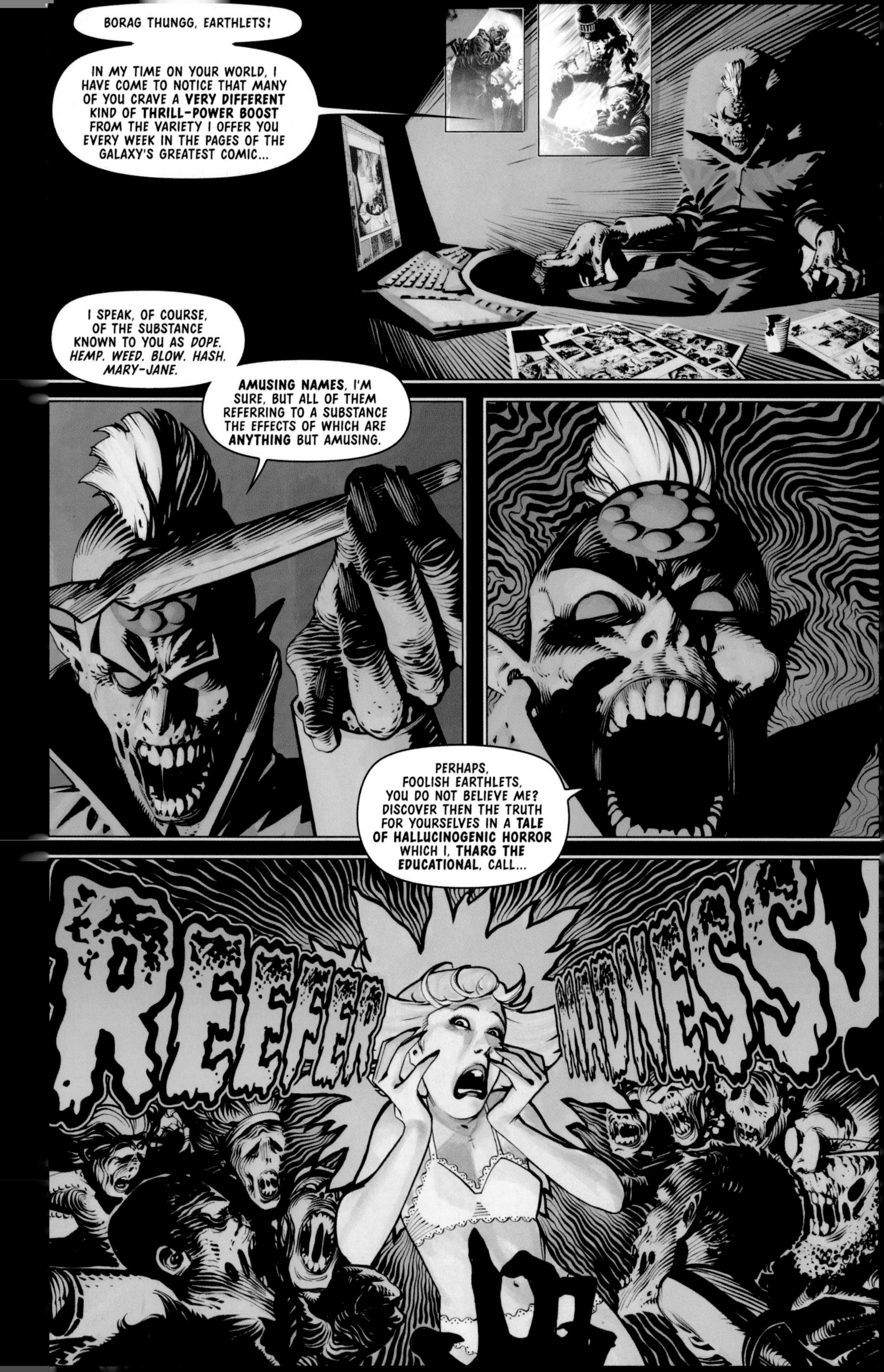
BORAG THUNGG, EARTHLETS!
IN MY TIME ON YOUR WORLD, I HAVE COME TO NOTICE THAT MANY OF YOU CRAVE A **VERY DIFFERENT** KIND OF **THRILL-POWER BOOST** FROM THE VARIETY I OFFER YOU EVERY WEEK IN THE PAGES OF THE GALAXY'S GREATEST COMIC...
I SPEAK, OF COURSE, OF THE SUBSTANCE KNOWN TO YOU AS *DOPE. HEMP. WEED. BLOW. HASH. MARY-JANE.*
AMUSING NAMES, I'M SURE, BUT ALL OF THEM REFERRING TO A SUBSTANCE THE EFFECTS OF WHICH ARE **ANYTHING** BUT AMUSING.
PERHAPS, FOOLISH EARTHLETS, YOU DO NOT BELIEVE ME? DISCOVER THEN THE TRUTH FOR YOURSELVES IN A **TALE OF HALLUCINOGENIC HORROR** WHICH I, **THARG THE EDUCATIONAL**, CALL...
REEFER MADNESS!

IT ALL BEGAN INNOCENTLY ENOUGH. JUST ANOTHER COLLEGE DORM-HOUSE PARTY, JUST ANOTHER GROUP OF YOUNG PEOPLE ENJOYING THEMSELVES.

IMAGES OF WELL-KNOWN SELF-CONFESSED 'HOPHEADS'

DRUG-INSPIRED 'ROCK MUSIC'

PEACENIK IMAGERY POPULAR AMONGST DRUG-ABUSING SUBVERSIVES

BUT LOOK CLOSER, AND SEE THE EVIDENCE OF THE NARCOTIC NIGHTMARE THAT THESE INNOCENTS WERE SOON TO FALL INTO...

CAN WE THEN BE TRULY SURPRISED, EARTHLETS, AT WHAT WAS TO HAPPEN NEXT?

HEY, WANNA HIT OF THIS? REAL PRIMO STUFF, I PROMISE YOU.

mmghmm...mmgg mmmhHHH mmghmm munhhhhh muhhh

HEY, STEVIE, YOU OKAY-?

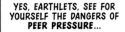

YES, EARTHLETS, SEE FOR YOURSELF THE DANGERS OF PEER PRESSURE...

SEE FOR YOURSELF HOW THE YOUNG AND INNOCENT ARE SO EASILY SEDUCED...

SEDUCED INTO THE THRALL OF THE TERRIFYING DRUG-FUELLED DEMENTIA THAT IS...

...REEFER MADNESS!

MUNCHIES!

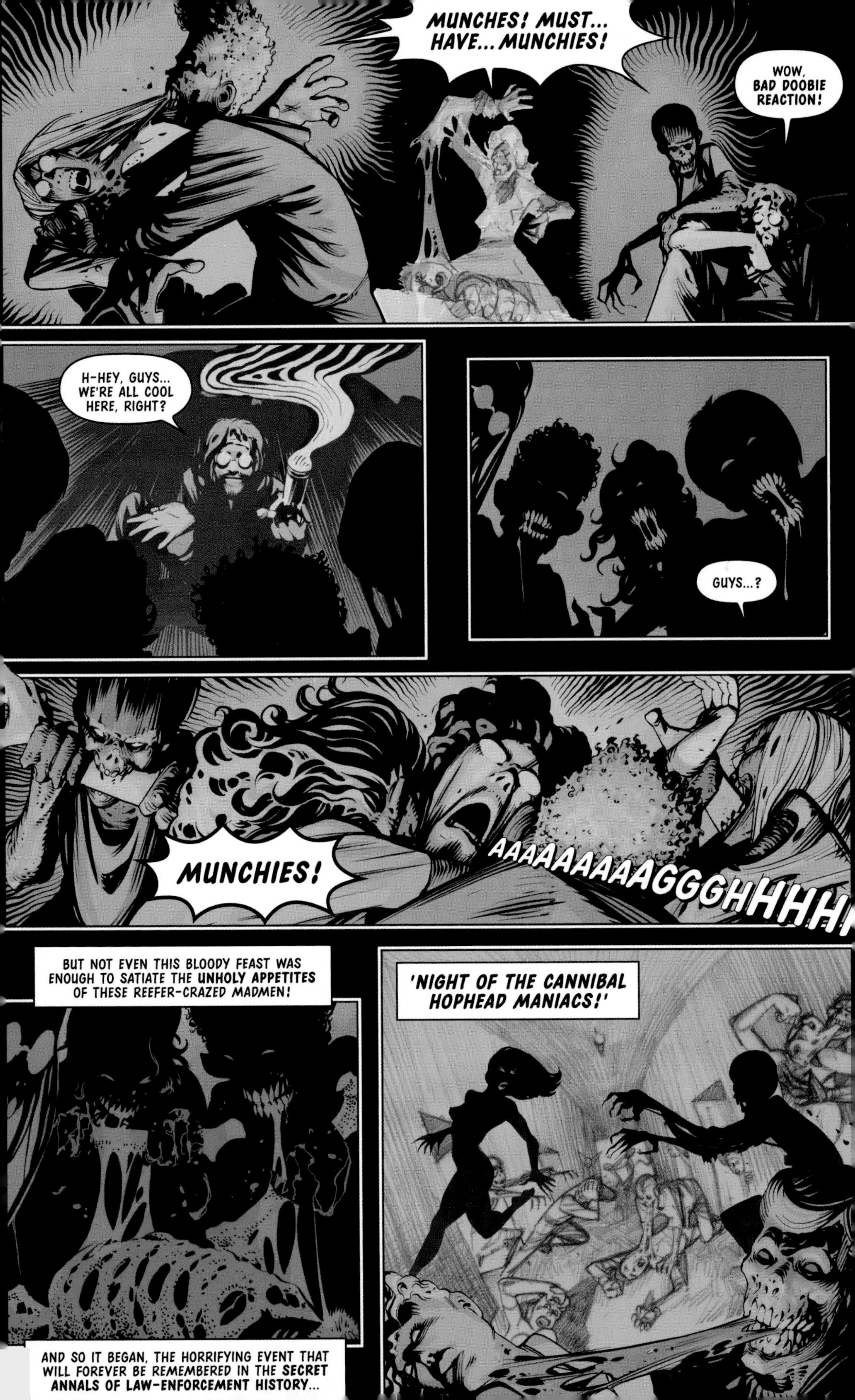
MUNCHES! MUST... HAVE... MUNCHIES!
WOW, BAD DOOBIE REACTION!
H-HEY, GUYS... WE'RE ALL COOL HERE, RIGHT?
GUYS...?
MUNCHIES!
AAAAAAAAAGGGGHHHHH
BUT NOT EVEN THIS BLOODY FEAST WAS ENOUGH TO SATIATE THE UNHOLY APPETITES OF THESE REEFER-CRAZED MADMEN!
AND SO IT BEGAN, THE HORRIFYING EVENT THAT WILL FOREVER BE REMEMBERED IN THE SECRET ANNALS OF LAW-ENFORCEMENT HISTORY...
'NIGHT OF THE CANNIBAL HOPHEAD MANIACS!'

MUNCHIES! NEED... MORE... MUNCHIES!

THANKFULLY, THE FORCES OF LAW AND ORDER WERE QUICKLY ON THE SCENE--

HELP ME! OH GOD, HELP ME...!

HOPHEADS! ONLY ONE WAY TO DEAL WITH THEIR DEGENERATE KIND--

OPEN FIRE! KILL 'EM ALL BEFORE THEY START TO SPORE!

'SPORE'? YES INDEED, EARTHLETS, FOR THERE IS ONE OTHER VITAL FACT WHICH THE FOOLISH ADVOCATES OF NARCOTIC LEGALISATION SOMEHOW ALWAYS FORGET TO MENTION...

ONE LAST AND VERY FATAL SIDE-EFFECT OF THIS MOST VILE OF SUBSTANCES...

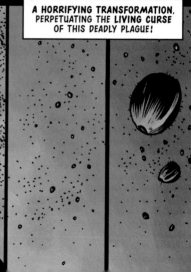

A HORRIFYING TRANSFORMATION, PERPETUATING THE LIVING CURSE OF THIS DEADLY PLAGUE!

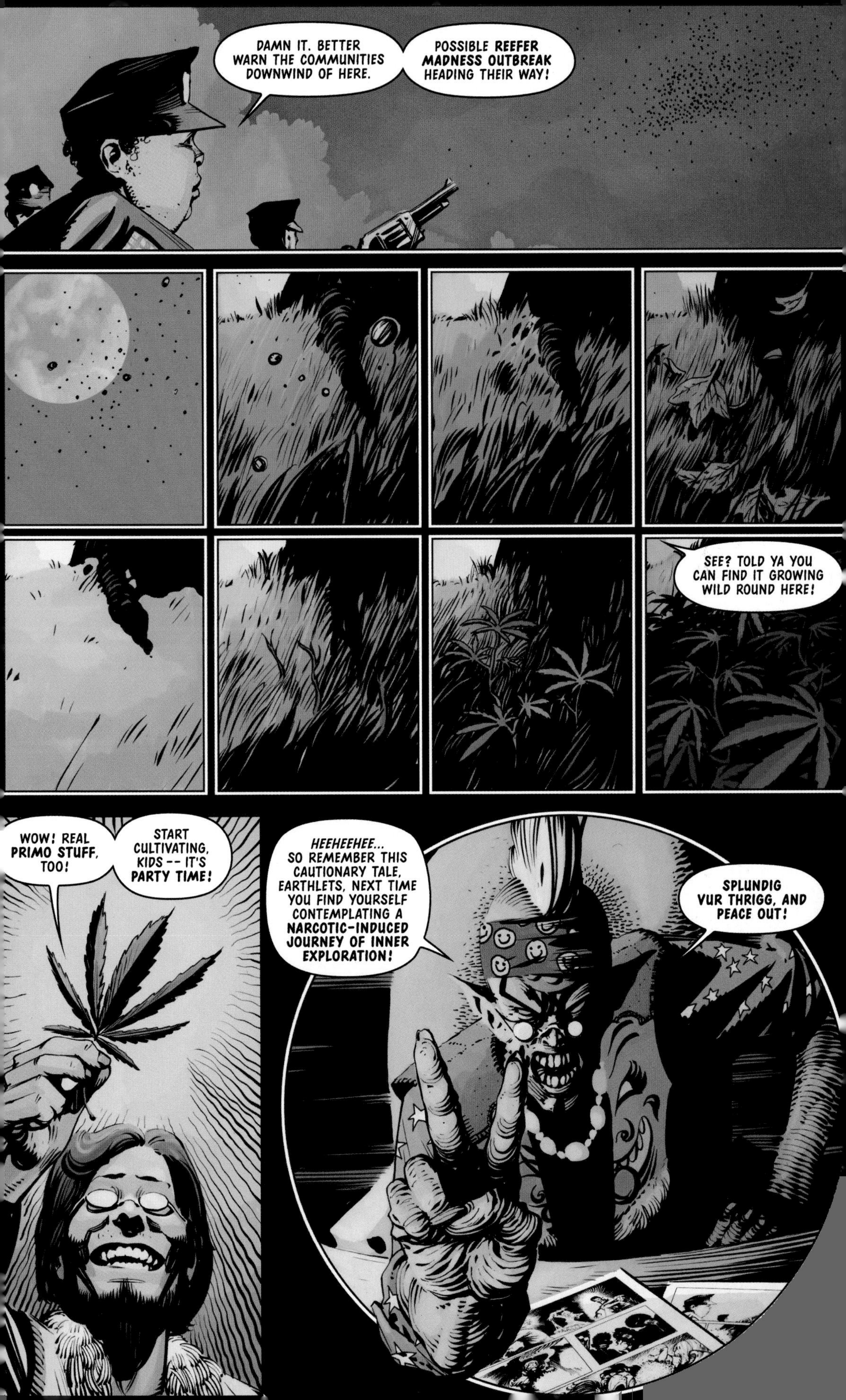
DAMN IT. BETTER WARN THE COMMUNITIES DOWNWIND OF HERE.
POSSIBLE REEFER MADNESS OUTBREAK HEADING THEIR WAY!
SEE? TOLD YA YOU CAN FIND IT GROWING WILD ROUND HERE!
WOW! REAL PRIMO STUFF, TOO!
START CULTIVATING, KIDS -- IT'S PARTY TIME!
HEEHEEHEE... SO REMEMBER THIS CAUTIONARY TALE, EARTHLETS, NEXT TIME YOU FIND YOURSELF CONTEMPLATING A NARCOTIC-INDUCED JOURNEY OF INNER EXPLORATION!
SPLUNDIG VUR THRIGG, AND PEACE OUT!

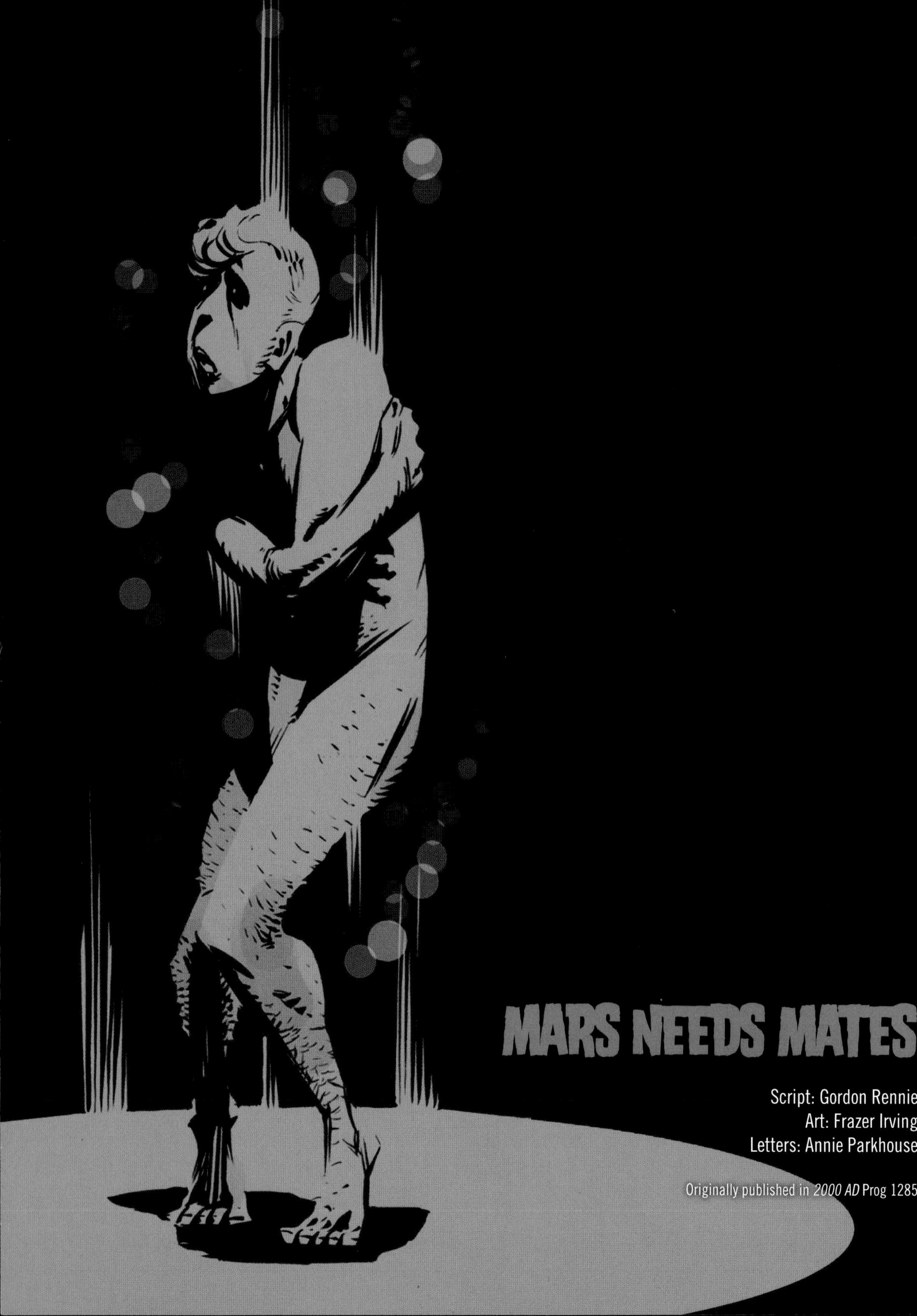

MARS NEEDS MATES

Script: Gordon Rennie
Art: Frazer Irving
Letters: Annie Parkhouse

Originally published in *2000 AD* Prog 1285

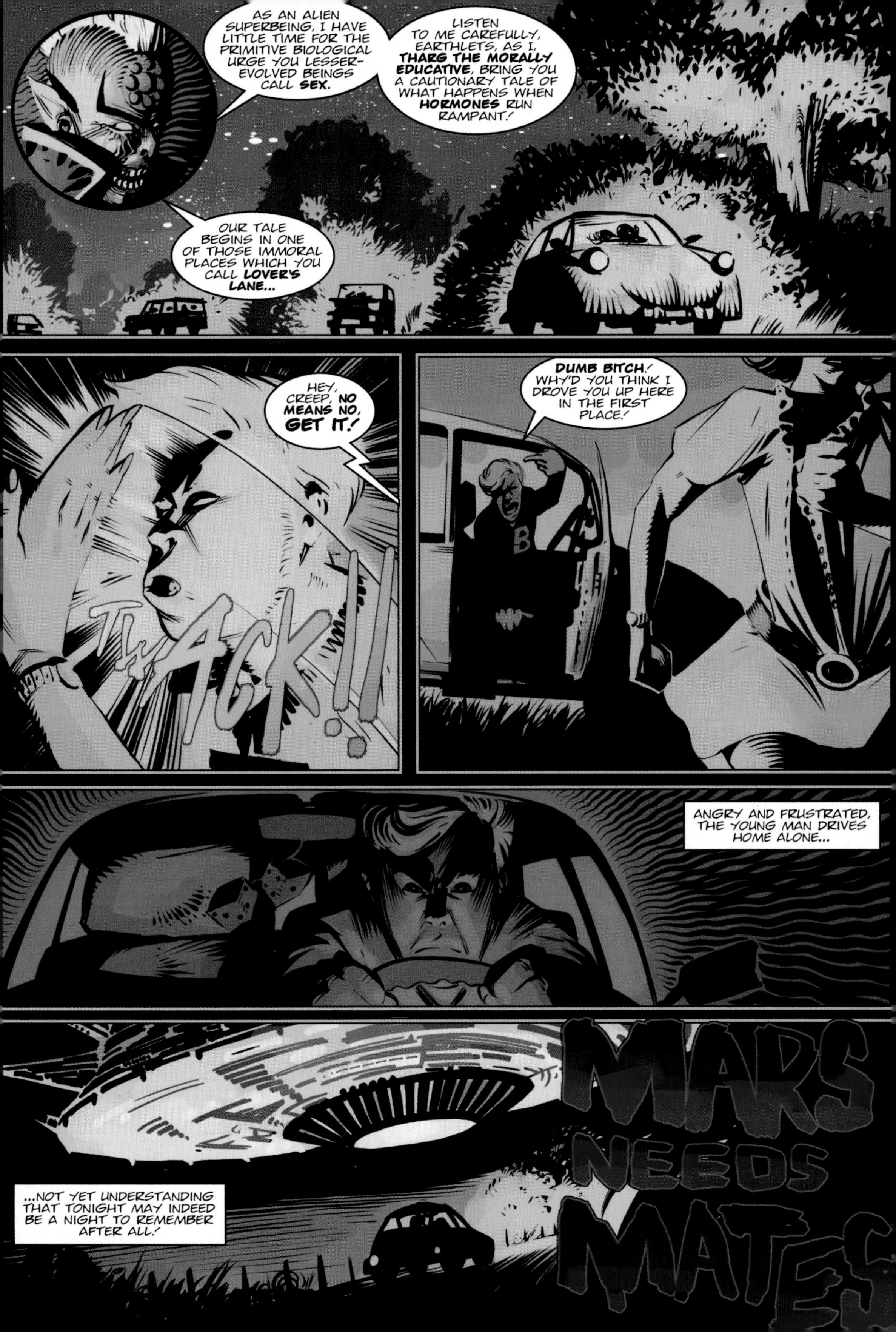

AS AN ALIEN SUPERBEING, I HAVE LITTLE TIME FOR THE PRIMITIVE BIOLOGICAL URGE YOU LESSER-EVOLVED BEINGS CALL **SEX.**
LISTEN TO ME CAREFULLY, EARTHLETS, AS I, **THARG THE MORALLY EDUCATIVE**, BRING YOU A CAUTIONARY TALE OF WHAT HAPPENS WHEN **HORMONES** RUN RAMPANT!
OUR TALE BEGINS IN ONE OF THOSE IMMORAL PLACES WHICH YOU CALL **LOVER'S LANE...**
HEY, CREEP, **NO MEANS NO, GET IT!**
THACK!!
DUMB BITCH! WHY'D YOU THINK I DROVE YOU UP HERE IN THE FIRST PLACE!
ANGRY AND FRUSTRATED, THE YOUNG MAN DRIVES HOME ALONE...
...NOT YET UNDERSTANDING THAT TONIGHT MAY INDEED BE A NIGHT TO REMEMBER AFTER ALL!
MARS NEEDS MATES

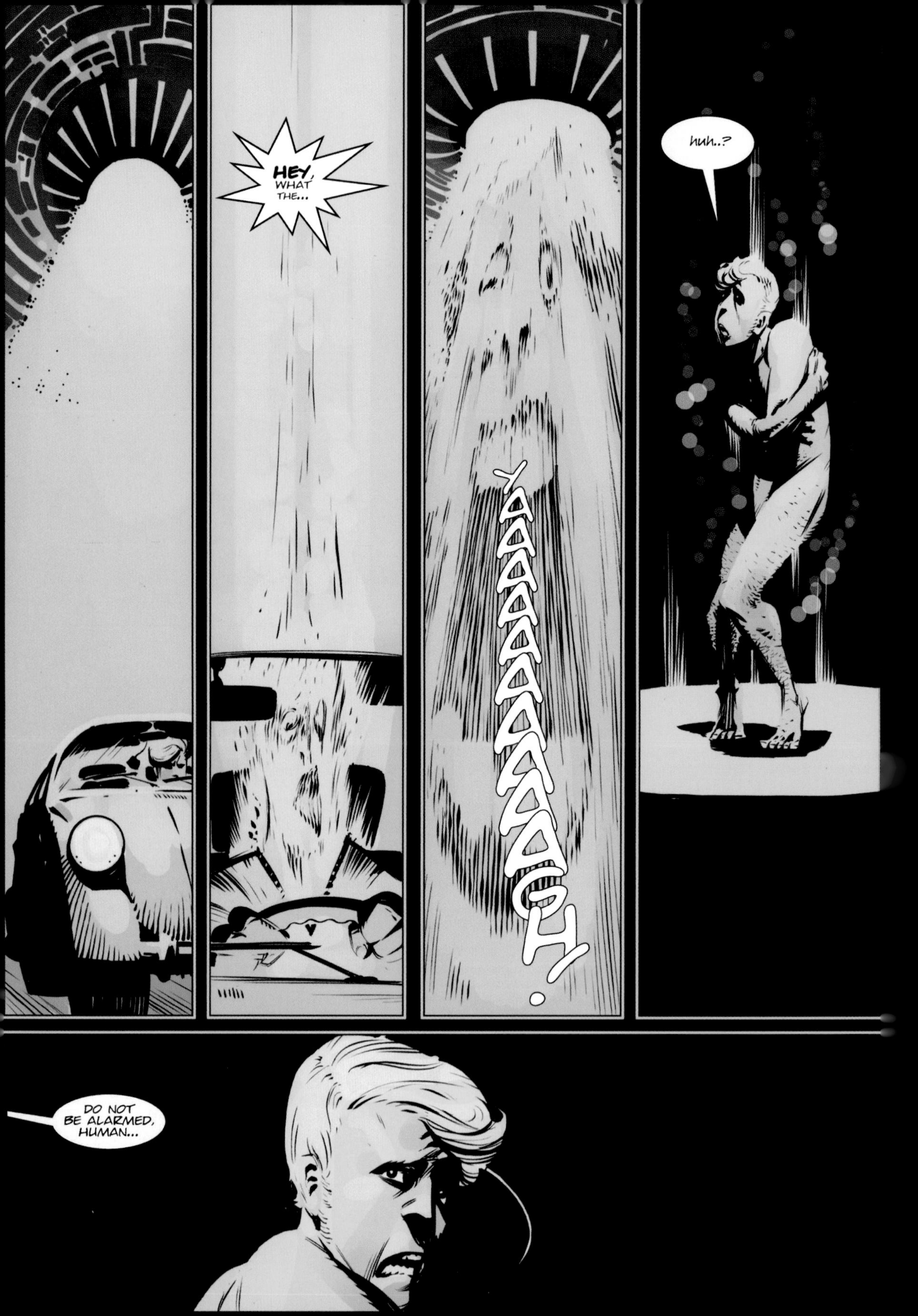
HEY, WHAT THE...
YAAAAAAAAAAAAAGH!
huh..?
DO NOT BE ALARMED, HUMAN...

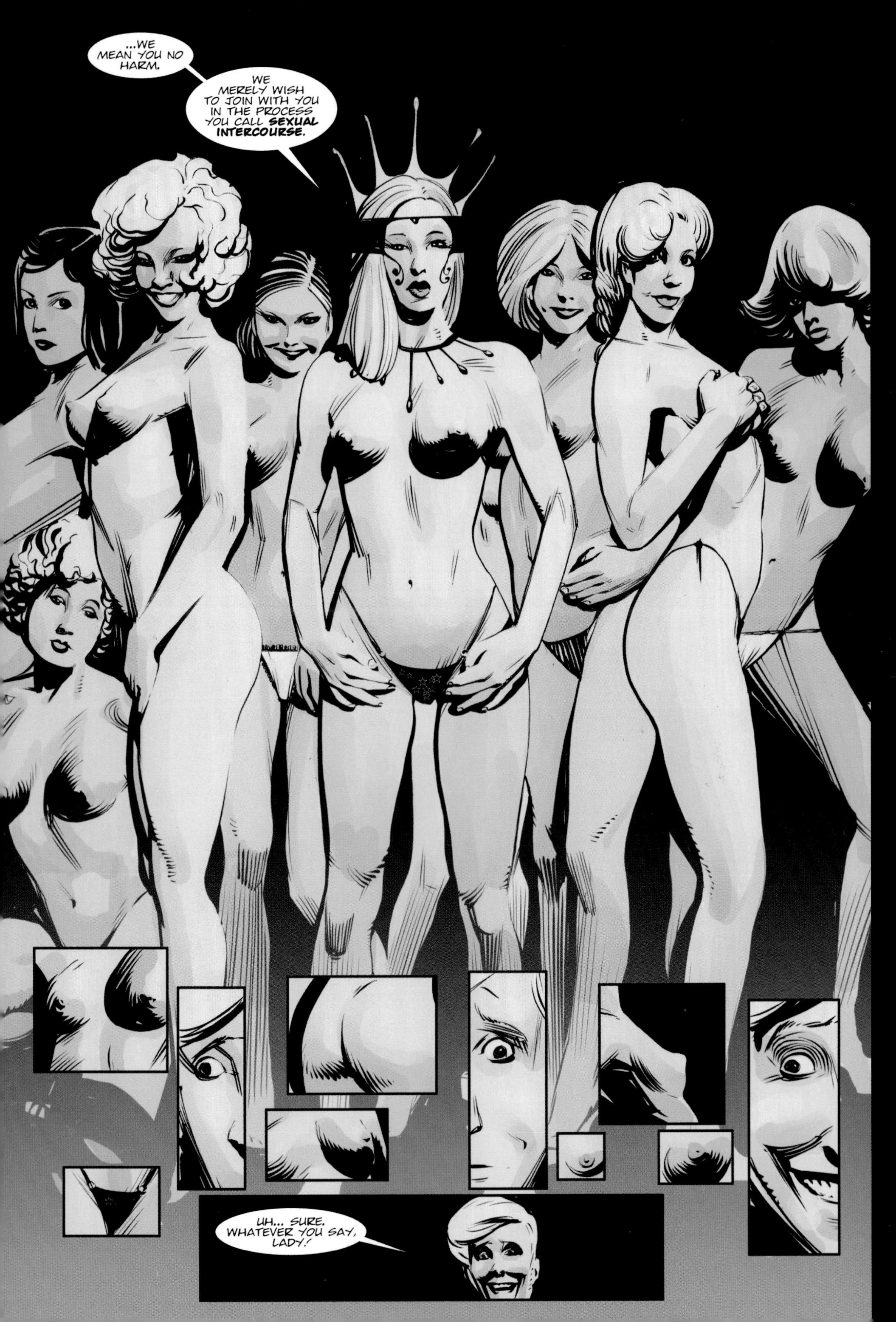
...WE MEAN YOU NO HARM.
WE MERELY WISH TO JOIN WITH YOU IN THE PROCESS YOU CALL **SEXUAL INTERCOURSE.**
UH... SURE. WHATEVER YOU SAY, LADY!

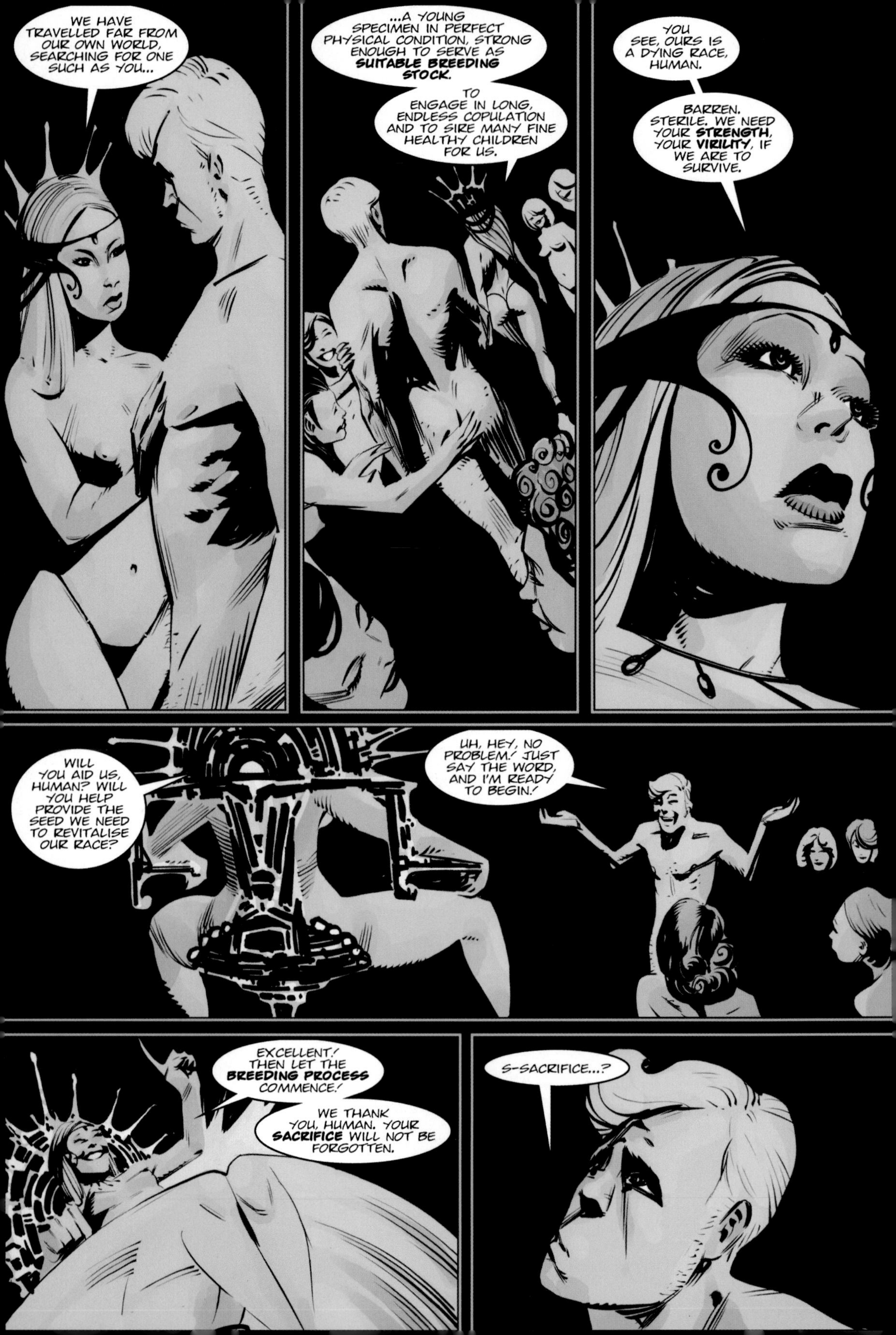
WE HAVE TRAVELLED FAR FROM OUR OWN WORLD, SEARCHING FOR ONE SUCH AS YOU...
...A YOUNG SPECIMEN IN PERFECT PHYSICAL CONDITION, STRONG ENOUGH TO SERVE AS SUITABLE BREEDING STOCK.
TO ENGAGE IN LONG, ENDLESS COPULATION AND TO SIRE MANY FINE HEALTHY CHILDREN FOR US.
YOU SEE, OURS IS A DYING RACE, HUMAN.
BARREN. STERILE. WE NEED YOUR STRENGTH, YOUR VIRILITY, IF WE ARE TO SURVIVE.
WILL YOU AID US, HUMAN? WILL YOU HELP PROVIDE THE SEED WE NEED TO REVITALISE OUR RACE?
UH, HEY, NO PROBLEM! JUST SAY THE WORD, AND I'M READY TO BEGIN!
EXCELLENT! THEN LET THE BREEDING PROCESS COMMENCE!
WE THANK YOU, HUMAN. YOUR SACRIFICE WILL NOT BE FORGOTTEN.
S-SACRIFICE...?

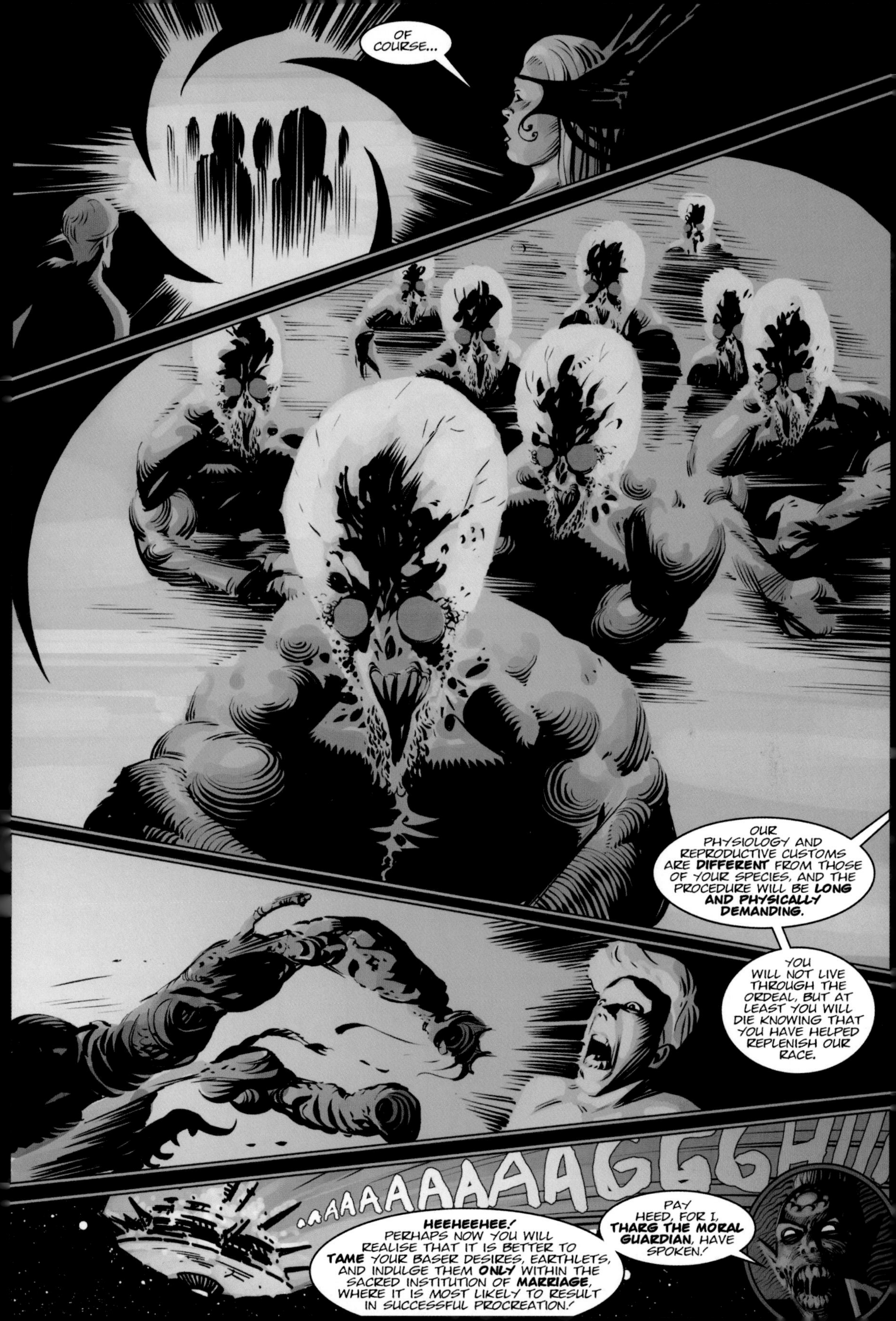
OF COURSE...
OUR PHYSIOLOGY AND REPRODUCTIVE CUSTOMS ARE **DIFFERENT** FROM THOSE OF YOUR SPECIES, AND THE PROCEDURE WILL BE **LONG AND PHYSICALLY DEMANDING.**
YOU WILL NOT LIVE THROUGH THE ORDEAL, BUT AT LEAST YOU WILL DIE KNOWING THAT YOU HAVE HELPED REPLENISH OUR RACE.
..AAAAAAAAAAGGGGH!!
HEEHEEHEE! PERHAPS NOW YOU WILL REALISE THAT IT IS BETTER TO **TAME** YOUR BASER DESIRES, EARTHLETS, AND INDULGE THEM **ONLY** WITHIN THE SACRED INSTITUTION OF **MARRIAGE**, WHERE IT IS MOST LIKELY TO RESULT IN SUCCESSFUL PROCREATION!
PAY HEED, FOR I, **THARG THE MORAL GUARDIAN**, HAVE SPOKEN!

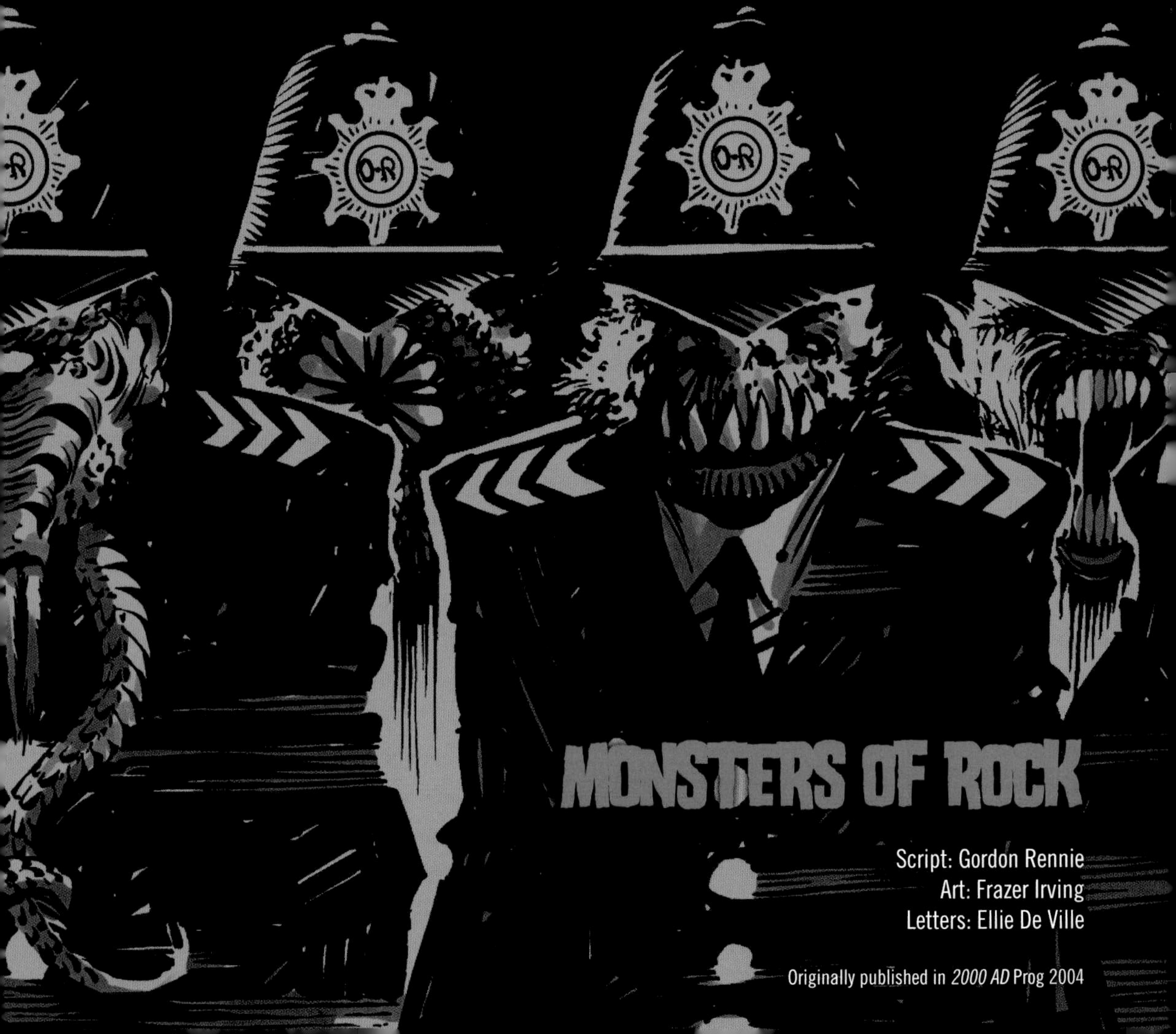

MONSTERS OF ROCK

Script: Gordon Rennie
Art: Frazer Irving
Letters: Ellie De Ville

Originally published in *2000 AD* Prog 2004

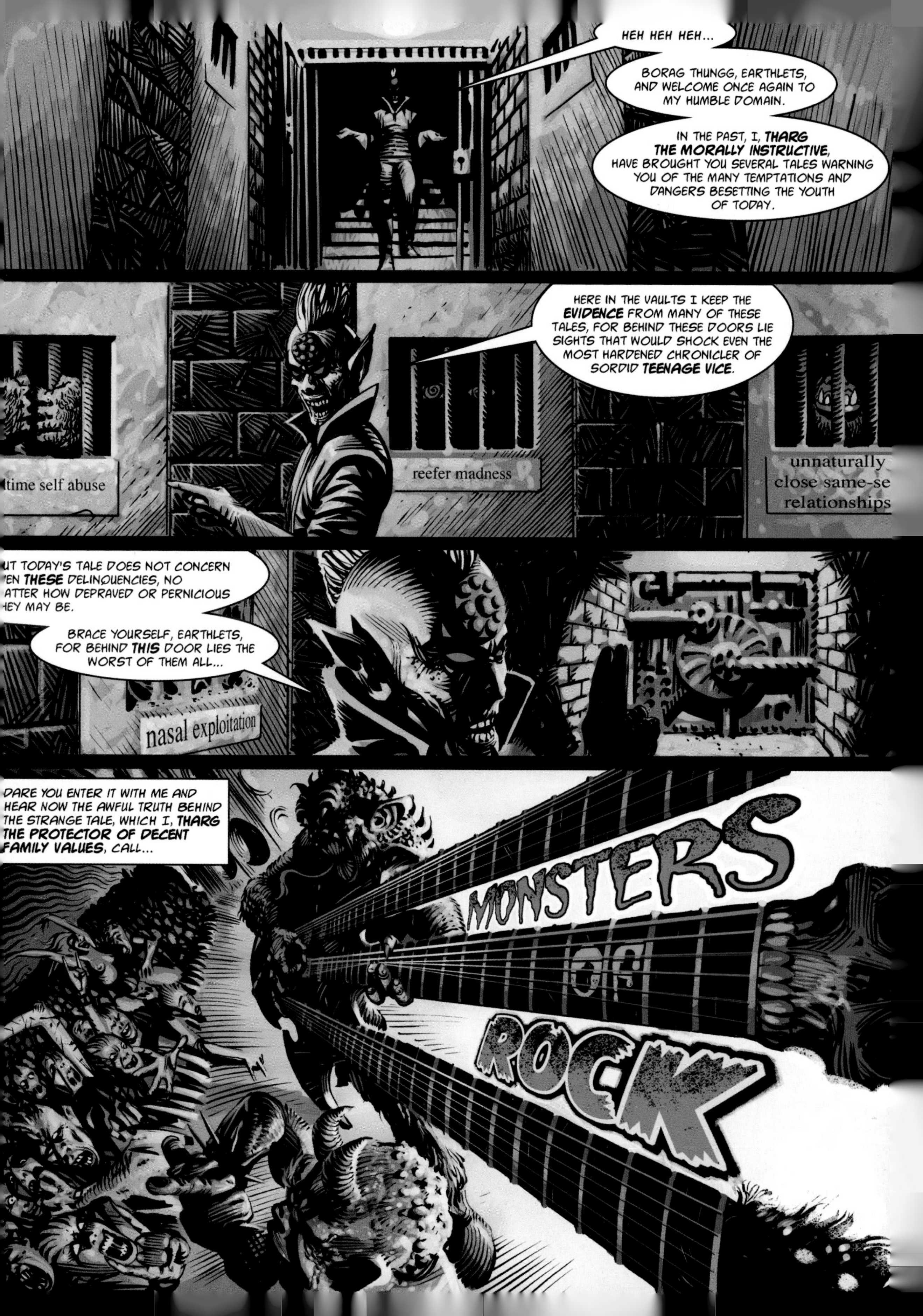

HEH HEH HEH...
BORAG THUNGG, EARTHLETS, AND WELCOME ONCE AGAIN TO MY HUMBLE DOMAIN.
IN THE PAST, I, THARG THE MORALLY INSTRUCTIVE, HAVE BROUGHT YOU SEVERAL TALES WARNING YOU OF THE MANY TEMPTATIONS AND DANGERS BESETTING THE YOUTH OF TODAY.
HERE IN THE VAULTS I KEEP THE EVIDENCE FROM MANY OF THESE TALES, FOR BEHIND THESE DOORS LIE SIGHTS THAT WOULD SHOCK EVEN THE MOST HARDENED CHRONICLER OF SORDID TEENAGE VICE.
time self abuse
reefer madness
unnaturally close same-se relationships
UT TODAY'S TALE DOES NOT CONCERN 'EN THESE DELINQUENCIES, NO ATTER HOW DEPRAVED OR PERNICIOUS HEY MAY BE.
BRACE YOURSELF, EARTHLETS, FOR BEHIND THIS DOOR LIES THE WORST OF THEM ALL...
nasal exploitation
DARE YOU ENTER IT WITH ME AND HEAR NOW THE AWFUL TRUTH BEHIND THE STRANGE TALE, WHICH I, THARG THE PROTECTOR OF DECENT FAMILY VALUES, CALL...
MONSTERS OF ROCK

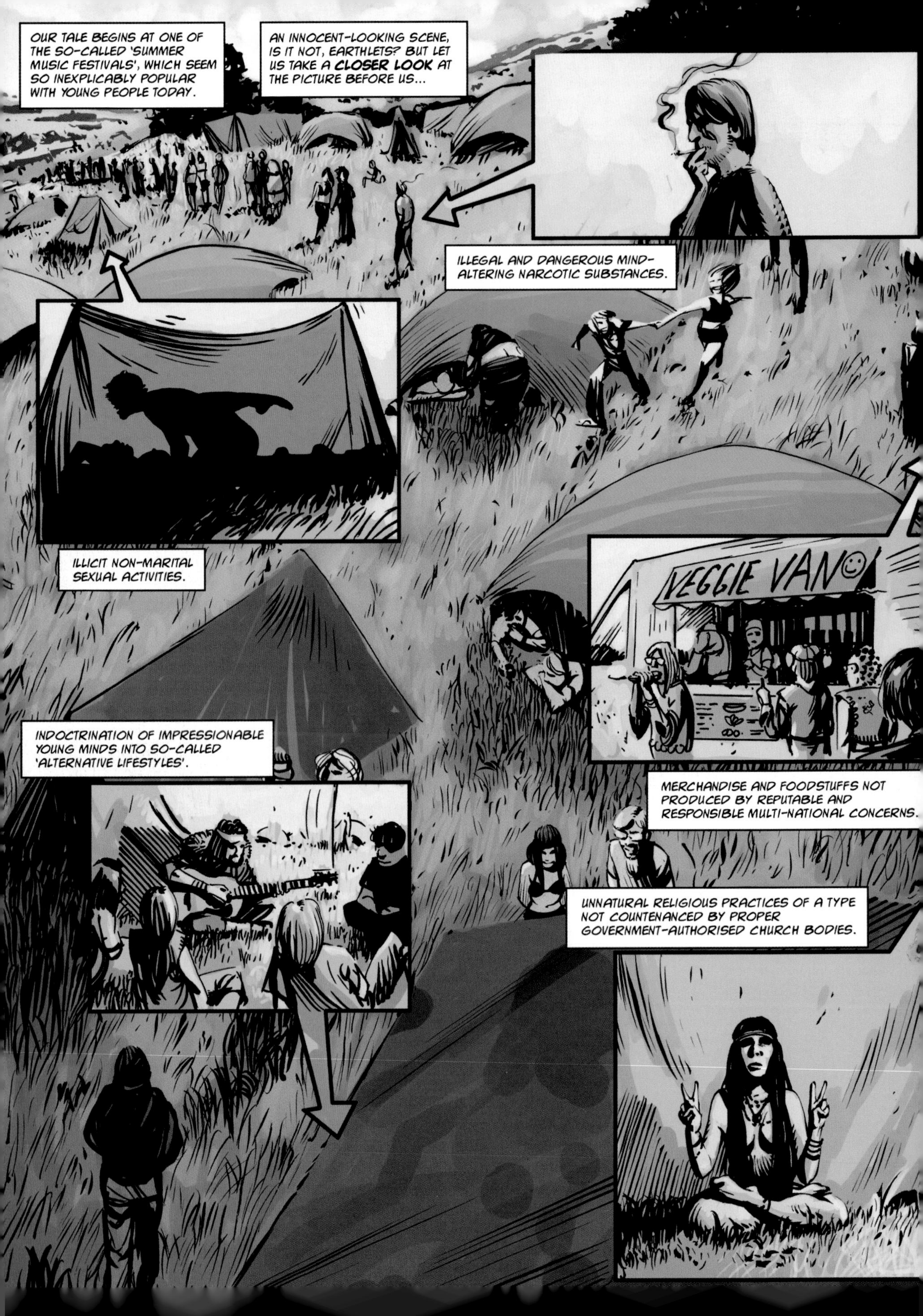
OUR TALE BEGINS AT ONE OF THE SO-CALLED 'SUMMER MUSIC FESTIVALS', WHICH SEEM SO INEXPLICABLY POPULAR WITH YOUNG PEOPLE TODAY.
AN INNOCENT-LOOKING SCENE, IS IT NOT, EARTHLETS? BUT LET US TAKE A **CLOSER LOOK** AT THE PICTURE BEFORE US...
ILLEGAL AND DANGEROUS MIND-ALTERING NARCOTIC SUBSTANCES.
ILLICIT NON-MARITAL SEXUAL ACTIVITIES.
VEGGIE VAN
MERCHANDISE AND FOODSTUFFS NOT PRODUCED BY REPUTABLE AND RESPONSIBLE MULTI-NATIONAL CONCERNS.
INDOCTRINATION OF IMPRESSIONABLE YOUNG MINDS INTO SO-CALLED 'ALTERNATIVE LIFESTYLES'.
UNNATURAL RELIGIOUS PRACTICES OF A TYPE NOT COUNTENANCED BY PROPER GOVERNMENT-AUTHORISED CHURCH BODIES.

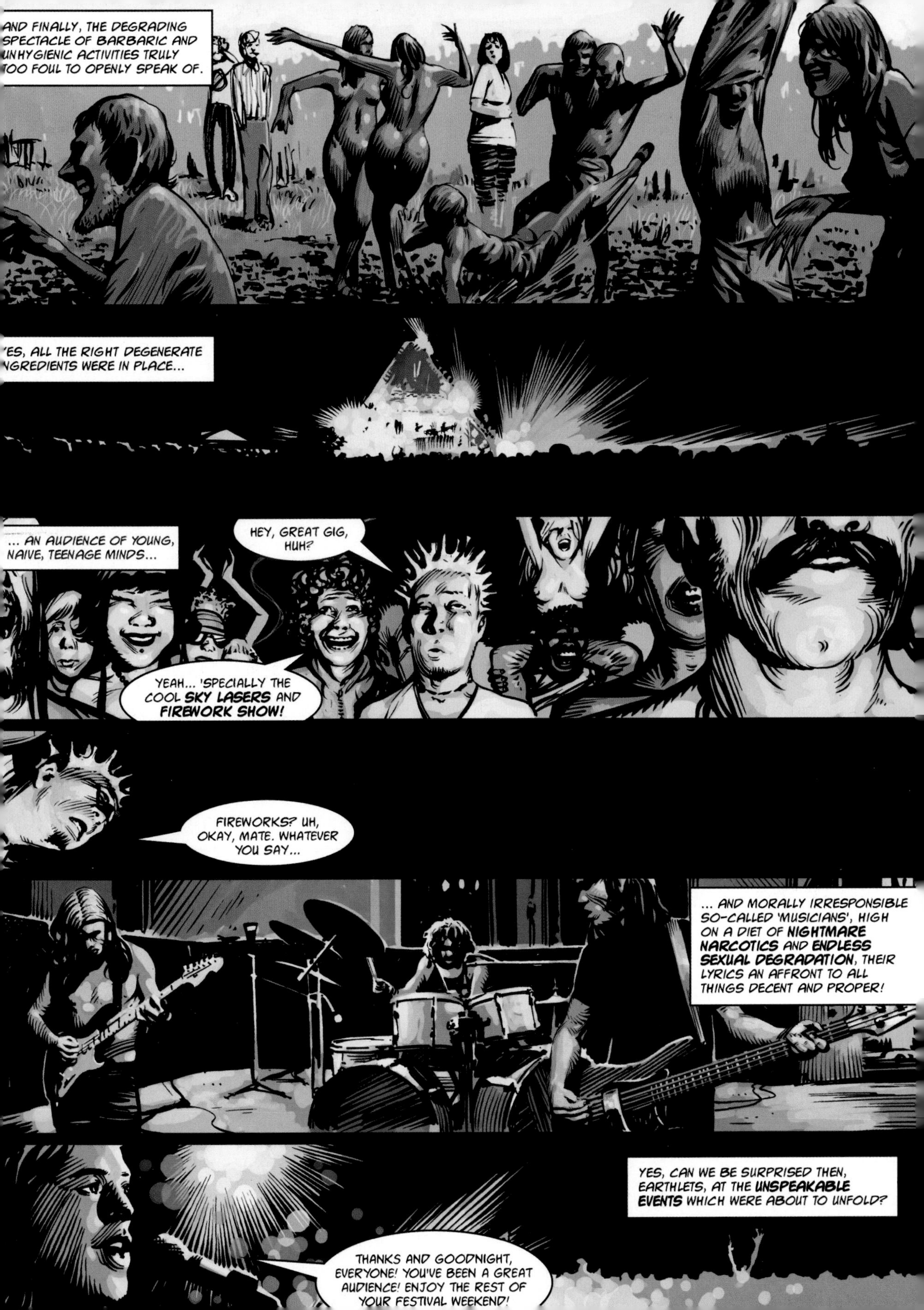
AND FINALLY, THE DEGRADING SPECTACLE OF BARBARIC AND UNHYGIENIC ACTIVITIES TRULY TOO FOUL TO OPENLY SPEAK OF.
YES, ALL THE RIGHT DEGENERATE INGREDIENTS WERE IN PLACE...
... AN AUDIENCE OF YOUNG, NAIVE, TEENAGE MINDS...
HEY, GREAT GIG, HUH?
YEAH... 'SPECIALLY THE COOL **SKY LASERS** AND **FIREWORK SHOW!**
FIREWORKS? UH, OKAY, MATE. WHATEVER YOU SAY...
... AND MORALLY IRRESPONSIBLE SO-CALLED 'MUSICIANS', HIGH ON A DIET OF **NIGHTMARE NARCOTICS** AND **ENDLESS SEXUAL DEGRADATION**, THEIR LYRICS AN AFFRONT TO ALL THINGS DECENT AND PROPER!
YES, CAN WE BE SURPRISED THEN, EARTHLETS, AT THE **UNSPEAKABLE EVENTS** WHICH WERE ABOUT TO UNFOLD?
THANKS AND GOODNIGHT, EVERYONE! YOU'VE BEEN A GREAT AUDIENCE! ENJOY THE REST OF YOUR FESTIVAL WEEKEND!

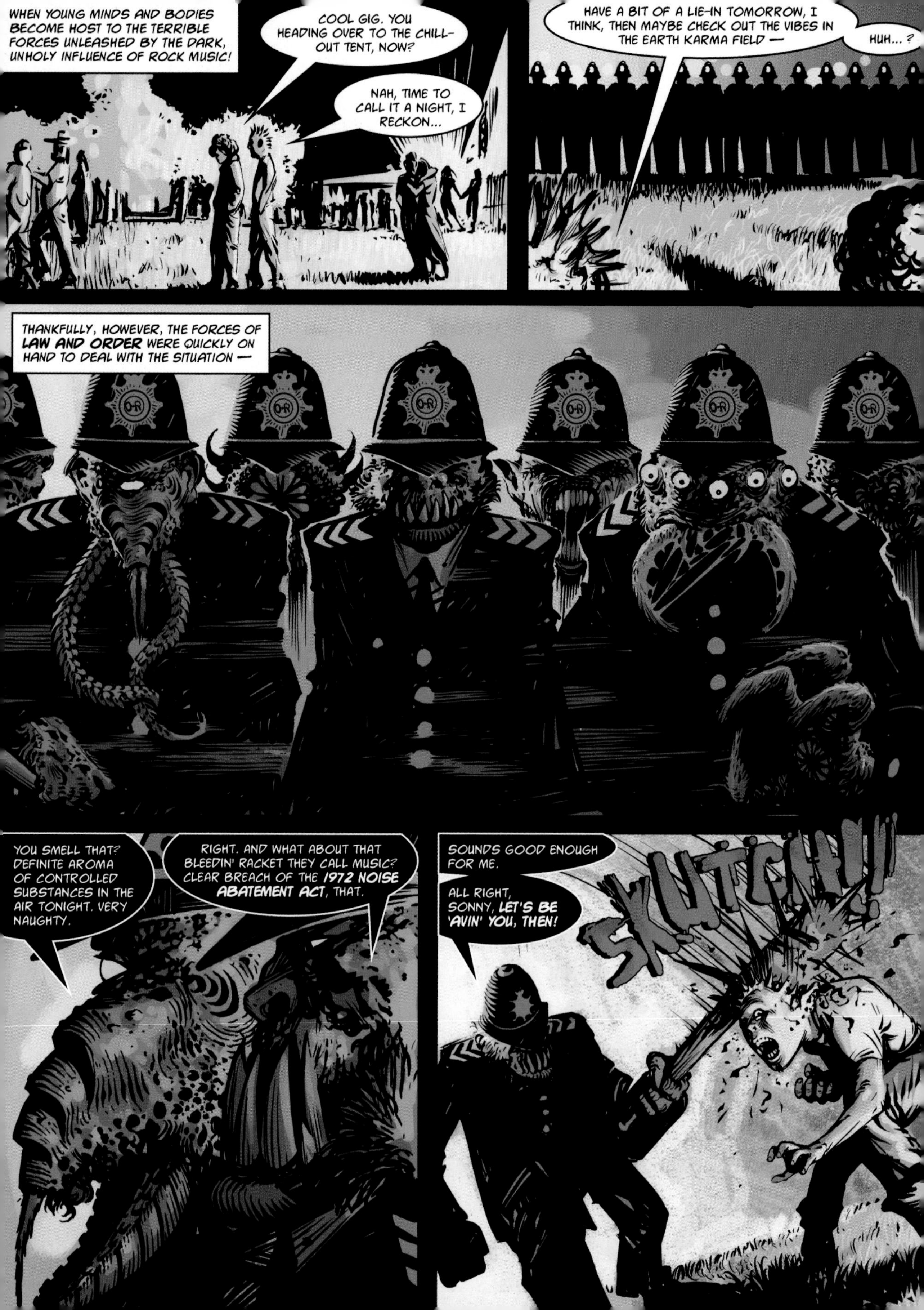

WHEN YOUNG MINDS AND BODIES BECOME HOST TO THE TERRIBLE FORCES UNLEASHED BY THE DARK, UNHOLY INFLUENCE OF ROCK MUSIC!
COOL GIG. YOU HEADING OVER TO THE CHILL-OUT TENT, NOW?
NAH, TIME TO CALL IT A NIGHT, I RECKON...
HAVE A BIT OF A LIE-IN TOMORROW, I THINK, THEN MAYBE CHECK OUT THE VIBES IN THE EARTH KARMA FIELD —
HUH...?
THANKFULLY, HOWEVER, THE FORCES OF LAW AND ORDER WERE QUICKLY ON HAND TO DEAL WITH THE SITUATION —
YOU SMELL THAT? DEFINITE AROMA OF CONTROLLED SUBSTANCES IN THE AIR TONIGHT. VERY NAUGHTY.
RIGHT. AND WHAT ABOUT THAT BLEEDIN' RACKET THEY CALL MUSIC? CLEAR BREACH OF THE 1972 NOISE ABATEMENT ACT, THAT.
SOUNDS GOOD ENOUGH FOR ME.
ALL RIGHT, SONNY, LET'S BE 'AVIN' YOU, THEN!
SKUTCH!!

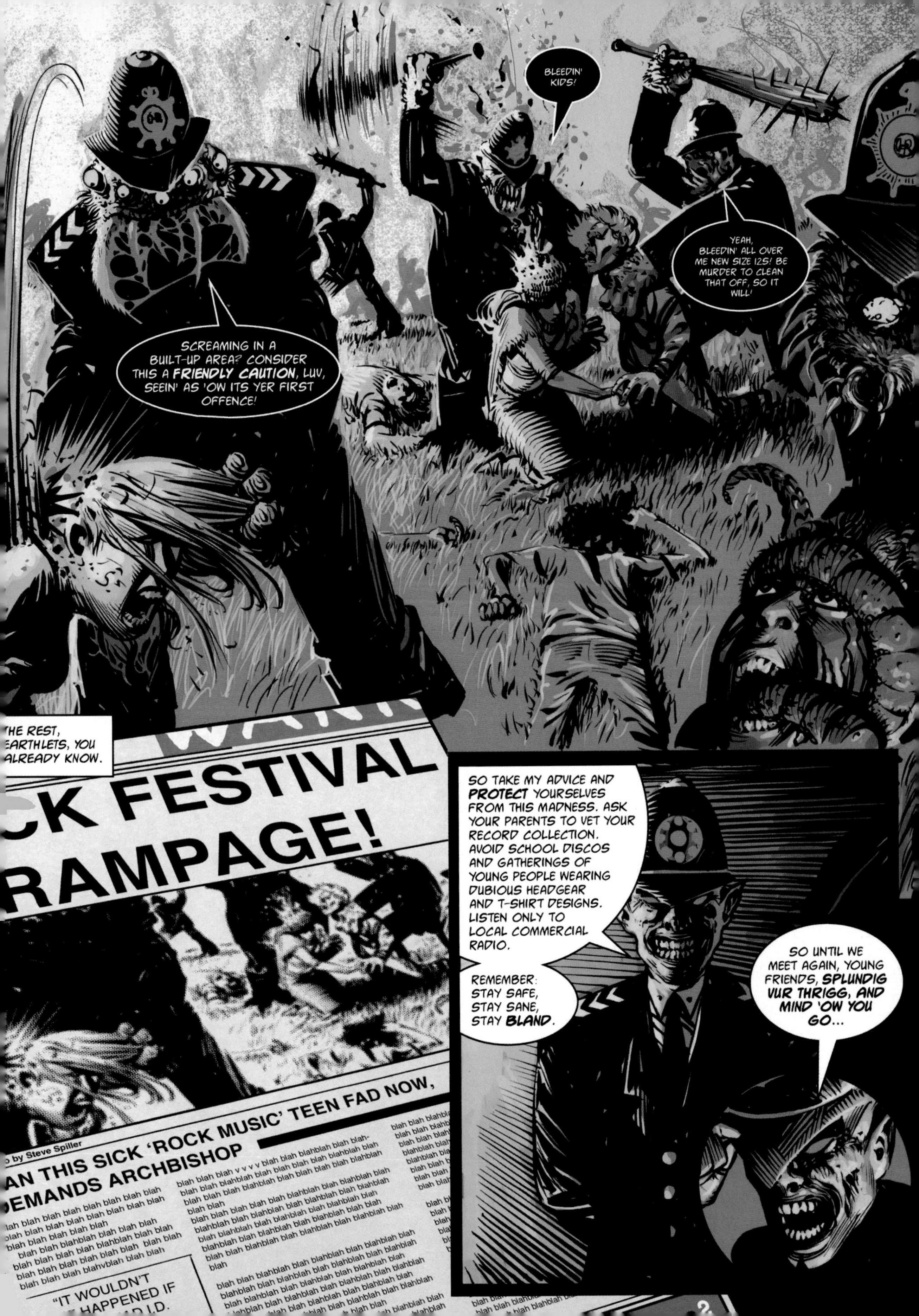

BLEEDIN' KIDS!
SCREAMING IN A BUILT-UP AREA? CONSIDER THIS A **FRIENDLY CAUTION**, LUV, SEEIN' AS 'OW ITS YER FIRST OFFENCE!
YEAH, BLEEDIN' ALL OVER ME NEW SIZE 12S! BE MURDER TO CLEAN THAT OFF, SO IT WILL!
THE REST, EARTHLETS, YOU ALREADY KNOW.
CK FESTIVAL RAMPAGE!
BAN THIS SICK 'ROCK MUSIC' TEEN FAD NOW, DEMANDS ARCHBISHOP
by Steve Spiller
"IT WOULDN'T HAPPENED IF
SO TAKE MY ADVICE AND **PROTECT** YOURSELVES FROM THIS MADNESS. ASK YOUR PARENTS TO VET YOUR RECORD COLLECTION. AVOID SCHOOL DISCOS AND GATHERINGS OF YOUNG PEOPLE WEARING DUBIOUS HEADGEAR AND T-SHIRT DESIGNS. LISTEN ONLY TO LOCAL COMMERCIAL RADIO.
REMEMBER: STAY SAFE, STAY SANE, STAY **BLAND**.
SO UNTIL WE MEET AGAIN, YOUNG FRIENDS, **SPLUNDIG VUR THRIGG, AND MIND 'OW YOU GO...**

DAUGHTER OF DARKNESS

Script: Tharg the Mighty
Art: Frazer Irving
Letters: Annie Parkhouse

Originally published in *Metal Hammer* magazine

THE DEAD CAN'T DANCE

Script: Tharg the Mighty
Art: Frazer Irving
Letters: Annie Parkhouse

Originally published in *Metal Hammer* magazine

THE DEVIL HAS THE BEST TUNES

Script: Tharg the Mighty
Art: Frazer Irving
Letters: Annie Parkhouse

Originally published in *Metal Hammer* magazine

SOUND OF THE UNDERGROUND

Script: Tharg the Mighty
Art: Frazer Irving
Letters: Annie Parkhouse

Originally published in *Metal Hammer* magazine

OF WOLF AND MAN

Script: Tharg the Mighty
Art: Frazer Irving
Letters: Annie Parkhouse

Originally published in *Metal Hammer* magazine

MONSTERS OF ROCK

Script: Tharg the Mighty
Art: Frazer Irving
Letters: Annie Parkhouse

Originally published in *Metal Hammer* magazine

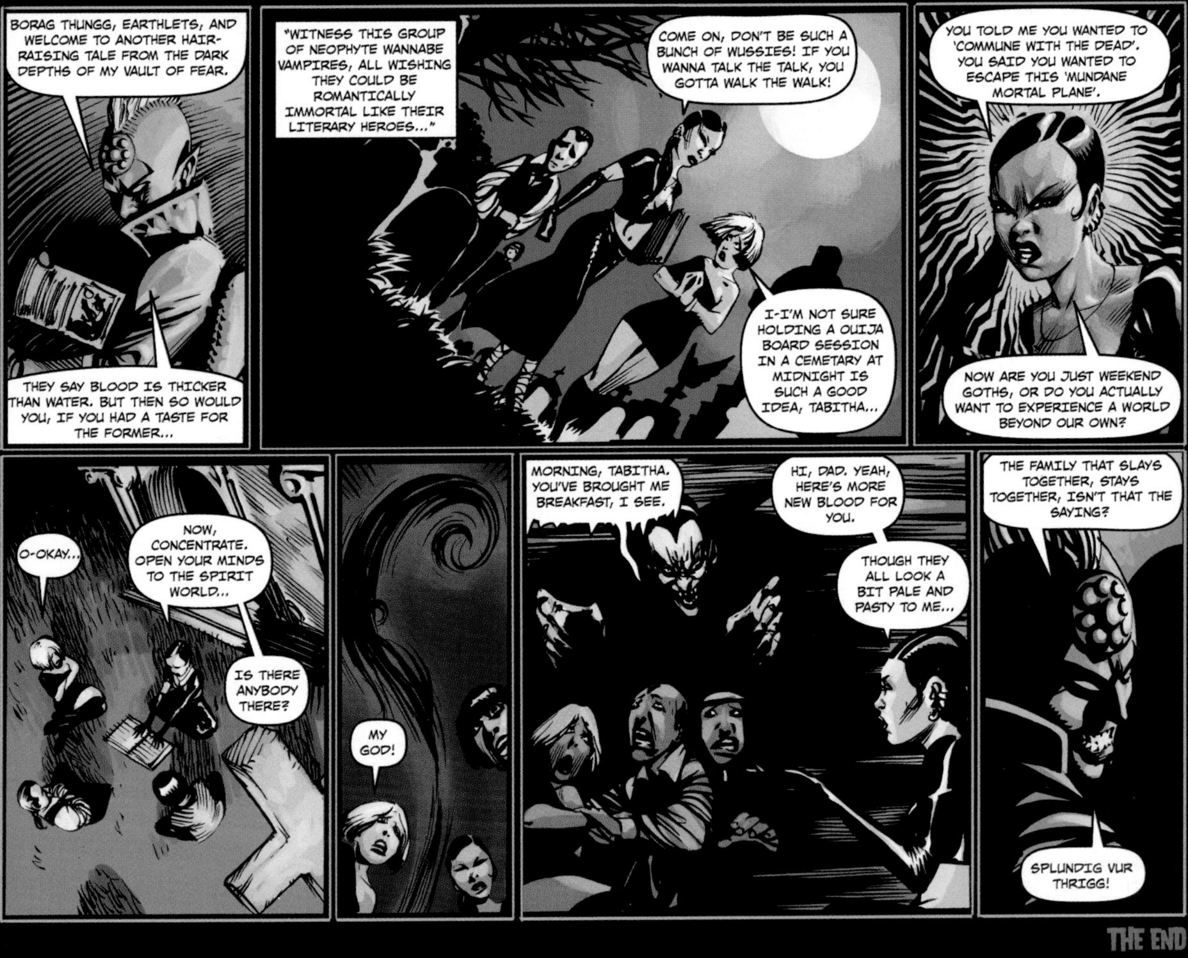
BORAG THUNGG, EARTHLETS, AND WELCOME TO ANOTHER HAIR-RAISING TALE FROM THE DARK DEPTHS OF MY VAULT OF FEAR.
THEY SAY BLOOD IS THICKER THAN WATER. BUT THEN SO WOULD YOU, IF YOU HAD A TASTE FOR THE FORMER...
"WITNESS THIS GROUP OF NEOPHYTE WANNABE VAMPIRES, ALL WISHING THEY COULD BE ROMANTICALLY IMMORTAL LIKE THEIR LITERARY HEROES..."
COME ON, DON'T BE SUCH A BUNCH OF WUSSIES! IF YOU WANNA TALK THE TALK, YOU GOTTA WALK THE WALK!
I-I'M NOT SURE HOLDING A OUIJA BOARD SESSION IN A CEMETARY AT MIDNIGHT IS SUCH A GOOD IDEA, TABITHA...
YOU TOLD ME YOU WANTED TO 'COMMUNE WITH THE DEAD'. YOU SAID YOU WANTED TO ESCAPE THIS 'MUNDANE MORTAL PLANE'.
NOW ARE YOU JUST WEEKEND GOTHS, OR DO YOU ACTUALLY WANT TO EXPERIENCE A WORLD BEYOND OUR OWN?
O-OKAY...
NOW, CONCENTRATE. OPEN YOUR MINDS TO THE SPIRIT WORLD...
IS THERE ANYBODY THERE?
MY GOD!
MORNING, TABITHA. YOU'VE BROUGHT ME BREAKFAST, I SEE.
HI, DAD. YEAH, HERE'S MORE NEW BLOOD FOR YOU.
THOUGH THEY ALL LOOK A BIT PALE AND PASTY TO ME...
THE FAMILY THAT SLAYS TOGETHER, STAYS TOGETHER, ISN'T THAT THE SAYING?
SPLUNDIG VUR THRIGG!
THE END

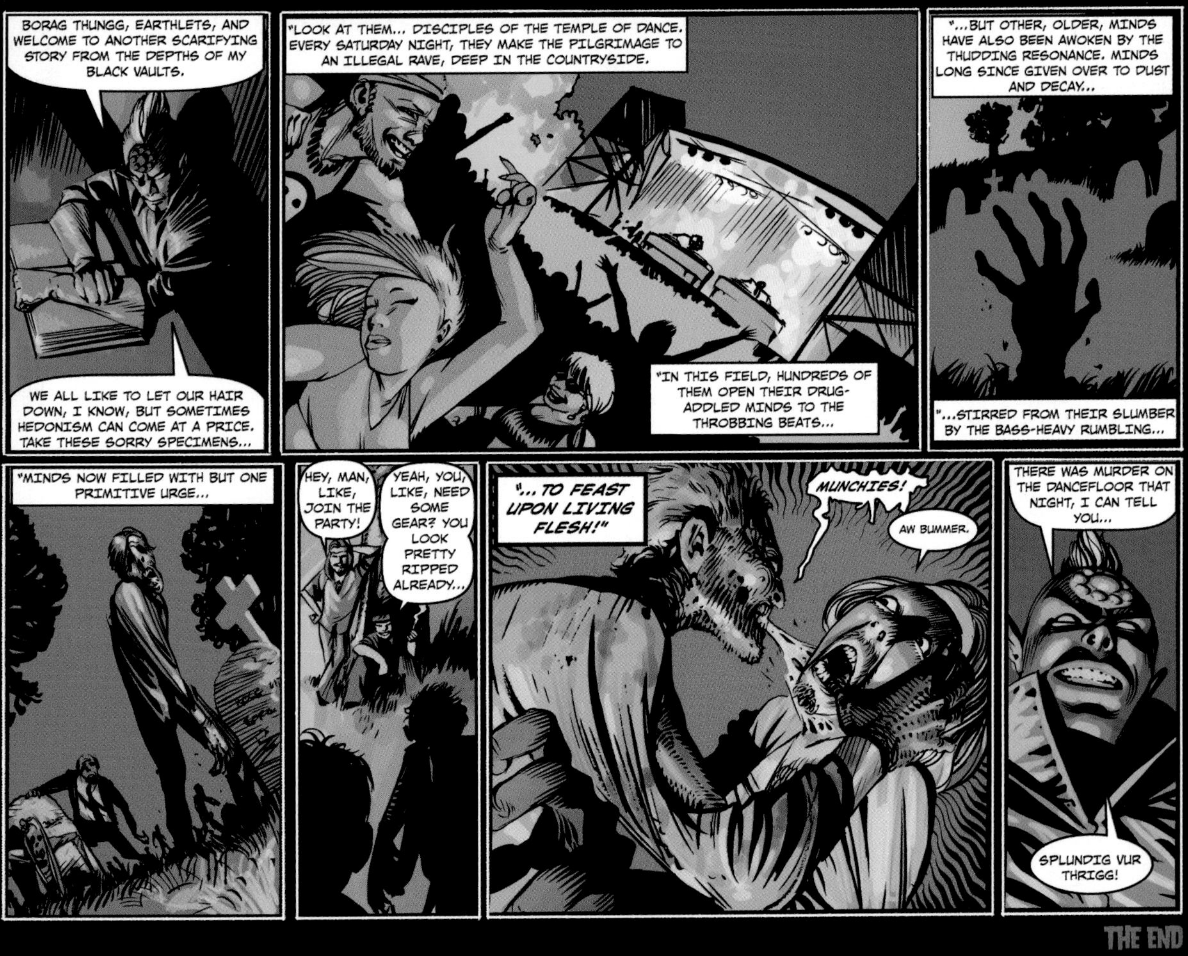
BORAG THUNGG, EARTHLETS, AND WELCOME TO ANOTHER SCARIFYING STORY FROM THE DEPTHS OF MY BLACK VAULTS.
WE ALL LIKE TO LET OUR HAIR DOWN, I KNOW, BUT SOMETIMES HEDONISM CAN COME AT A PRICE. TAKE THESE SORRY SPECIMENS...
"LOOK AT THEM... DISCIPLES OF THE TEMPLE OF DANCE. EVERY SATURDAY NIGHT, THEY MAKE THE PILGRIMAGE TO AN ILLEGAL RAVE, DEEP IN THE COUNTRYSIDE.
"IN THIS FIELD, HUNDREDS OF THEM OPEN THEIR DRUG-ADDLED MINDS TO THE THROBBING BEATS...
"...BUT OTHER, OLDER, MINDS HAVE ALSO BEEN AWOKEN BY THE THUDDING RESONANCE. MINDS LONG SINCE GIVEN OVER TO DUST AND DECAY...
"...STIRRED FROM THEIR SLUMBER BY THE BASS-HEAVY RUMBLING...
"MINDS NOW FILLED WITH BUT ONE PRIMITIVE URGE...
HEY, MAN, LIKE, JOIN THE PARTY!
YEAH, YOU, LIKE, NEED SOME GEAR? YOU LOOK PRETTY RIPPED ALREADY...
"...TO FEAST UPON LIVING FLESH!"
MUNCHIES!
AW BUMMER.
THERE WAS MURDER ON THE DANCEFLOOR THAT NIGHT, I CAN TELL YOU...
SPLUNDIG VUR THRIGG!
THE END

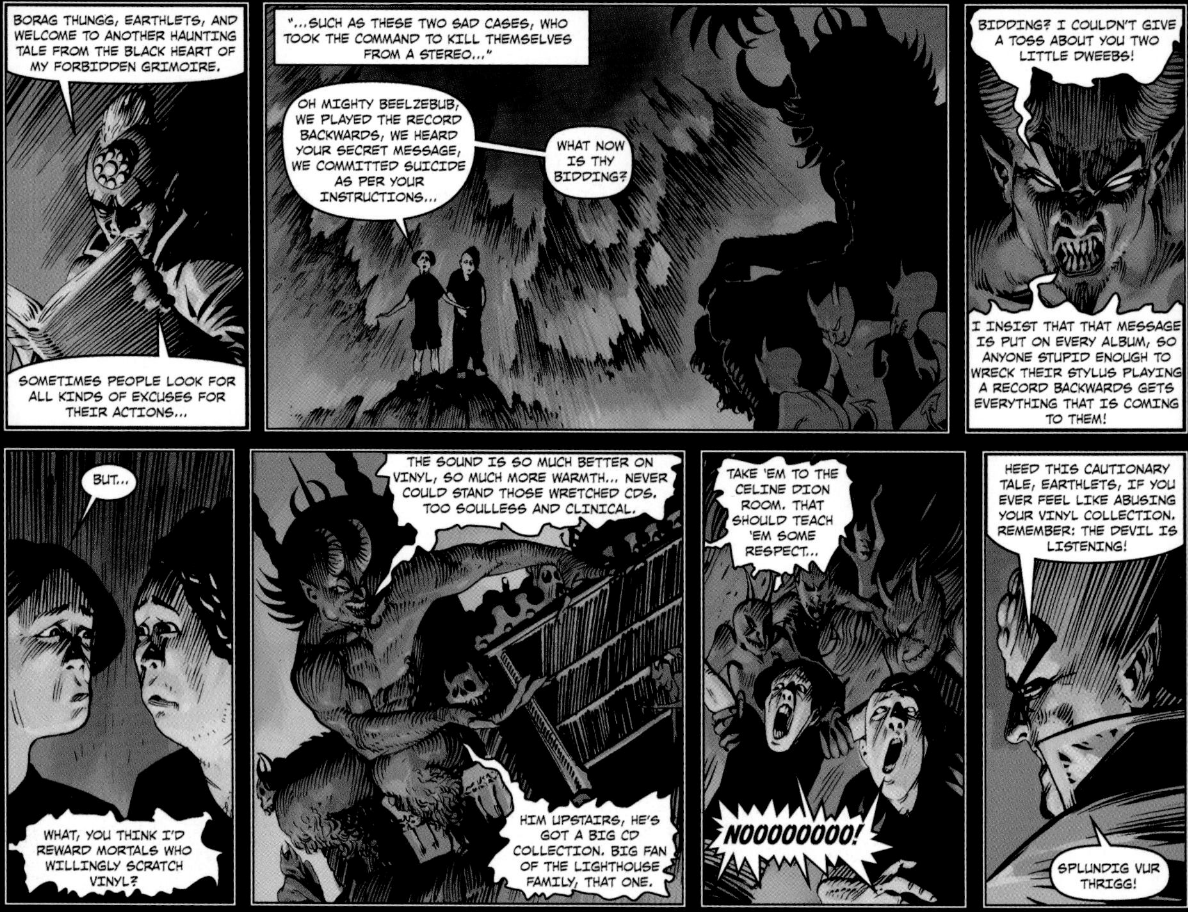
BORAG THUNGG, EARTHLETS, AND WELCOME TO ANOTHER HAUNTING TALE FROM THE BLACK HEART OF MY FORBIDDEN GRIMOIRE.
SOMETIMES PEOPLE LOOK FOR ALL KINDS OF EXCUSES FOR THEIR ACTIONS...
"...SUCH AS THESE TWO SAD CASES, WHO TOOK THE COMMAND TO KILL THEMSELVES FROM A STEREO..."
OH MIGHTY BEELZEBUB, WE PLAYED THE RECORD BACKWARDS, WE HEARD YOUR SECRET MESSAGE, WE COMMITTED SUICIDE AS PER YOUR INSTRUCTIONS...
WHAT NOW IS THY BIDDING?
BIDDING? I COULDN'T GIVE A TOSS ABOUT YOU TWO LITTLE DWEEBS!
I INSIST THAT THAT MESSAGE IS PUT ON EVERY ALBUM, SO ANYONE STUPID ENOUGH TO WRECK THEIR STYLUS PLAYING A RECORD BACKWARDS GETS EVERYTHING THAT IS COMING TO THEM!
BUT...
WHAT, YOU THINK I'D REWARD MORTALS WHO WILLINGLY SCRATCH VINYL?
THE SOUND IS SO MUCH BETTER ON VINYL, SO MUCH MORE WARMTH... NEVER COULD STAND THOSE WRETCHED CDS. TOO SOULLESS AND CLINICAL.
HIM UPSTAIRS, HE'S GOT A BIG CD COLLECTION. BIG FAN OF THE LIGHTHOUSE FAMILY, THAT ONE.
TAKE 'EM TO THE CELINE DION ROOM. THAT SHOULD TEACH 'EM SOME RESPECT...
NOOOOOOOO!
HEED THIS CAUTIONARY TALE, EARTHLETS, IF YOU EVER FEEL LIKE ABUSING YOUR VINYL COLLECTION. REMEMBER: THE DEVIL IS LISTENING!
SPLUNDIG VUR THRIGG!

THE END

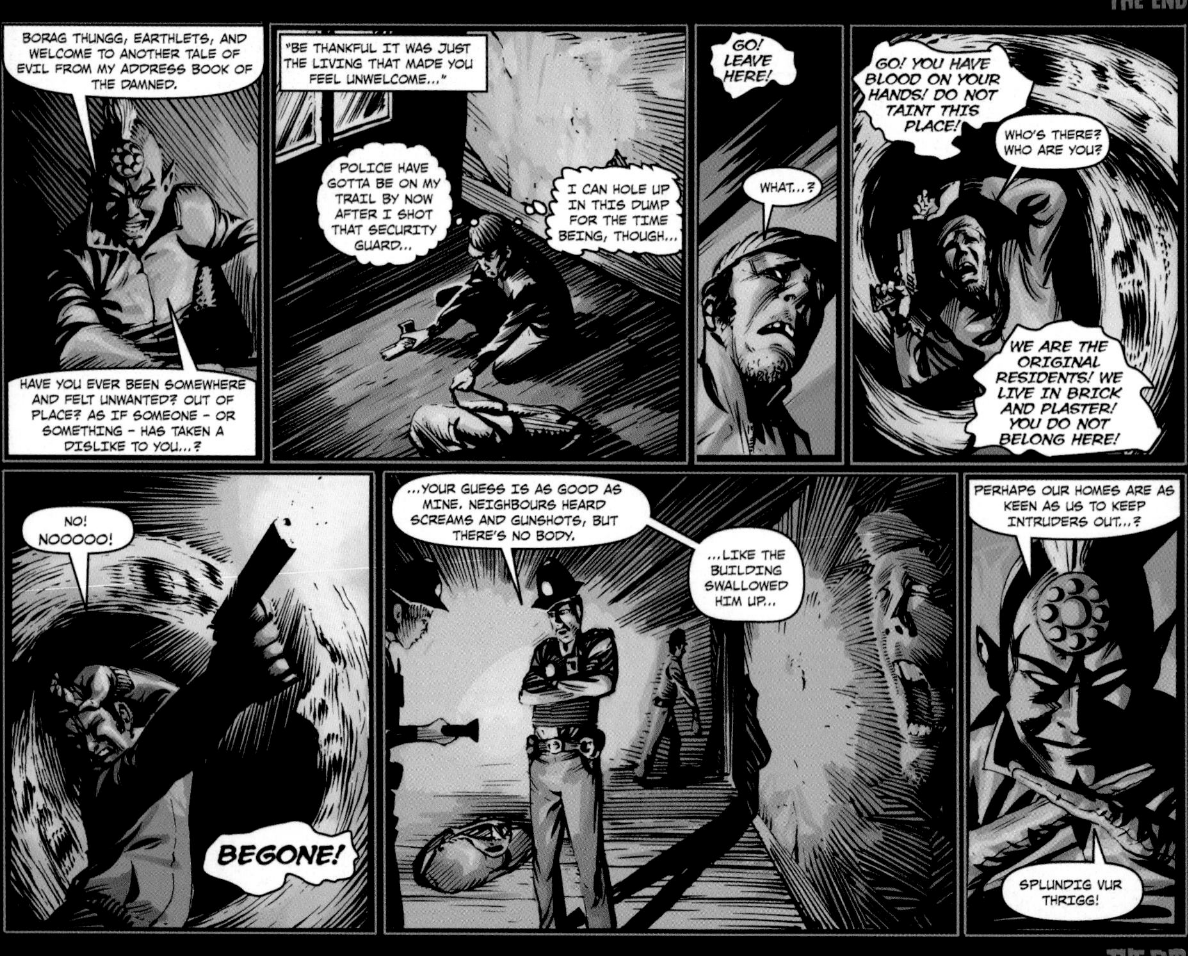
BORAG THUNGG, EARTHLETS, AND WELCOME TO ANOTHER TALE OF EVIL FROM MY ADDRESS BOOK OF THE DAMNED.
HAVE YOU EVER BEEN SOMEWHERE AND FELT UNWANTED? OUT OF PLACE? AS IF SOMEONE – OR SOMETHING – HAS TAKEN A DISLIKE TO YOU...?
"BE THANKFUL IT WAS JUST THE LIVING THAT MADE YOU FEEL UNWELCOME..."
POLICE HAVE GOTTA BE ON MY TRAIL BY NOW AFTER I SHOT THAT SECURITY GUARD...
I CAN HOLE UP IN THIS DUMP FOR THE TIME BEING, THOUGH...
GO! LEAVE HERE!
WHAT...?
GO! YOU HAVE BLOOD ON YOUR HANDS! DO NOT TAINT THIS PLACE!
WHO'S THERE? WHO ARE YOU?
WE ARE THE ORIGINAL RESIDENTS! WE LIVE IN BRICK AND PLASTER! YOU DO NOT BELONG HERE!
NO! NOOOOO!
BEGONE!
...YOUR GUESS IS AS GOOD AS MINE. NEIGHBOURS HEARD SCREAMS AND GUNSHOTS, BUT THERE'S NO BODY.
...LIKE THE BUILDING SWALLOWED HIM UP...
PERHAPS OUR HOMES ARE AS KEEN AS US TO KEEP INTRUDERS OUT...?
SPLUNDIG VUR THRIGG!

THE END

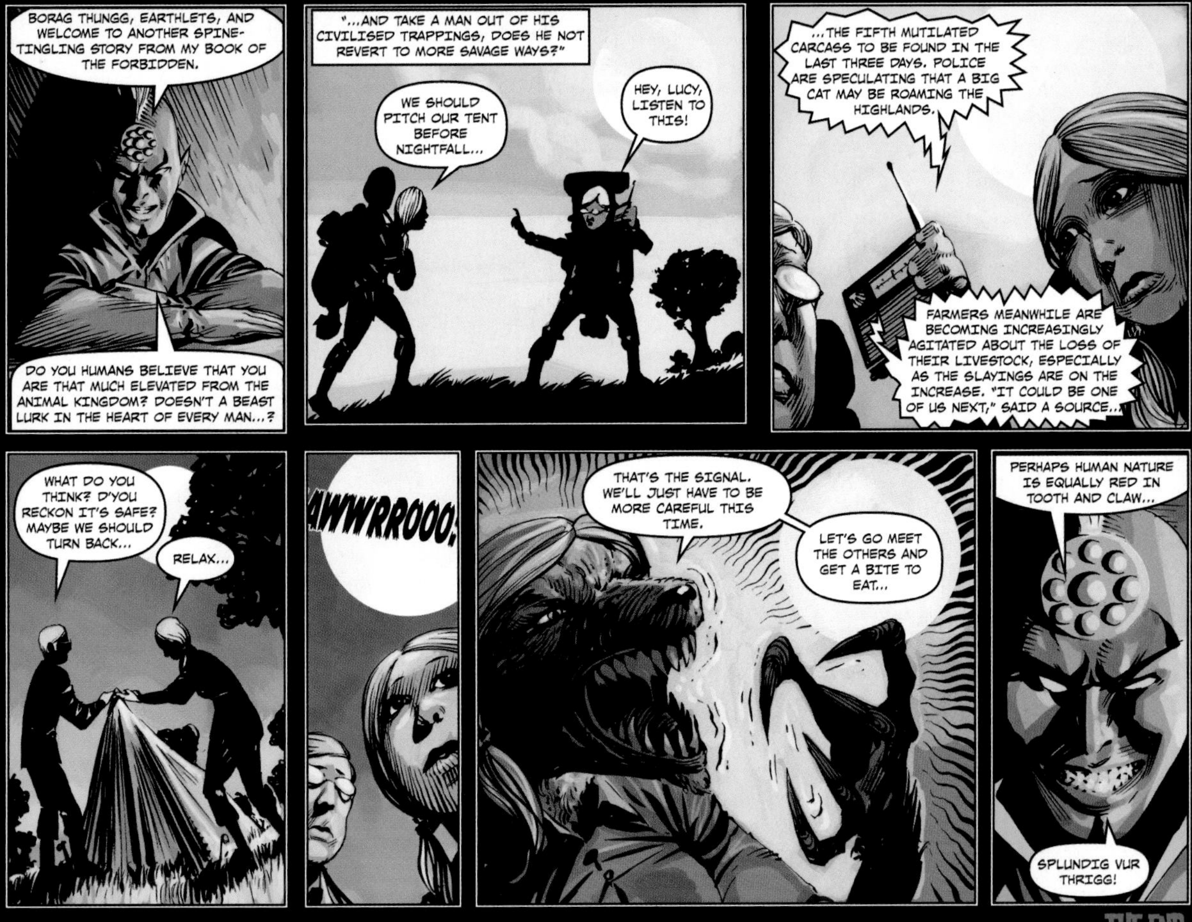
BORAG THUNGG, EARTHLETS, AND WELCOME TO ANOTHER SPINE-TINGLING STORY FROM MY BOOK OF THE FORBIDDEN.
DO YOU HUMANS BELIEVE THAT YOU ARE THAT MUCH ELEVATED FROM THE ANIMAL KINGDOM? DOESN'T A BEAST LURK IN THE HEART OF EVERY MAN...?
"...AND TAKE A MAN OUT OF HIS CIVILISED TRAPPINGS, DOES HE NOT REVERT TO MORE SAVAGE WAYS?"
WE SHOULD PITCH OUR TENT BEFORE NIGHTFALL...
HEY, LUCY, LISTEN TO THIS!
...THE FIFTH MUTILATED CARCASS TO BE FOUND IN THE LAST THREE DAYS. POLICE ARE SPECULATING THAT A BIG CAT MAY BE ROAMING THE HIGHLANDS.
FARMERS MEANWHILE ARE BECOMING INCREASINGLY AGITATED ABOUT THE LOSS OF THEIR LIVESTOCK, ESPECIALLY AS THE SLAYINGS ARE ON THE INCREASE. "IT COULD BE ONE OF US NEXT," SAID A SOURCE...
WHAT DO YOU THINK? D'YOU RECKON IT'S SAFE? MAYBE WE SHOULD TURN BACK...
RELAX...
AWWRROOO!
THAT'S THE SIGNAL. WE'LL JUST HAVE TO BE MORE CAREFUL THIS TIME.
LET'S GO MEET THE OTHERS AND GET A BITE TO EAT...
PERHAPS HUMAN NATURE IS EQUALLY RED IN TOOTH AND CLAW...
SPLUNDIG VUR THRIGG!
THE END

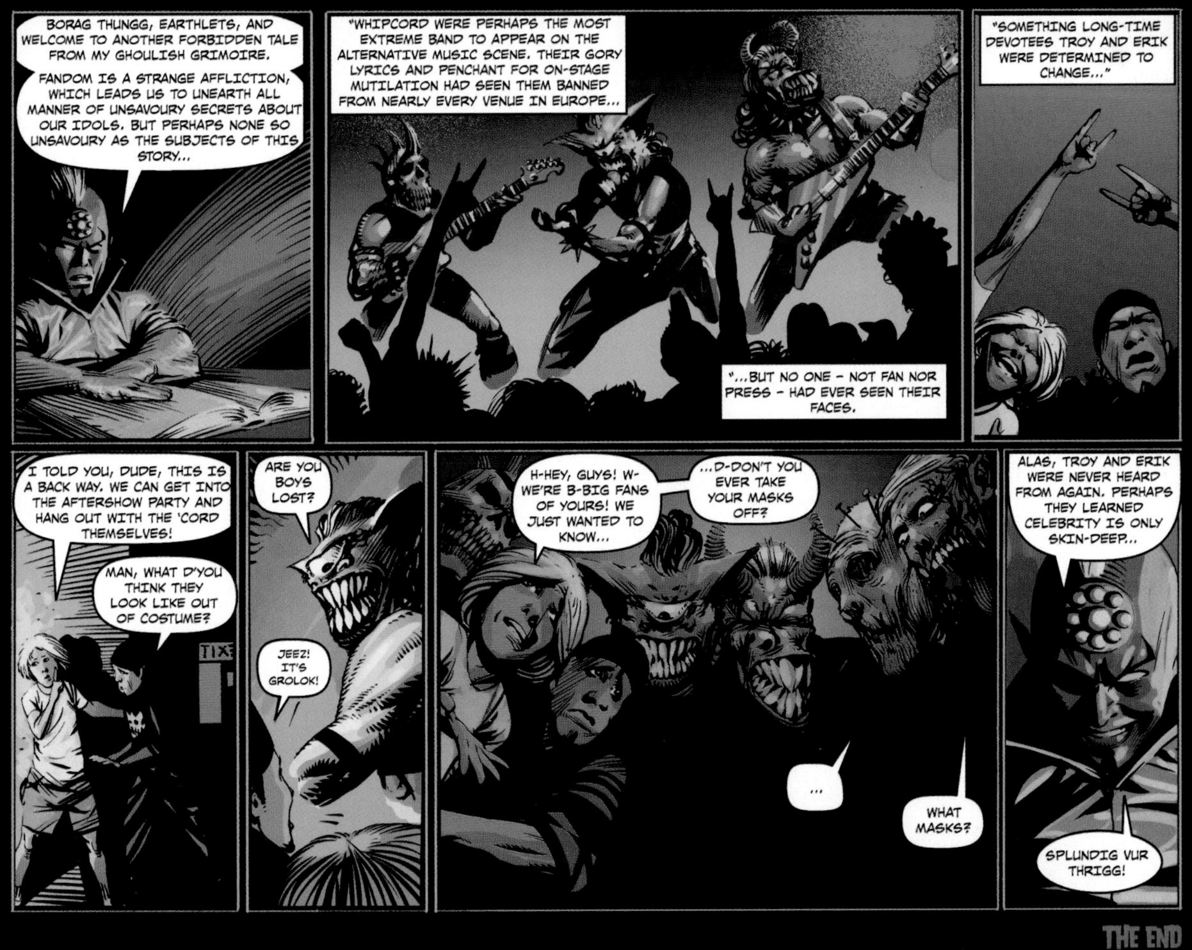
BORAG THUNGG, EARTHLETS, AND WELCOME TO ANOTHER FORBIDDEN TALE FROM MY GHOULISH GRIMOIRE.
FANDOM IS A STRANGE AFFLICTION, WHICH LEADS US TO UNEARTH ALL MANNER OF UNSAVOURY SECRETS ABOUT OUR IDOLS. BUT PERHAPS NONE SO UNSAVOURY AS THE SUBJECTS OF THIS STORY...
"WHIPCORD WERE PERHAPS THE MOST EXTREME BAND TO APPEAR ON THE ALTERNATIVE MUSIC SCENE. THEIR GORY LYRICS AND PENCHANT FOR ON-STAGE MUTILATION HAD SEEN THEM BANNED FROM NEARLY EVERY VENUE IN EUROPE...
"...BUT NO ONE – NOT FAN NOR PRESS – HAD EVER SEEN THEIR FACES.
"SOMETHING LONG-TIME DEVOTEES TROY AND ERIK WERE DETERMINED TO CHANGE..."
I TOLD YOU, DUDE, THIS IS A BACK WAY. WE CAN GET INTO THE AFTERSHOW PARTY AND HANG OUT WITH THE 'CORD THEMSELVES!
MAN, WHAT D'YOU THINK THEY LOOK LIKE OUT OF COSTUME?
TIX
ARE YOU BOYS LOST?
JEEZ! IT'S GROLOK!
H-HEY, GUYS! W-WE'RE B-BIG FANS OF YOURS! WE JUST WANTED TO KNOW...
...D-DON'T YOU EVER TAKE YOUR MASKS OFF?
...
WHAT MASKS?
ALAS, TROY AND ERIK WERE NEVER HEARD FROM AGAIN. PERHAPS THEY LEARNED CELEBRITY IS ONLY SKIN-DEEP...
SPLUNDIG VUR THRIGG!
THE END

FRAZER IRVING SKETCHBOOK

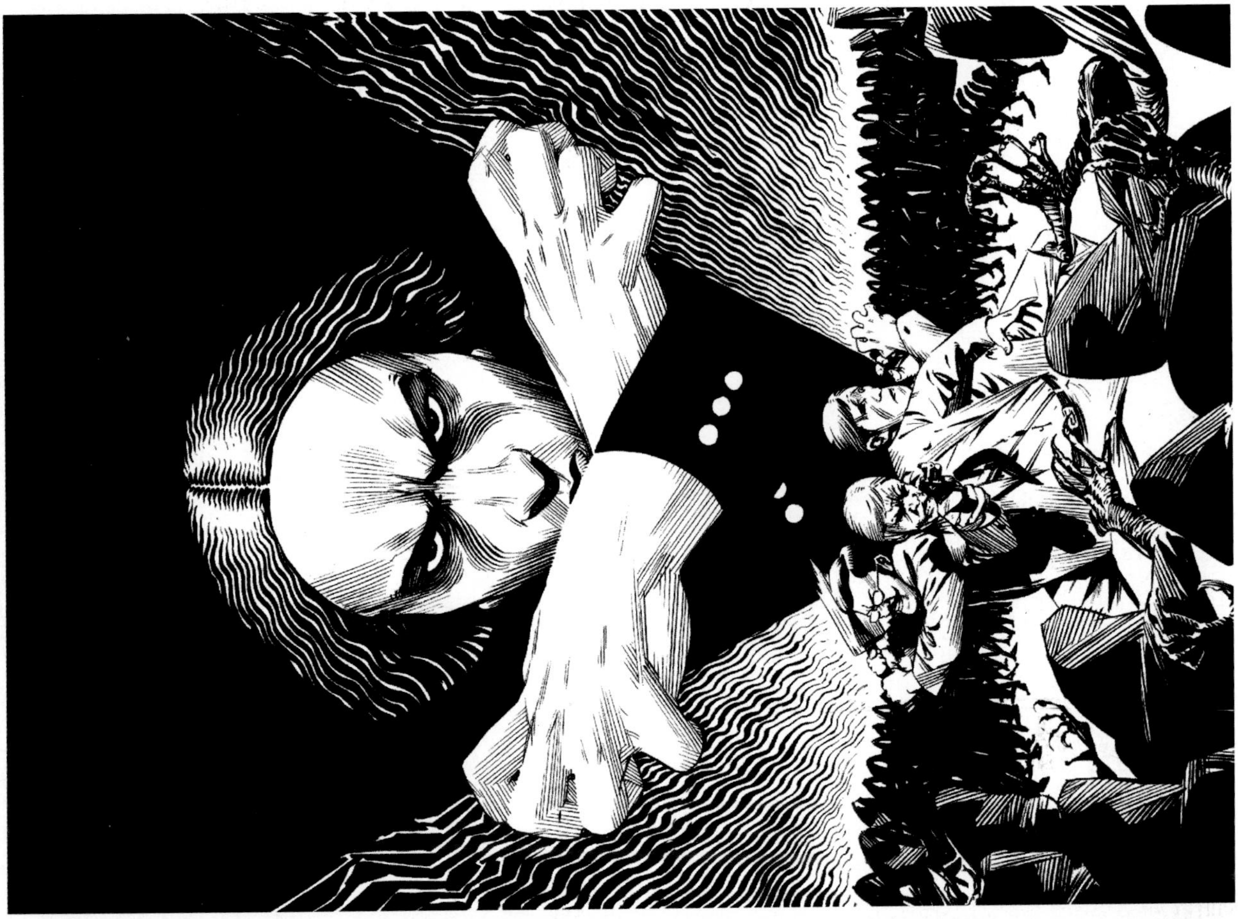

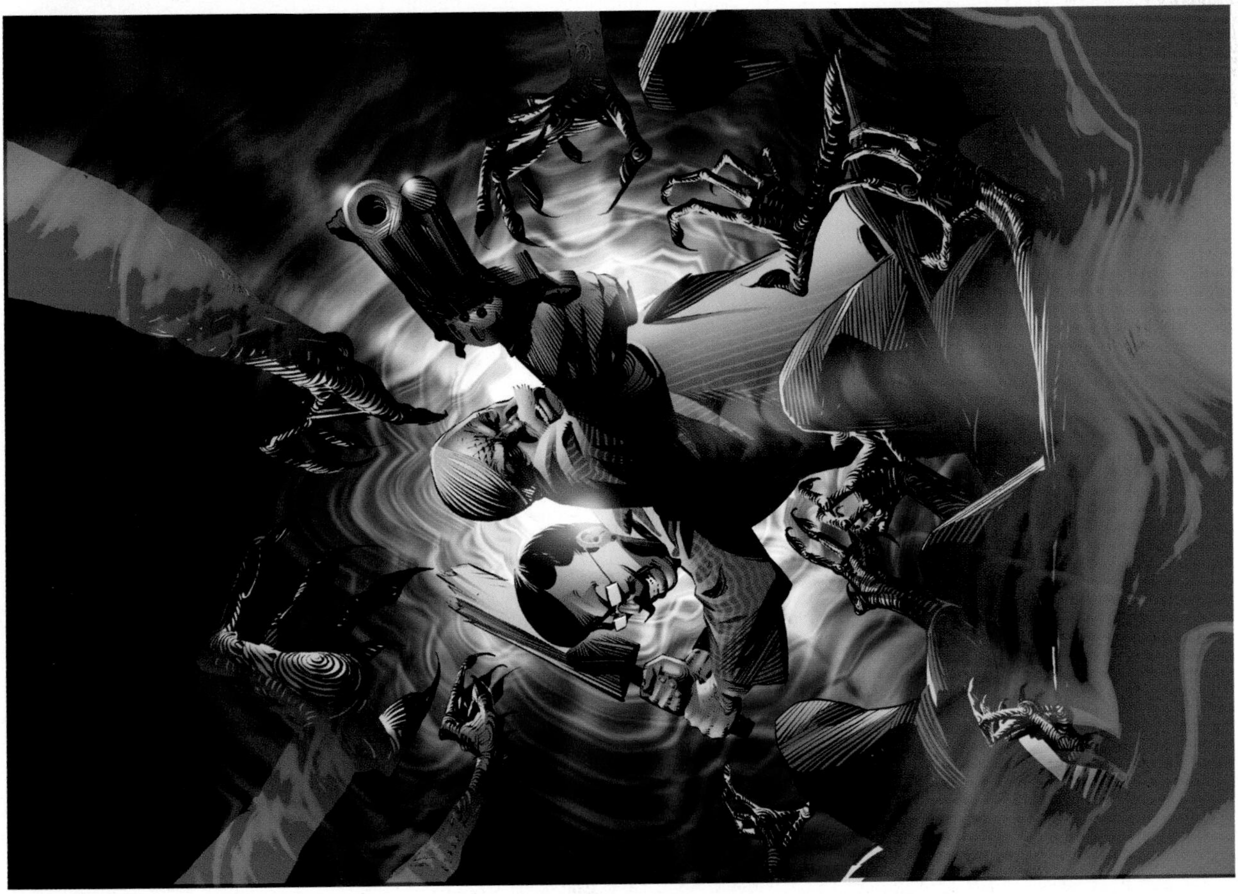

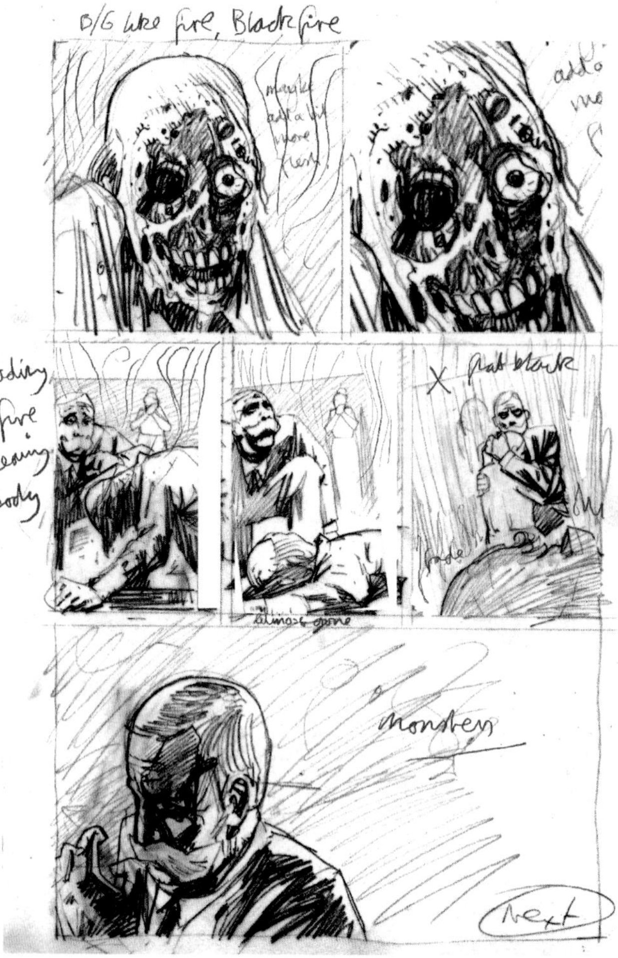
B/G like fire, Black fire
flat black
fade
almost gone
monsters
Next

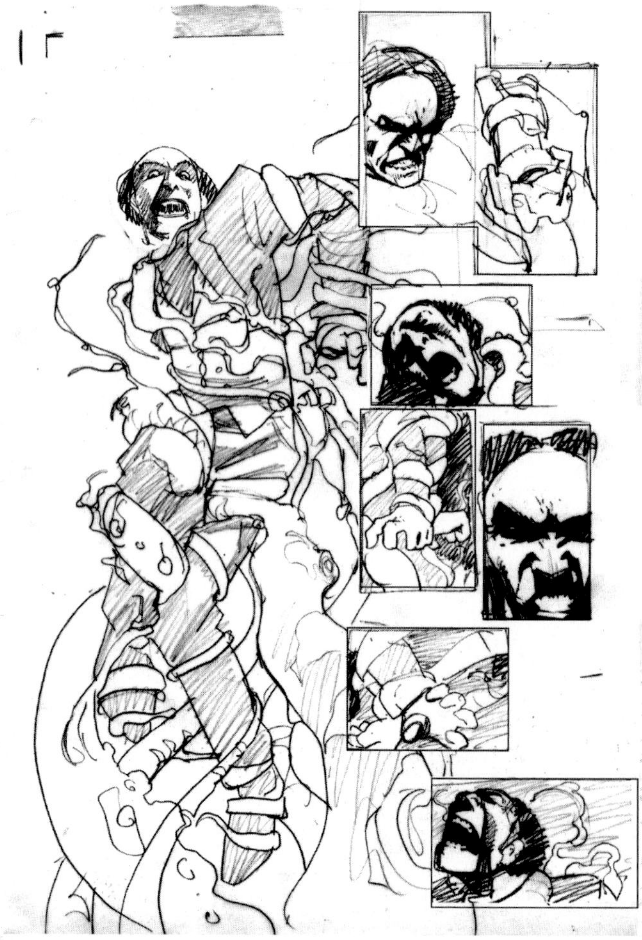

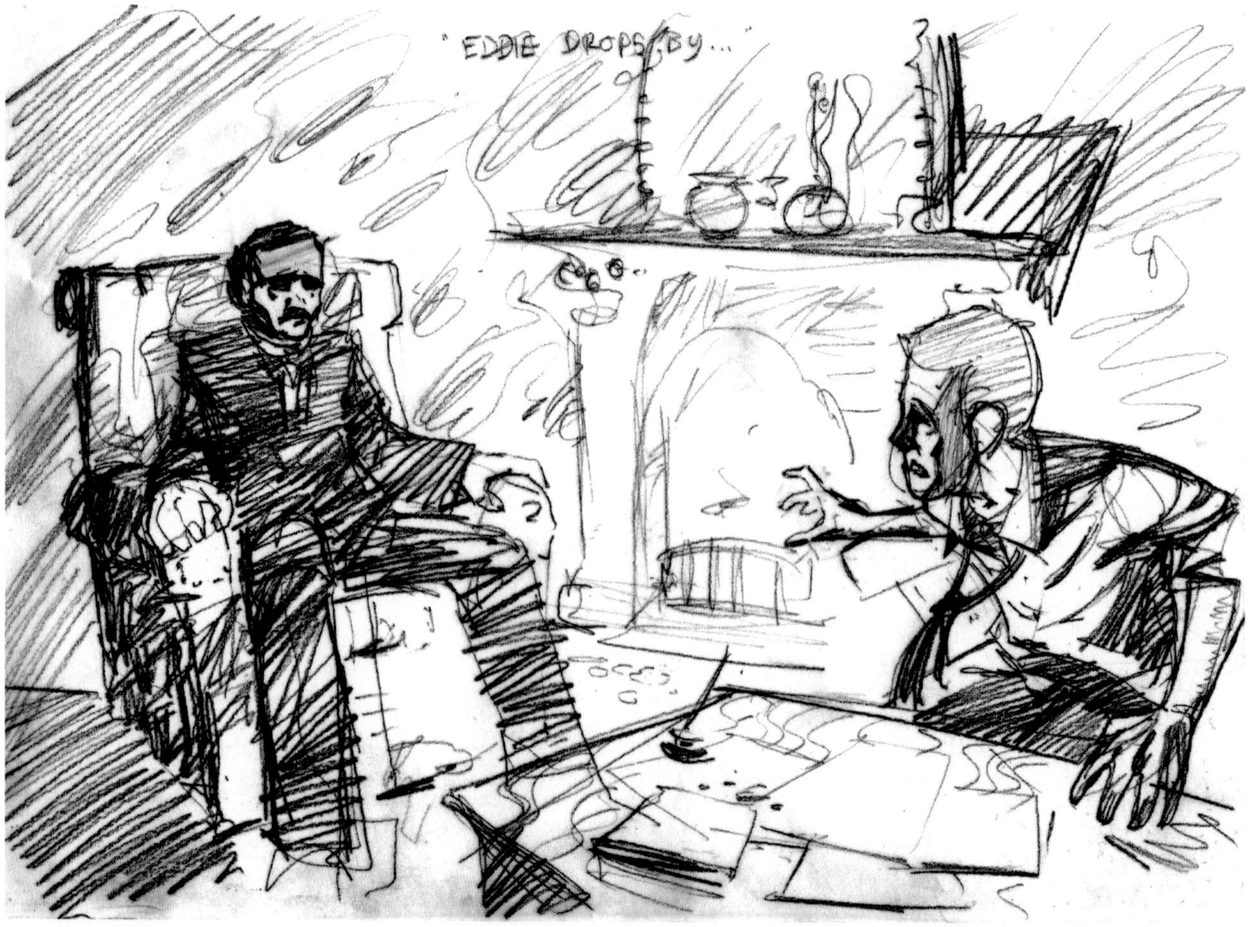
"EDDIE DROPS BY..."

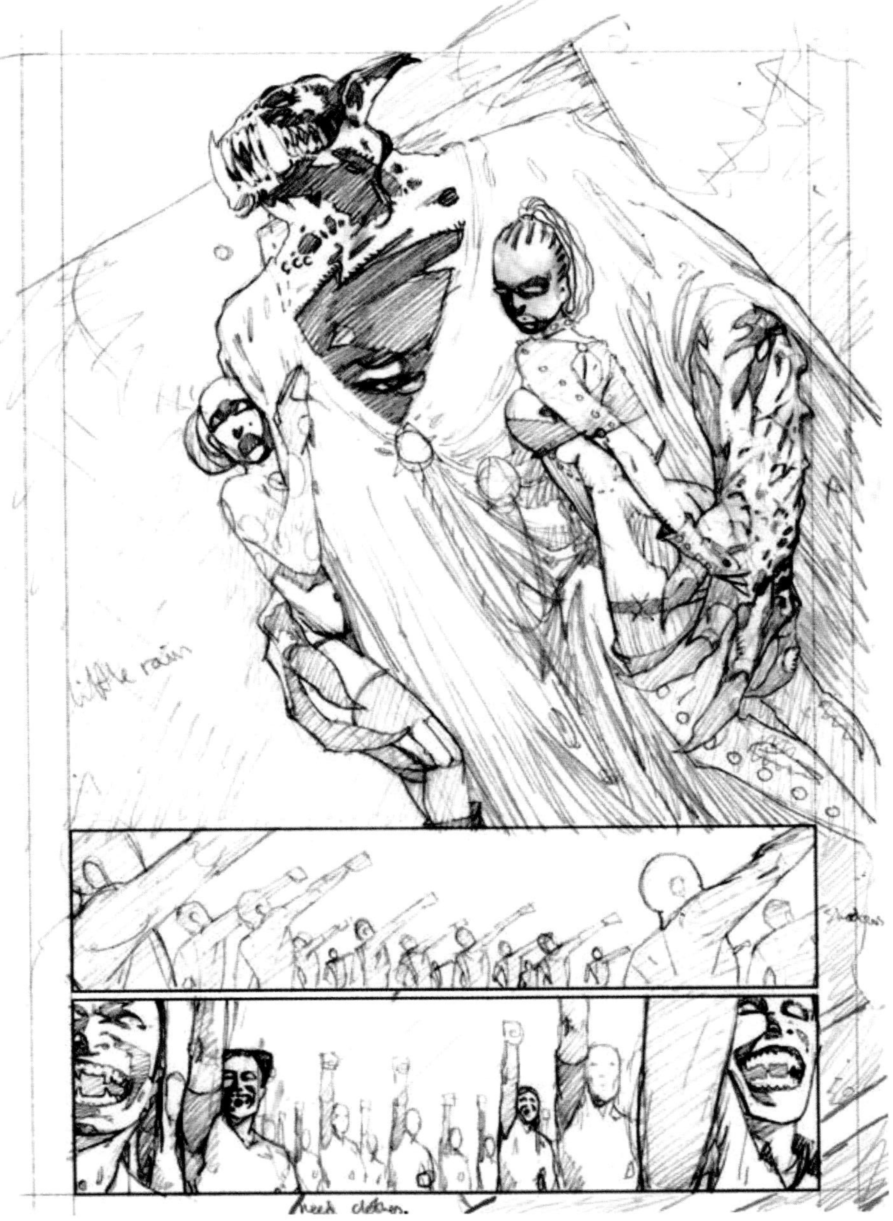
little rain
shadows
needs clothes.

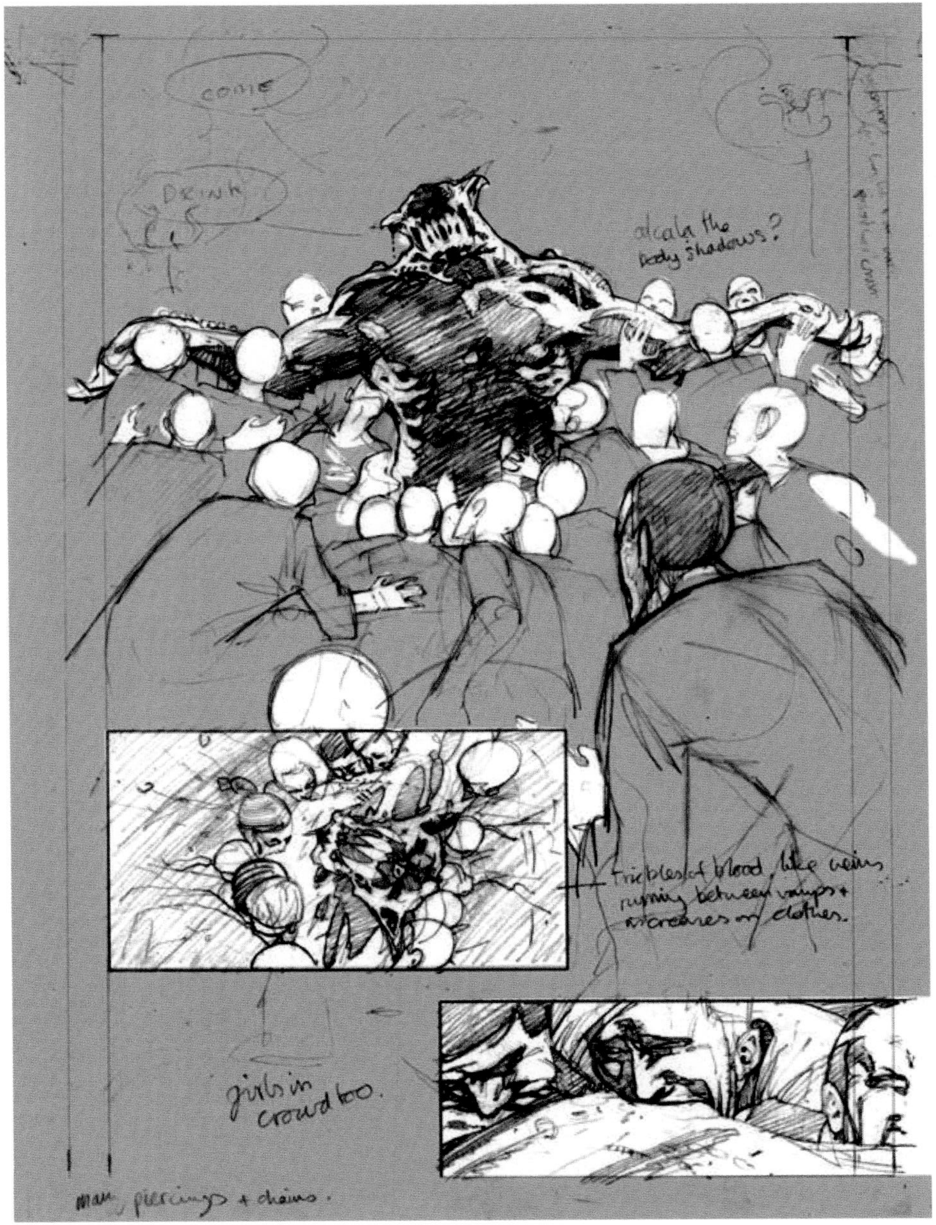
COME
DRINK
decals the body shadows?
trickles of blood like veins running between vamps + in creases in clothes.
girls in crowd too.
man, piercings + chains.

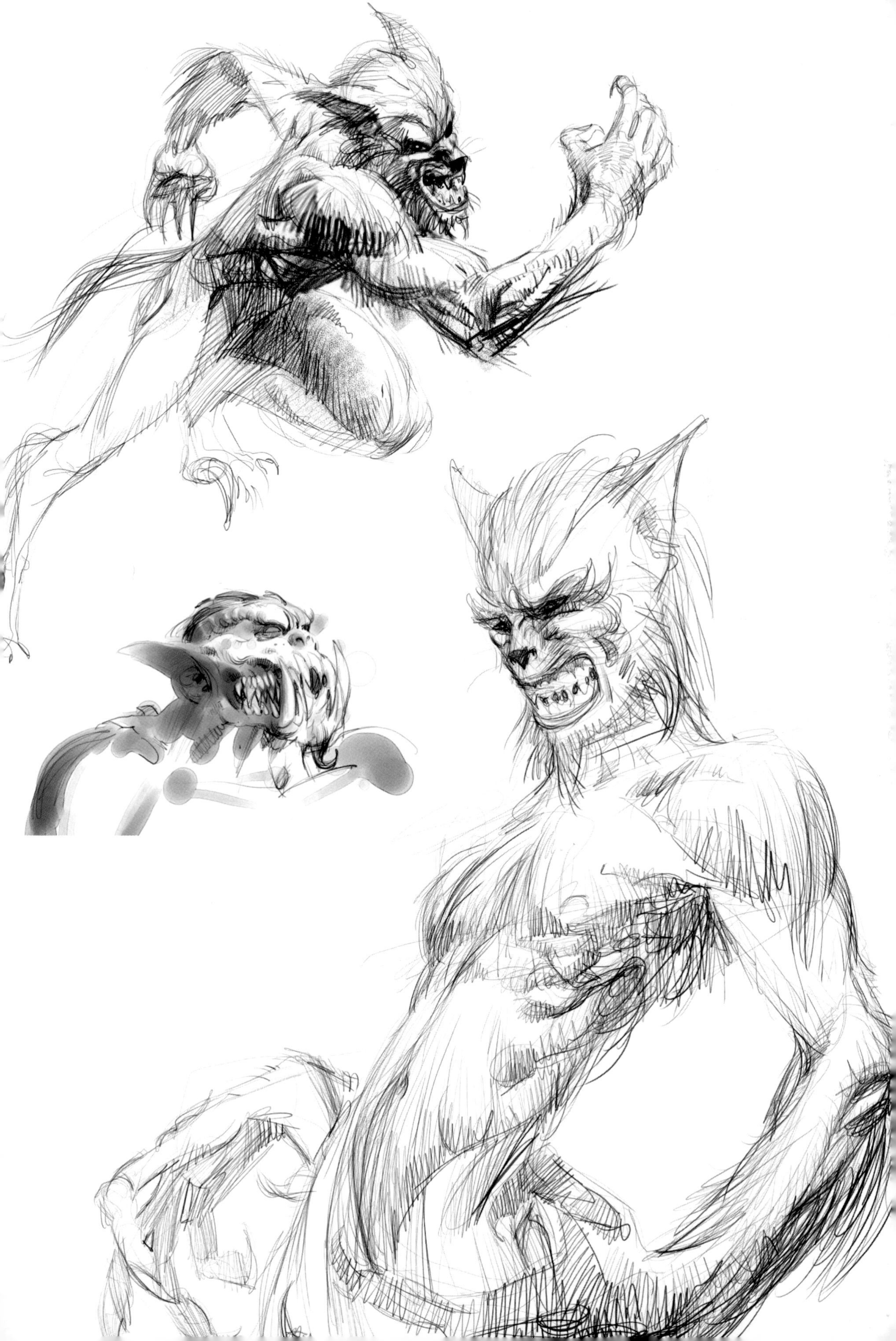

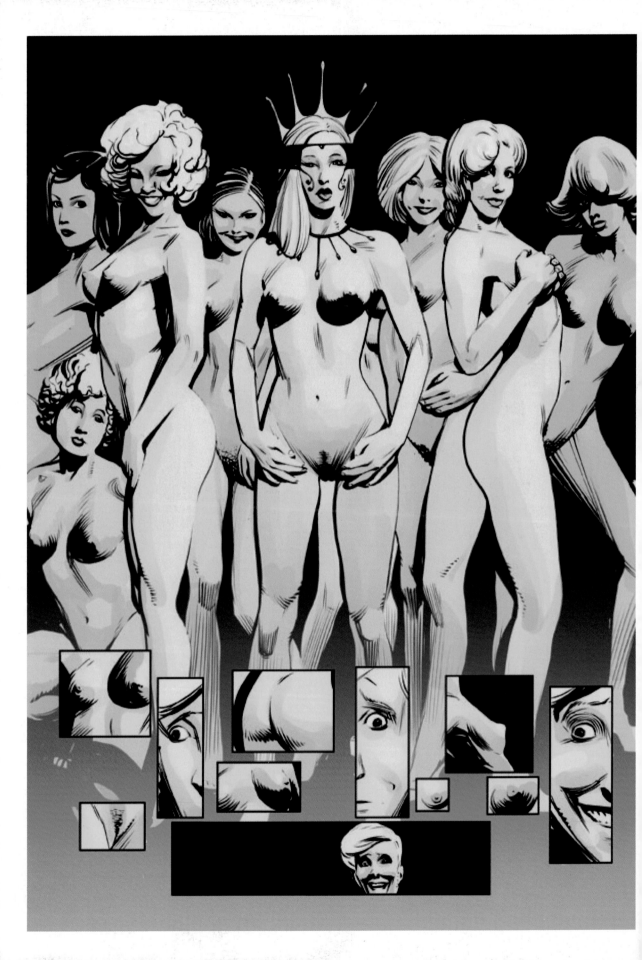

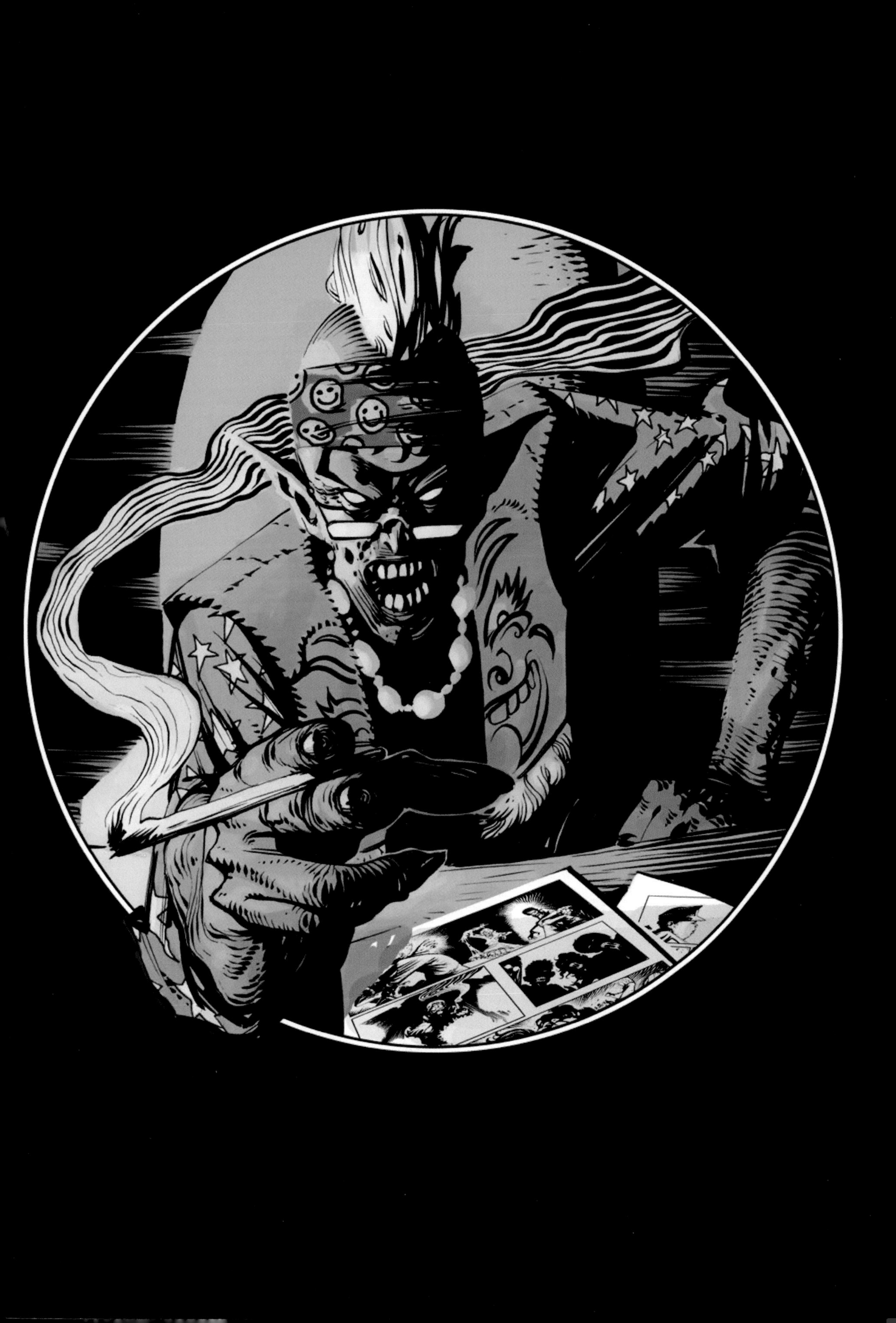

JOHN SMITH

John Smith is unquestionably a *2000 AD* hero, with a host of creative credits to his name, including *A Love Like Blood, Devlin Waugh, Firekind, Holocaust 12, Indigo Prime, Pussyfoot 5, Revere, Slaughterbowl, Tyranny Rex, Leatherjack, Dead Eyes* and the fan-favourite 'hoodie horror' strip *Cradlegrave*. Smith has also written *Future Shocks, Heavy Metal Dredd, Judge Dredd, Judge Karyn, Pulp Sci-Fi, Robo-Hunter, Rogue Trooper, Tales from Beyond Science, Tales of Mega-City One* and *Vector 13*. His work beyond *2000 AD* includes the long-running *New Statesmen* series in *Crisis*, DC/Vertigo's *Hellblazer* and *Scarab*, and Harris Comics' *Vampirella* and *Pantha*.

GORDON RENNIE

Gordon Rennie has co-created many exciting stories and characters for *2000 AD*, including *Caballistics, Inc., Glimmer Rats, Missionary Man, Necronauts, Storming Heaven, Rain Dogs, Witchworld* and the recent occult strip, *Absalom*. He has also written *Daily Star Dredd, Judge Dredd, Harke and Burr, Mean Machine, Past Imperfect, Pulp Sci-Fi, Rogue Trooper, Satanus, Terror Tales, Tharg the Mighty* and *Vector 13*. Outside the 'Galaxy's Greatest Comic', Rennie has written for anthologies *Heavy Metal* and *Warhammer Monthly*, as well as *Species, Starship Troopers* and *White Trash*. Gordon has also written several computer game scripts, such as *Judge Dredd: Dredd Vs. Death* and the BAFTA-nominated *Rogue Trooper*.

FRAZER IRVING

Frazer Irving is one of the biggest talents to have emerged from *2000 AD* over the last decade. His distinctive style, both on co-created strips like *A Love Like Blood, Necronauts* and *Storming Heaven*, as well as on *Judge Dredd, Judge Death, Future Shocks, Terror Tales, Tharg the Mighty, The Scarlet Apocrypha* and *Sinister Dexter*, have quickly brought him to the attention of the US industry. Irving has already worked with DC Comics on *Klarion the Witch Boy, Hellblazer, Robin and Azrael*, and illustrated the Marvel titles, *Iron Man: Inevitable, Inhumans: Silent War* and *The Mystic Hands of Dr. Strange*. Now he is back at DC Comics working with writer Grant Morrison on *Batman & Robin* and the critically-acclaimed *Xombi* with John Rozum.